# THE IRISH SHORT STORY

Declan Kiberd, Patrick Rafroidi, David Norris, Maurice Harmon, André Boué,
Jean Lozès, Guy Fehlmann, Donald T. Torchiana, John Cronin, Anne Clune, Sean Lucy,
Brendan Kennelly, Roger Chatalic, Guy Le Moigne, Alec Reid, Seamus Deane,
John Foster, Henri-Dominique Paratte, Terence Brown.

Patrick Rafroidi, Terence Brown
*editors*

# THE IRISH SHORT STORY

1979
Colin Smythe Ltd., Gerrards Cross, Buckinghamshire
Humanities Press Inc., Atlantic Highlands, N.J. 07716

Copyright © 1979, by Presses Universitaires de Lille
(C.E.R.I.U.L.) and Colin Smythe Ltd.
First published in England by Colin Smythe Ltd, P.O. Box 6,
Gerrards Cross, Buckinghamshire in 1979

**British Library Cataloguing in Publication Data**

The Irish short story.
   1. Short stories, English — Irish authors
   — History and criticism
   I. Rafroidi, Patrick II. Brown, Terence
   823'.01       PR8797

   ISBN 0-86140-022-4

Published in U.S.A. and Canada by Humanities Press Inc., 171 First Avenue, Atlantic Highlands, N.J. 07716
ISBN 0-391-01703-9

Printed in France
by the Press of the University of Lille III
and bound by Leighton Straker Bookbinders, London N.W. 10

# TABLE OF CONTENTS

# FOREWORD

In as far, at any rate, as the contemporary period is concerned, the present volume is a companion to the previous ' Cahier Irlandais `: *The Irish Novel in Our Time* published in 1976 of which a revised and updated version is, we hope, shortly to be issued.

In *The Irish Novel in Our Time* no study appeared of writers who were best approached, in our opinion, through their short-stories, hence the fact that no paper was included on, say, Mary Lavin, Frank O'Connor or Sean O'Faolain who figure pre-eminently in this work.

On the other hand, authors who were dealt with at length in our 1976 publication, like Edna O'Brien, have not normally been re-valued here whatever their merits in the genre considered.

In a few cases, finally, writers of fiction who could be examined with equivalent profit through their longer or their shorter works have been artificially placed in one context or another according to the lights of the editors or to the wishes of the contributors.

The only important thing seemed to us that the two volumes put together should give an overall picture of fictional literature in Ireland, providing a sense of its roots and its present achievements.

As Bibliographies of over 80 novelists and short-story writers are to be found in *The Irish Novel in Our Time*, we have left them out in the present study and advise the readers of *The Irish Short Story* to consult the previous volume.

*The Editors.*

# GENERAL SURVEY

# STORY-TELLING : THE GAELIC TRADITION

## Declan KIBERD

In 1888, that prince of literary diplomats, Henry James, observed with some tact that « the little story is but scantily relished in England, where readers take their fiction rather by the volume than by the page » (1). Pondering this text almost seventy years later, Seán Ó Faoláin remarked with a kind of baffled triumph that « the Americans and Irish do seem to write better stories » (2). The short story as a literary form has flourished in many countries besides Ireland and America. Even highly developed, the shorter form has had gifted exponents such highly developed, the shorter from has had gifted exponents such as Katherine Mansfield. The Russians of the past century are rightly regarded as masters of the genre and Chekhov is justly celebrated as the master of the Russians. France, too, has produced many great story-tellers in the tradition of Daudet and Maupassant. In his study of the genre, Mr. Ó Faoláin attempted to explain why the English, who have given the world so many great novels, should have failed so spectacularly to master the short story. He concluded that English readers preferred the social scope of the novel to the more private concerns of the short story. English writers, he believed, found a natural form for expressing their social philosophy in the extended narrative. The short story, on the other hand, was « an emphatically personal exposition » (3). Mr. Ó Faoláin offered various explanations for the strength of the shorter genre in other countries. The form had prospered in the United States because « American society is still unconventionalized », in Ireland because her people were still « an unconventional and comparatively human people », and in France which was « the breeding ground of the personal and original way of looking at things » (4). These are pleasant arguments but there may be deeper reasons for the success of the form in such countries.

It seems, at least to the present author, that the short story has flourished in those countries where a vibrant oral culture is suddenly challenged by the onset of a sophisticated literary tradition. The short story is the natural result of a fusion between the ancient form of the folk-tale and the preoccupations of modern literature. We can, with some accuracy, even begin to identify the place and time of such a fusion. For example, the frontier in nineteenth-century America gave us the « tall tale » of Mark Twain's west, in stories such as « The Man that Corrupted Hadleyburg » or « The Celebrated Jumping Frog of Calaveras County ». It was this tradition which provided the basis for the episodic narrative art of *Huckleberry Finn*. In this work, a sequence of anecdotes told in folk idiom became the classic novel of a young nation and, according to Ernest Hemingway, the source of subsequent American literature. The same might be observed of the frontier in Australia and New Zealand, where an indigenous folk culture came into creative conflict with a developing literary tradition. In Russia the vibrant culture of the peasants inspired Nikolai Leskov to write superb short stories at a time of national upheaval. In more settled countries, such as France, it is no accident that the form was pioneered by writers such as Maupassant, who hailed from Normandy where an oral tradition was still a force in the lives of the people. Indeed, many of Maupassant's finest stories take as their theme that very clash between ancient and modern standards in regional communities which made the development of the genre possible.

For the past eighty years in Ireland, the short story has been the most popular of all literary forms with readers. It has also been the form most widely exploited by writers. Whereas the great Anglo-Irish writers of the Literary Revival, such as Yeats and Synge, excelled in poetry and drama, the short story has been mainly pioneered by the « risen people » — the O'Kellys, O'Flahertys, Ó Faolains and O'Connors. The genre had a particular appeal for the writers of the emerging Catholic bourgeoisie who hailed from regional towns. To take a clear example, Seán Ó Faoláin and Frank O'Connor both grew up in Cork, strategically poised between the folk and the literary tradition. From lending libraries in the city, they could read the classic works of English literature ; but in the countryside all around Cork, the folk story-tellers still delighted peasant audiences around cottage firesides and blacksmiths' forges. Even in the heart of the city itself, one or two old people — immigrants from the surrounding country-side — plied the story-teller's art. It was inevitable that such a town would produce, in the twentieth century, some of the nation's greatest exponents of the short story, a genre which was poised, like its authors, between the profane world of contemporary literature and the pious world of the folk. By nature of its origins, the form was admirably suited to the task of reflecting the disturbances in Irish society as it painfully shed its ancient traditions. O'Connor himself has observed that without the concept of a normal society, the novel is impossible (5) ; but the short story is particularly appropriate to a society in which revolutionary upheavals have shattered the very idea of normality. In the years in which the modern Irish nation took shape, the short story was the form in which many writers chose to depict their vision of the emerging Ireland. In the earliest phase of the Literary Revival, at the beginning of this century, many of these writers looked to the Gaelic folk tradition for inspiration.

The art of oral story-telling in Ireland goes back over a thousand years and is very similar to that of Brittany. Léon Marillier, in his introduction to Anatole Le Braz's collection, *La Légende de la Mort en Basse-Bretagne*, draws a classic distinction between two types of folk narrative. On the one hand, there is the « conte », a tale of international provenance with a durable form which scarcely varies from one country to the next. On the other hand, there is the « légende », which is infinitely variable and deals with more homely matters (6). The tellers of the « contes » put little of their own personalities into their remote and marvellous tales, but the « légendes » arose from the lives of ordinary people and were rooted in a particular place (7). In Ireland, the same distinction holds good and a discrimination is made between two types of story teller. The « sgéalaí » enjoys higher status as narrator of the « sean-sgéal » or international tale, while the « seanchaí » narrates local tales and lore concerning familiar places, family genealogies, fairies and ghosts (8). The

« sgéalaí » was always a man but the « seanchaí » could be male or female. The tales told by the « sgéalaí » were long and difficult to remember, filled with amazing adventures and remote wonders narrated neutrally in the third person. The « seanchaí » told his story as if he himself had witnessed it. These stories were sometimes translated into English, but the versions in the native language were far superior, as J.M. Synge discovered on the Aran Islands (9).

Perhaps the finest account of the Gaelic story-teller and his art was given by Seán Mac Giollarnáth in his collection published under the title *Peadar Chois Fhairrge* (10). As a rule, stories were told at night around the winter fire from the end of the harvest until the middle of March. The stories held in highest esteem were tales of heroes such as Oisín and the Fianna, full of astonishing feats and marvellous incidents. Many of the old story-tellers believed in these marvels and would suppress the questions of cynical youths in their audience with the exclamation : « Bhíodh draíocht ann sa tsean-shaol ! » (« There was magic in the old times ») (11). The tales were often told round the fireside of the « sgéalaí » himself and folk from the surrounding countryside would crowd into his house to listen. Audiences were critical and not slow to correct a teller who stumbled and made a mistake. They loved to hear a familiar story again and again, having a deep admiration for the skill with which it was told. They became deeply involved in the plot, murmuring with apprehension or sighing with fear as the story progressed. The tellers were often shy, sensitive artists who had to be coaxed into a performance and who did not like to perform before a harsh or unfriendly audience. One famous lady story-teller was so shy of her more critical neighbours that she always locked her kitchen door before starting a story. Very often, a pipe was passed around before the entertainment began and then the « sgéalaí » would sit back in his chair and prepare himself for delivery. Sometimes the person next to him would hold his hand as he spoke by way of encouragement. A most moving account of a Kerry teller in his eighties was given by Tadhg Ó Murchú in the 1930s :

His piercing eyes are on my face, his lips are trembling, as, immersed in his story, and forgetful of all else, he puts his very soul into the telling. Obviously much affected by his narrative, he uses a great deal of gesticulation, and by the movement of his body, hand, and head, tries to convey hate and anger, fear and humour, like an actor in a play (12).

The Cork in which Daniel Corkery was born in 1878 was surrounded by a countryside in which traditions of story-telling were still a powerful force. Corkery was a teacher and a writer, a man equally at home by the story-teller's fireside or in the scholar's library. Like his future disciples, Ó Faoláin and O'Connor, he found in the short story the form most suited to his purposes. He saw his role as that of an artist mediating between two cultures. In 1916, a reviewer in the *Times Literary Supplement* wrote that « Mr. Corkery's stories read as if he had heard them from old Irish peasants and set them down in his own way ... very deftly, so that the endings of his tales come with a queer, unexpected, epigrammatic turn » (13). Many of the techniques employed by Corkery in his stories are closely related to those of the folktale. For example, in « The Spancelled », a story from *A Munster Twilight*, we read at the start of a paragraph : « Now, as to the spancelled man who was to meet this spancelled woman. John Keegan his name was ... (14). The opening three words, « now as to ... », were frequently used by oral story-tellers to introduce sequences of action, just as passages in the native language were often introduced by phrases such as « nós iomarra » or « maidir le » or « iomthúsa », after a digression on the part of the speaker. The second sentence reproduces the exact order of the words as they would be spoken by a teller, but they would certainly never be written in this way in standard English.

A number of Corkery's stories were unashamedly introduced by their « author » with the information that they had been gleaned from the folk. There is a sense in which Corkery presented himself not as an artist, but as a collector of folklore, recording the stories of the people and examining the very way in which a story was told. A revealing passage at the close of « The Lady of the Glassy Palace », from *A Munster Twilight*, runs as follows :

Of course, Watchpole found humour in it, but not for a few days. In this way he now begins the tale ; « Did ye ever hear tell of how Mick Hosford kilt two birds with the wan stone ? » As a matter of fact, he killed only one, though at the wake Hawky Sullivan did conduct himself with the reserve that befits one who has had a narrow escape (15).

In this way, Corkery reasserts his authorial presence and corrects exaggerations in the folk anecdotes with a witty and acid turn of phrase. Each of his oral tales is framed by a literary reference in this fashion. This device is used even with a series of tales, such as those grouped under the collective title, *The Cobbler's Den*.

Corkery was the forerunner of a host of Munster writers who set out to base their stories on folk idiom and belief. In the Irish language, this attempt to preserve the continuity of the Munster folk tradition in the transition to a written literature was even more powerful. The leader of this movement, an tAthair Peadar Ua Laoghaire, explained his policy : « In order to preserve Irish as a spoken tongue, we must preserve our spoken Irish. That is to say we must write and print exactly what the people speak... I am determined to write down most carefully every provincialism I can get hold of. Then I shall be sure to have the people's language » (16). Even within the language movement, however, there were many writers who dissented from this principle. Aodh de Blácam called instead for a modernist literature which would express « the individual mind » (17). The most influential apostle of Gaelic Modernism was Patrick Pearse. In a major statement in the Gaelic League paper, *An Claidheamh Soluis*, as early as May 1906, he explained why a vital modern literature could never be founded on the folk-tale :

We hold the folk tale to be a beautiful and gracious thing only in its own time and place ... and its time and place are the winter fireside, or the spring sowing time, or the country road at any season. Thus, we lay down the proposition that a living literature *cannot* (and if it could, should not) be built up on the folk tale. The folk tale is an echo of old mythologies : literature is a deliberate criticism of actual life ... This is the twentieth century ; and no literature can take root in the twentieth century which is not of the twentieth century. We want no Gothic revival (18).

One month later, Pearse insisted with uncanny accuracy that the future of Irish literature lay not with the folk tale but with the short story : « We foresee for this type of composition a mighty future in Irish and indeed in European literature » (19). Three years later, he defended his own famous story, « Iosagán », against the traditionalists : « 'Iosagán has been described as a 'Standard of Revolt'... It is the standard of definite art form as opposed to the folk form » (20).

What can Pearse have meant ? In the statement of May 1906, he asserted that « personality » was the quality which distinguished the individual artist from the folk tradition. This was an elaboration of a point which he had made as far back as 1903 : « Style after all is another name for personality. One cannot always stick to the folk formula and genealogies are out of fashion » (21). For Pearse the virtue of the short story was that it permitted intense self-expression. Because he lacked the social scope of the novelist, the writer of short stories was bound to select a single aspect of life through which he might reveal his personality. Seán Ó Faoláin was to make the same observation many years later in his study of the genre :

> What one searches for and what one enjoys in a short story is a special distillation of personality, a unique sensibility which has recognized and selected at once a subject that, above all other subjects, is of value to the writer's temperament and to his alone — his counterpart, his perfect opportunity to express himself (22).

It is this scope for self-expression which distinguishes the short story from the folk-tale. The folk-tale was impersonal, magical, and recited to a credulous audience in a public manner. The short story is personal, credible, and written in private for the critical solitary reader. The folk story-teller could win the assent of his listeners to the most impossible of plots. The modern writer is confronted with an audience of lonely sceptics who insist on a literature which reflects their everyday lives. James Delargy has described folklore as « the literature of escape » through which « the oppressed and downtrodden could leave the grinding poverty of their surroundings, and in imagination rub shoulders with the great, and sup with kings and queens, and lords and ladies, in the courts of fairyland » (23). When Lady Gregory went to collect tales in a Galway workhouse, she was « moved by the strange contrast between the poverty of the tellers and the splendours of the tales » (24). In the modern short story, however, the teller no longer seeks to flee from his humdrum surroundings, but rather to confront them in all their banality. His motto is that of Katherine Mansfield who promised to tell how the laundry-basket squeaked. Such a literature describes no longer the exploits of kings and princes, but rather the minor triumphs and small sadnesses of the commonplace man. Frank O'Connor has even gone so far as to assert that the short story marks « the first appearance in fiction of the Little Man » (25). In the opening chapter of *The Lonely Voice*, O'Connor articulates his belief that the short story is characterised by its treatment of « submerged population groups » (26), of those lonely people who live on the fringes of society because of spiritual emptiness or material deprivation. America is offered as an example of a society composed almost entirely of « submerged population groups » in their respective ethnic ghettoes after immigration from Europe. This takes us back to the present writer's contention that the short story flourishes on any cultural frontier, where solitary men daily confront the ambiguities of a changing society which is based on rival folk and cosmopolitan traditions. O'Connor goes on to assert that the short story grew out of folklore and that such stories are « drastic adaptations of a primitive art to modern conditions — to printing, science, and individual religion » (27). In the work of writers as diverse as Carleton, O'Kelly, Colum, Stephens, Corkery, O'Connor, Lavin and MacMahon, we find undeniable signs of that adaptation. For example, many of these writers employ in their stories a style which verges on the conversational and this mode of delivery characterised not only the ancient sagas but also the modern Irish folk-tale (28). To a greater or lesser extent, each of these writers has been conditioned by the Gaelic tradition of story-telling.

Having said that much, it is only just to add that the greatest collection of short stories to come out of Ireland, Joyce's *Dubliners*, bears positively no trace of the oral tradition. Where the oral tradition took the spectacular as its subject, Joyce finds poetry in the commonplace. Where the oral tales climaxed in blood-baths and supernatural reversals, Joyce's epiphanies describe nothing more momentous than the passing of a coin. Nor is Joyce alone in this proud immunity to the Gaelic tradition. George Moore and John McGahern might also be cited as writers of real class whose work bears no trace of the folklore of the rural Ireland in which they grew up. One reason for this may lie in the fact that « tales which had previously been told in the Irish language passed over into English only to a very small extent » (29).

In such a situation, it might have been expected that the Gaelic tradition of story-telling would have exerted its most profound influence on writers in the Irish language. The work of Mícheál Ó Siochfhradha (An Seabhac) in *An Baile Seo Againne* is an impressive example of this kind of writing. All too often, however, those who relied on folk-tales for inspiration did so because they had no art or theme of their own. Anyone who looks back over the literature of the past seventy years will find that the prophecies of Pearse have been vindicated. The finest short stories in Irish have been written by Pádraic Ó Conaire, Liam O'Flaherty and Máirtín Ó Cadhain, not one of whom relied on the art of the folk tradition which was their logical inheritance. Ó Conaire dealt most often in his stories with the middle class rather than the peasants and he rigorously excluded all idiosyncrasies of folk dialect from his prose. Some of his finest collections, like Joyce's *Dubliners* or Sherwood Anderson's *Winesburg Ohio*, are built around a single theme. For instance, the short stories in *Seacht mBua an Éirí Amach* all deal with the ways in which the Easter Rising impinged on the lives of ordinary people. Ó Conaire began to write at the start of the century under the influence of European Realists. With later writers such as O'Flaherty and Ó Cadhain, the short story in Irish became unashamedly modernist. Ó Cadhain even denied that it was a « story » as such, preferring to see it is a dramatisation of an incident, of a state of mind, or of a person simply passing on the road. For Ó Cadhain, the form is intensely compressed, like that of a lyric poem. More is left unsaid than is said. The story can cover only a short period of time, an hour, a day, a week, and, like the classical drama, it calls for a unity of time, place and action (30). By these searching criteria, few stories in modern Irish, apart from O'Flaherty's and Ó Cadhain's, would survive the test. O'Flaherty's simple lyric descriptions of children, of animals, and of evanescent moments in a human relationship, mark off *Dúil* as the finest collection of short stories in the Irish language. These stories have also been published in English, the language in which O'Flaherty composed all his subsequent writing. This leaves Ó Cadhain as the undisputed master of modern prose in Irish. Although his masterpiece is the novel, *Cré na Cille*, his short stories betray similar evidence of his gift for dramatising the human consciousness. Ō Cadhain loved folklore and collected and published many superb tales from story-tellers in Galway ; but he did not believe that folk-tales should be made the basis of a modern literature. In a radio broadcast on the short story, he observed wearily that he would prefer to read a single folk-tale in its original form than twenty listless adaptations of that tale in the shape of the short story. In such versions, the distinctive art of the folk-tale is not so much adapted as destroyed.

This leads to a final point. Too many bad short stories are written in Ireland today and too few good novels. Foolish people convince themselves that the short story is easily written and that it requires little effort. They know that rewards from newspapers, radio and television are handsome, so they sit down to write. The truth is that the short story, like the lyric poem, is one of the most difficult forms in literature, requiring a concentration and intense economy of effect possible only to a true artist. Nevertheless, a particularly fatuous type of story, which claims to record « the pieties of the folk », has recently enjoyed a sudden revival. Every town in the west of Ireland has produced some schoolmaster who fancies himself to be a past master of the art. Summer festivals are held in these towns and foreign tourists flock into public houses to applaud the maudlin performances of these rustic geniuses. These men write as if Daniel Corkery were the only model to follow in Irish literature, as if Joyce and Ō Cadhain had never put pen to paper. Such ignoble exercises, carried out on the fringes of the tourist industry, have no artistic value for the contemporary Irish writer or reader. Nevertheless, the phenomenon is worth pondering. It was Corkery himself, in that controversial opening chapter of *Synge and Anglo-Irish Literature*, who declared that every Irish writer is faced with a decision — whether to express Ireland or exploit her (31). The choice lies between expressing the life of the nation to itself or exploiting that life for the delectation of a « superior » foreign audience. In Corkery's time, that audience was composed mainly of upper-class English readers who chortled over novels which recorded the foibles of the peasants. In our own day, the nature of that audience has changed, but not the nature of the attendant temptation. The current audience is composed mainly of Irish-American tourists who come to confirm their fondest hope that the fairies are still at the bottom of the garden. Those writers who entertain these tourists by teasing the beautiful old folk-tales into shapeless short stories are exploiting their native culture rather than expressing it. They do a signal disservice to the integrity of the folk-tales which they travesty.

The folk-tale was a valid and beautiful means by which the Gaelic story-teller expressed the Irish people to themselves at a certain phase in their history. That phase lasted for hundreds of years, but it is now past. The vibrant tradition of oral story-telling was one major reason for the triumph of the short story as a characteristic Irish literary form. Seeing this, many writers, with varying degrees of success, applied in the short story the techniques of the folk-tale. Some minor writers even tried to adapt folk anecdotes to the form of the short story in the years of national upheaval at the start of this century. This, too, was a valid means of expressing the nation to itself at a time of self-conscious cultural revival. That period, also, is past. It is now clear that the greatest short stories, in both Irish and English, owe more to the narrative genius of their authors than to the Gaelic tradition of story-telling. Pearse's prophecy is fulfilled and it is the modernist artists who have written, in Joyce's lucid phrase, a chapter of the moral history of their country.

# NOTES

1. Henry James : *Partial Portraits*, London, 1888, p. 264.
2. Seán Ó Faoláin : *The Short Story*, 2nd ed. Cork, 1972, p. 43.
3. *Ibid.*, p. 44.
4. *Ibid*, pp. 44-5.
5. Frank O'Connor : *The Lonely Voice : A Study of the Short Story*, London, 1963, p. 17.
6. Léon Marillier : Introduction to *La Légende de la Mort en Basse Bretagne* by Anatole Le Braz, Paris, 1892, p. XVIII.
7. *Ibid.*, p. X.
8. *Ibid.*, pp. V, XIII, and XIV.
9. J.M. Synge : *The Aran Islands* in *Collected Works : Prose*, ed. Alan Price, Oxford, 1966, p. 61.
10. Seán Mac Giollarnáth, ed. : *Peadar Chois Fhairrge*, Dublin, 1934.
11. James Delargy : « The Gaelic Storyteller » in *Proceedings of the British Academy*, Vol. XXXI, London, 1945, p. 8.
12. Quoted by Delargy : « The Gaelic Storyteller », p. 16.
13. Quoted in frontispiece to Daniel Corkery : *The Threshold of Quiet*, Dublin, 1917.
14. Daniel Corkery : *A Munster Twilight*, Cork, 1967, p. 57.
15. *Ibid.*, p. 51.
16. Quoted by T.F. O'Rahilly : *Papers on Irish Idiom*, Dublin, 1920, p. 138.
17. Aodh de Blácam : « Gaelic and Anglo-Irish Literature Compared », in *Studies*, March 1924, p. 71.
18. Patrick Pearse : « About Literature » in *An Claidheamh Soluis*, 26 May 1906, p. 6.
19. Patrick Pearse : « Literature, Life, and the Oireachtas Competition » in *An Claidheamh Soluis*, 2 June 1906, p. 6.
20. Quoted by Máirtín Ó Cadhain : « Conradh na Gaeilge agus an Litríocht » in *The Gaelic League Idea*, ed. Seán Ó Tuama, Cork, 1972, p. 59.
21. Patrick Pearse : « Reviews » in *An Claidheamh Soluis,* 14 March 1903, p. 3.
22. O Faoláin : *The Short Story*, p. 44.
23. Delargy : « The Gaelic Storyteller », p. 24.
24. Lady Gregory : *Poets and Dreamers : Studies and Translations from the Irish,* Dublin, 1903, p. 129.
25. O'Connor : *The Lonely Voice*, p. 15.
26. *Ibid.*, p. 18.
27. *Ibid.*, p. 45.
28. Delargy : « The Gaelic Storyteller », p. 33.
29. Seán O'Sullivan : *The Folklore of Ireland,* London, 1974, p. 15.
30. Máirtín Ó Cadhain : « An Gearrscéal sa nGaeilge », Radio Éireann, 1967.
31. Daniel Corkery : *Synge and Anglo-Irish Literature*, Cork, 1931, pp. 10-11.

# THE IRISH SHORT STORY IN ENGLISH.
# THE BIRTH OF A NEW TRADITION

Patrick RAFROIDI

The remarkable success of the short story in Ireland has been variously explained.

*Sociologically.* As the echo of a collective consciousness, the immediate mirror of a feeling of alienation, the short story, more than the synthetic form of the novel, can easily become the voice of those whom Frank O'Connor calls « submerged population groups » (1).

*Aesthetically.* With some notable exceptions Irish writers are ill at ease in the longer genre (2), especially in so far as it is less open to the suggestion of a face to face relationship between an author and a reader, reminiscent of a storyteller of the past speaking to an audience.

*Historically.* In the Gaelic nation, where urbanization is so recent, a fundamental place must be assigned to the immemorial tradition of the storyteller, the sgéalaí or seanchaí who every year from Hallowe'en to the night of Saint Patrick's Day, was the very soul of the ceili, as people gathered around the fireplace in mansions or cottages to enjoy a performance from a repertory of 350 items or more.

Although this last reason, the most inspiring, is not to be understated (the texture of the Irish story often if not always suggests the influence of fireside gatherings) it does nevertheless require qualification. In Ireland as elsewhere an evolutionary shift marks the passage from the legend or the traditional story to the modern short story. The latter is a short narrative based on a single isolated subject, referring to experience in its reality and even in its banality. It is quickly and economically presented and its structure is dominated by a privileged moment. At the same time it resembles its ancestor in its frequent reliance on the direct testimony of its narrator or author (3).

Furthermore the first Irish practitioners of the new genre not only wrote in a language other than that of the traditional story-tellers, they also preferred themes and structures that, at first sight at least, seem to mark a major break with those of the Gaelic tradition.

This departure can be seen in the use of the *fantastic* by such romantic Anglo-Irish writers as Charles Robert Maturin, Joseph Sheridan Le Fanu, Fitzjames O'Brien, Bram Stoker. In their work there would appear to be little that is typically Irish. Its *content* tends to be identical to that of the work of foreign contemporaries. One finds, for instance, the same preference for exaggeration and for a figurative expression that invites a literal reading. This is the case in « Leixlip Castle » by the first named author when the killer of his brother draws a dagger from its sheath and throws it into the sea while praying that « the guilt of his brother's blood might be as far from his soul as he could fling that weapon from his body » (4). The blood could not be wiped away however, and neither could the weapon.

Here as elsewhere, the *mode of presentation* implies a narrator who, by speaking in the first person, seeks to give more authority to his true story. One thinks of the first words of « the Wonder-smith » (5) by Fitzjames O'Brien :

A small lane, the name of which I have forgotten, or do not choose to remember, slants suddenly off from Catham Street, (before that headlong thoroughfare rushes into the Park), and retreats suddenly down towards the East River, as if it were disgusted with the smell of old clothes, and had determined to wash itself clean.

or of the second sentence of Bram Stoker's terrible story, « The Squaw » (6) :

Nurnberg at the time was not so much exploited as it has been since then. Irving had not been playing *Faust*, and the

very name of the old town was hardly known to the great bulk
of the travelling public. My wife and I being in the second
week of our honeymoon, naturally wanted someone else to join
our party, so that when the cheery stranger, Elias P.
Hutcheson, hailing from Isthmian City, Bleeding Gulch, Maple
Tree County, Neb., turned up at the station at Frankfort, and
casually remarked that he was going on to see the most all-
fired old Methuselah of a town in Yurrup, and that he guessed
that so much travelling alone was enough to send an intelligent, active citizen into the melancholy ward of a daft
house, we took the pretty broad hint and suggested that we
should join forces.

Even when a first person narrator is not immediately involved
the third person narration refers to him at least indirectly as can
be seen again in « Leixlip Castle » :

The incidents of the following tale are not merely founded on
fact, they are facts themselves, which occurred at no very
distant period in *my* own family.

The sense of an eye-witness record can be achieved by such
devices as documents or an intimate diary inherited from a friend.
This is the simplest procedure of the « circumstantial method »
without which it is impossible to provoke the Coleridgeian
suspension of disbelief exploited by Le Fanu throughout the
whole of *In a Glass Darkly* (7) where each story of the collection
is introduced as an item taken from his files by Dr. Hesselius, a
German specialist in psychic cases.

   In the stories of the above-mentioned writers the *narrative
structure* — the « syntax » of the structuralist critics —
conforms to the general pattern defined by Poe. Even when it is
not based on an indispensable « gradation » it always seeks a
single effect towards which all the components of the work must
contribute.

   The *semantics* of these stories show the same attraction for the
themes that Mario Praz (8), Roger Caillois (9) and Tzvetan
Todorov (10) were able to find in the fictional production of
writers in Romantic Europe and beyond its shores. In broad
terms these are combinations like beauty/ugliness, beauty/death,
the surfacing of murky desires (sadism, masochism), the concrete

manifestation of remorse, fear of the other, (woman-phantom or *belle dame sans merci* — objects which come alive), the fear of emptiness (the disappearance of the natural milieu, of the loved person, the halting of time), the terror of death and of supernatural beings (satanism, bargain with the devil).

Alongside these not particularly Irish semantic elements one can however find certain tendencies that give a specificity to the writers' work.

At the outset it should be described as no more than an *Anglo-Irish specificity* in the strictest sense of the term Anglo-Irish.

Anglo-Irish society, the most charming in the British Isles, was a guilty society

writes V.S. Pritchett (11) and a conviction of guilt accounts not only for the extraordinary flourishing of a taste for the supernatural in this milieu from Burke to Wilde, but also for the basic elements of the works themselves. They show the clear mark of political guilt (the theme of usurpation), of sociological guilt (the theme of the irresponsibility of the Planters as they womanize, brawl, drink, laze, spend and live by the sweat of others). Such works are weighed down by a feeling of futility and impotence in the present moment, by insecurity about the future and these inspire symbols whose intense qualities cannot be found in other, more secure civilizations. There is no other explanation for the motif of the powerful reincarnation of faults (e.g. « The Familiar » by Le Fanu), for the recurrence of the theme of the blood-sucking vampire (e.g. « Carmilla »), for the obsession with a cut-off hand (e.g. « The Haunting of the Tiled House » (12), these last two also by Le Fanu) the horror of attack by unidentified assailants (e.g. O'Brien « What Was It » (13) ) which faithfully embody the nocturnal terrors which the secret societies could visit at any time on the mansions of the Ascendancy. Guilt feelings are not the only manifestations of the special situation in which the ruling class found itself in nineteenth century Ireland. Ambivalent, anxious feelings about identity often reveal themselves in a fascination for portraits and images which retain a suggestion of a lost Golden Age when in fact the subject portrayed has become unrecognisably ugly.

The place of many Anglo-Irish writers in a « gothic » or

fantastic tradition may however give them, finally, a *specificity* that is *simply Irish*. Here, while using material of foreign origin, they discover some of the deeper tendencies of the race to which they were very imperfectly assimilated but whose qualities finally rubbed off on them. Among these was a feeling for the supernatural even in everyday reality as expressed in folklore.

Folklore as such ot course is not within the scope of this article, even if the period dealt with is one which sees its first transcriptions in the work of Thomas Crofton Croker, Thomas Keightley, Patrick Kennedy, Lady Wilde and other precursors of Douglas Hyde, Lady Gregory and Yeats whose *Irish Fairy and Folk Tales* (14) is a first timid effort of classification pointing the way towards the learned works that were yet to be written (15). The present study can only deal with works showing a personal creative imagination and it is obvious that a true writer cannot be content with just transcribing or adapting. Experience shows that adaptation quickly becomes unduly poetic or burlesque in tendency and this quickly undermines the realist bases of popular forms of fairylore or deprives it of its potential seriousness.

At the same time contact becomes revelation and imitation a liberating discipline. Out of the ancestral soil spring original plants that, in all likelihood, would never have seen the light of day in a land other than the one where they first took root. Some of Carleton's work or that of Griffin or the Banim brothers and later on in the century that of authors as different as Oscar Wilde, James Stephens and Yeats himself illustrate this point.

Again and again in *Traits and Stories of the Irish Peasantry* (1830, 1833), *Tales of Ireland* (1834), *The Fawn of Springvale* (1841) or *Tales and Sketches* (1845) afterwards called *Tales and Stories*, Carleton can be caught in the act of exploiting folk-lore material which he either refuses to transmute or which he treats comically. Nevertheless in other works he is the outstanding intermediary between the old order and the new, and the originator of a modern art.

In the narrative technique and themes of this writer the influence of popular tradition is unmistakable. One immediately thinks of « The Three Tasks » (16) where the motif reappears of an adventurous journey to a wonderful country akin to Tir na nOg in the Ossianic sagas and folklore, as well as the voyages (imrama) of Saint Brendan and others. But in such a work or in « A Legend of Knockmany » (17) one can find a transcription among whose values is an already greater realism (a point which will be dealt with later). Other stories also come to mind, like the extraordinary « The Donagh or the Horse Stealers » (18) which completely reverse the proportions of tradition and originality in this fantastic vein ; and there are those stories which deal realistically with everyday life.

Even if he is far from being the most artistically honest, Carleton is without doubt the most gifted of the storytellers of the first generation of the nineteenth century. Many of the stories of Gerald Griffin, « The Barber of Bantry » (19), for instance, could be examined from a similar point of view and if I am not delaying on the work of the Banim brothers it is because their relationship to the present subject is more readily apparent in novels than short stories.

It may appear surprising to find Oscar Wilde next on the list. Admittedly the son of Speranza seemed to feel no more than a middling attraction for an Ireland which in turn has been slow to claim him. Besides, his most famous attempt at a ghost story, « The Canterville Ghost », is a burlesque where he gives in to the fatal temptations that we have noted some other practitioners of the genre also experienced. Yet at the same time critics have often passed over the seriousness of his approach when, from folklore motifs (often common in his native country), he creates his own wonderful universe of kings (« The Young King »), of dwarfs (« The Birthday of the Infanta »), of giants (« The Selfish Giant »), of mermaids (« The Fisherman and his Soul »), of statues come to life (« The Happy Prince »), of animals with the power of speech (« The Star Child »). These he ultimately uses to reach an apparently contradictory double philosophy of aestheticism and mutual help.

James Stephens' novel *The Crock of Gold* (1912) and the not easily classified work *In The Land of Youth* (1924) show an abundant Gaelic influence. Neither one of them however is simply imitation, the personal themes of the author, like Time and the condemnation of Mercantilism, are always close to the surface or even dominant and the plot is always original. Straddling the frontier of the real and the imaginary, his short stories proper also betray his memory of his readings of ancestral legends. This is especially true of « Desire », the piece at the start of *Etched in Moonlight* (20).

The creative prose of W.B. Yeats has not attracted the same

cohorts of thesis writers as his poetry (21), yet it shows the same exemplary development. In a way his role as a collector of tales enabled him to skip the level of the profane (literal history) and to arrive immediately at the level of the sacred (the symbol of the human psyche) and even at that of an initiation (the hidden esoteric meaning which is the reflection of the collective sub-consciousness or the Memory of the World) in pieces like « The Tables of the Law » or « The Adoration of the Magi » collected in 1925 in the volume *Mythologies*.

A few more names could be added and a longer study would look at the work of Lord Dunsany and others. At the same time what has been argued above amply makes the point especially since neither the supernatural, the magical nor the esoteric constitute the richest themes of the Irish short story written in English during the following generations.

Nor indeed does the *heroic* inspiration inherited from the Gaelic tradition. It could be argued, it is true, that the hand of Cuchulainn can still be seen here and there, as in *The Green Rushes* by Maurice Walsh (22) and even more so his spirit in the work of Daniel Corkery, in Bryan MacMahon's « Kings Asleep in the Ground », and in Michael MacLaverty's « The Pigeons ». Yet if one reads the stories found alongside the two last mentioned titles in David Marcus' recent anthology (23) one becomes aware that the dominant mood is one of relativism, of weariness, of disgust, of a feeling of absurdity. The same is true of the famous « Guests of the Nation » by Frank O'Connor, of « The Patriot Son » by Mary Lavin, of « Scoop » by James Plunkett (and one could have chosen the much more typical « The Wearin' of the Green » (24) by the same author), and of the unusual « An Aspect of the Rising » by Tom MacIntyre in which the Republican tradition is embodied in a prostitute who, before going to her gainful employment, stops under the official residence of President de Valera and abuses him as a traitor.

Before becoming the subject matter of the short story the theme of heroism has to pass through an individual sensibility, and rather than the praise of high deeds, authors now prefer a scepticism prompted by the spirit of the age. Moreover, the anecdote itself, heroic or otherwise, cannot be the whole of the short story and, after the fictional discourse has abandoned the hearth or the camp fire and settled down in the printed page, exceptional destinies and protagonists fade into the background.

Henceforth the genre is open only to material that springs from everyday life and eschews more exotic sources.

Carleton understood this lesson, in part at least. According to his biographer D.J. O'Donoghue he had a high opinion of the *realist truth* of his work :

> It is told of Carleton that when somebody said to him that his pictures of Irish life were « really more reliable than those of Mrs S.C. Hall » he boisterously answered « Why, of course, they are ! Did she ever live with the people as I did ? Did she ever dance and fight with them as I did ? Did she ever get drunk with them as I did ? » (25)

(This last question is of course highly rhetorical when one thinks of the energetic and extremely virtuous wife of Samuel Carter Hall ; a puritanical lady who practised Victorian charity and threw herself heart and soul into the Temperance Crusade).

Carleton expresses an opinion about some of his stories that is probably valid for all the others.

> My « Lough Derg Pilgrim »... resembles a coloured photograph... there is not a fact or incident which is not detailed with the minuteness of the strictest truth and authenticity (26).

If Carleton were to be taken literally then his work would not be pertinent to the present article. But the fact remains that he is at the source of a development, which, because of his lack of education and an absence of models, he was unable to exploit fully. Besides he had no immediate successors and he lucidly saw the reasons for this in the immediate aftermath of the Great Famine :

> Banim and Griffin are gone and I will soon follow them — *ultimus Romanorum*, and after that will come a lull, an obscurity of perhaps half a century, when a new condition of civil society and a new phase of manners and habits among the people — for this is a *transition* state — may introduce new fields and new tastes for other writers (27).

In fact the subsequent history of the short story in Ireland was going to know fewer than fifty barren years, at least if one thinks of the Irish cousins, Edith Somerville and Martin Ross whose work should not be too systematically contrasted with their great predecessor's. Like him they use rural material, they are as sensitive to laughter as to tears, and they show the same gift for rendering linguistic particularities. Such points of resemblance are more important than the obvious differences, of social class, which from another point of view would place the two aristocratic writers in the lineage of Maria Edgeworth or in that of William Hamilton Maxwell in his *Wild Sports of the West* (28) rather than in step with the peasant writers. But their class position does add a patronizing touch to their humour and introduces echoes of the insecurity of a doomed society.

The greatest gap between the short stories of the cousins and those of Carleton lies in the artistic education and consciousness of their authors. Somerville and Ross are anything but self-educated. They were acquainted with the English tradition in which they admired, among other storytellers, Kipling. While a student at the Ecole des Beaux-Arts in Paris Edith had, before George Moore, come into contact with the French tradition. Their compositions do not show the improvisation and inconsistency of those of the author of *Traits and Stories*. Each story has a coherent internal structure and each collection also shows a careful overall structure involving a common framework, a common protagonist (29) and variations on a theme that ultimately reveals its unity, that of the disharmony between man and the world which surrounds him. Details and isolated effects are all subordinated to a general design based on economy, progression, crisis and dénouement.

One wonders therefore at the way the work of these two writers is neglected while George Moore and James Joyce are proclaimed as the fathers of the modern Irish short story. Ignorance is not the only explanation of this state of affairs ; the windows of the Great Houses of Somerville and Ross were too tightly closed and their lands too strictly reserved for the horses and hounds. The formal perfection of their work could not make up for such deficiency.

George Moore, a scrupulous and sophisticated writer, opens his work to an outside world that is much wider and that his personal dialectics make him successively love and chastise, which situates him in a modern Irish tradition that expresses the disenchantment of individuals with a milieu (generally rural) which is narrow, gossipy, banal, priest-ridden, crushed by taboos and numb to feelings of beauty and pleasure.

He stated in his preface to *Celibate Lives* that he preferred « soul cries » to adventures. Nevertheless it is only with the work of Joyce that « adventures » either disappear totally or become a mere occasion for an internal vision which humanizes everything, even the city of Dublin perceived like a vast paralysed body remembering the various moments of its private and public life while death approaches — one has only to think of the title of the last story in *Dubliners*.

The new lineage, more accomplished and less prolific, is now, for better or worse, established.

Between them the two traditions exhaust nearly all the possibilities. Admittedly the new Irish short story will show the colours of various possibilities, become more daring and sometimes indiscreet, yet its metamorphoses will be more formal or ephemeral responding to vogues of technique and manners, than fundamental. But of course the century is not yet over.

# NOTES

1. Frank O'Connor : *The Lonely Voice*, 1962 ; London, Macmillan, 1965.
2. See my own study, « A Question of Inheritance », p. 27 of *The Irish Novel in Our Time*, P. Rafroidi and M. Harmon, eds., Lille, P.U.L., 1976.
3. See René Godenne : *La nouvelle française*, Paris, P.U.F., 1974.
4. Charles Robert Maturin : « Leixlip Castle », *The Literary Souvenir*, london, Hurst and Robinson, 1825.
5. Fitzjames O'Brien:« The Wondersmith » : *Poems and Stories of Fitzjames O'Brien*, ed. William Winter. Boston, J.R. Osgood and Co., 1881, p. 177.
6. Bram Stoker : « The Squaw » : *Dracula's Guest and Other Weird Stories*, London, Routledge and Sons, 1914, p. 45.
7. Joseph Sheridan Lefanu : *In A Glass Darkly*, London, Bentley, 1872.
8. Mario Praz : *The Romantic Agony*, Oxford University Press, 1933 ; 2nd edition, 1951, etc.
9. Roger Caillois : *Anthologie du fantastique*, Paris, Gallimard ; Club Français du Livre, 1958.
10. Tzvetan Todorov : *Introduction à la littérature fantastique*, Paris, Editions du Seuil, 1970.
11. V.S. Pritchett, Introduction to Lefanu's *In A Glass Darkly*, London, John Lehman, 1947.
12. Joseph Sheridan Lefanu, first published as part of *The House by the Churchyard* in the *Dublin University Magazine* for 1861-2. Republished separately later under the title « The Authentic Narrative of the Ghost of a Hand ».
13. Fitzjames O'Brien : « What Was It ? A Mystery » (signed « Harry Escott ») first published in *Harper's New Monthly Magazine*, XVIII, March 1859, pp. 504-9.
14. W.B. Yeats : *Fairy and Folk Tales of the Irish Peasantry* (1888), *Irish Fairy Tales* (1892).
15. E.g. :
Stith Thompson : *Motif Index of Folk Literature*, Bloomington, Indiana, 1955-8.
Antti Aarne and Stith Thompson : *The Types of the Folktale*, Helsinki, 1961.
O'Suilleabháin and Christiansen : *The Types of the Irish Folktale, ibid.*, 1963.
16. William Carleton : *Traits and Stories of the Irish Peasantry*, Dublin, W.M. Curry, 1830, vol. 1.
17. William Carleton : *Tales and Sketches*, Dublin, J. Duffy, 1845.
18. William Carleton : *Traits and Stories of the Irish Peasantry*, 2nd series, Dublin W.F. Wakeman, 1833, vol. 1.
19. Gerald Griffin : *Tales of My Neighbourhood*, London, Saunders and Otley, 1835, vol. 1.
20. James Stephens : *Etched in Moonlight*, London, Macmillan and Co., 1928.
21. See, however, Richard Finneran : *The Prose Fiction of W.B. Yeats*, Dublin, The Dolmen Press, 1973.
22. Maurice Walsh : *Green Rushes*, London and Edinburgh, W. and R. Chambers, 1927.
23. David Marcus : *Tears of the Shamrock*, London, Wolfe Publishing, 1972.
24. James Plunkett : *The Trusting and the Maimed*, London, Hutchinson, 1959.
25. Quoted by D.J. O'Donoghue : *The Life of William Carleton*, London, Downey and Co., 1896.
26. *Id.*
27. *Id.*

28. William Hamilton Maxwell : *Wild Sports of the West*, London, R. Bentley, 1832.

29. Major Yeates in *Experiences of an Irish R.M.*, London, Longmans, 1898, and *Further Experiences of an Irish R.M.*, ibid., 1908.

# IMAGINATIVE RESPONSE VERSUS AUTHORITY STRUCTURES. A THEME OF THE ANGLO-IRISH SHORT STORY

## David NORRIS

### BACKGROUND

The characteristic elements of the Anglo-Irish short story can be traced back in origin to a complex root-system of commingled social, political and cultural factors. I am, of course, conscious that the potential variety of which even so apparently constricting a form as the short story is capable in the hands of an artist, is great enough for there to be more than a hint of risk in my suggesting detectable special characteristics in our local specimen of the genre. Moreover, the example of E.M. Forster who consumed an entire volume in an attempt to « salt the tail » of his own chosen literary form, and emerged with an inexplosive formula for the novel as « a prose fiction of a certain length » is a salutary reminder that any enquiry as to *what is* the Anglo-Irish short story has a rhetorical flavour almost as strong as Captain Boyle's cosmic query anent the moon and the stars. A daarlin' question it may well indeed be but one to which the appropriate response is tentative rather than dogmatic, sensitive rather than mechanical.

Therefore I am concerned not to concoct « a receipt to make an Anglo-Irish short story » but instead to propose for examination a theme which, although treated with varying degrees of sophistication, is common to all significant writers in the form. This theme is that of the conflict between the individual's capacity for developing an imaginative response to his environment, and those forces I have characterized in my title as « authority structures » — which can be either the acknowledged public focus of organizational power represented by Church and State and their respective officers, or more frequently the subtle unacknowledged and internalized restrictions on personal growth inherent in us all. It is the universal tension between the dynamic and the static, between the accepting respectable members of a conventional society, and the outsider, the individualist, suspect because of his deliberate distance from received opinions, and his questioning either deliberately and directly, or implicitly by his quality of apartness of some of the traditional assumptions by which society believes itself to function.

What distinguishes our group of writers is not just their consensus in dealing with the subject of individuality, but also their common possession of a value system which places as touchstone in the human drama the existence or absence, survival or destruction in the central characters of their stories of qualities enabling them to respond positively, imaginatively, even creatively to the life that surrounds them. It is by this test, crudely speaking, that the sheep are separated from the goats, and it is fascinating to watch how a succession of writers stretching from Padraic O'Conaire and Seumas O'Kelly, through Somerville and Ross on up to Frank O'Connor, Sean O'Faolain and Mary Lavin, cross the boundaries of what we may assume to be their background preconceptions about class, religion and politics, to endorse those figures in their work who come closest to embodying this trait. The question of imaginative response is pervasive, almost a general condition which suffuses the atmosphere of many stories with its own subtle colouring. It underlies a whole system of imagery in which suggestions of energy, brightness, movement and organic growth are used to indicate the presence of an inner imaginative life. It finds expression in the presence at the centre of these stories of characters who, seen perhaps in some vivid moment of joy or grief, perceptions undimmed by the antiseptic anodynes of convention and cliché, bring a heightened sensitivity to this and each subsequent encounter with reality.

Frank O'Connor describes the subject of the short story as being not a hero, but what he terms a « submerged population group » (1). This is one natural resource in which our country is unusually rich. By the middle of the last century, for a complexity of historical factors known sometimes in patriotic shorthand as « the 700 years of brutal British oppression », but for our purposes more conveniently if nearly as simplistically regarded as a battle between forces that were on the one hand Gaelic tribal and imaginative, and on the other British imperial and rational, the Irish people as a whole could be regarded as constituting just such a group. In the turbulence of nineteenth century Ireland, the different traditions in the Island were preparing for a final decisive clash, not only on the political front but also at a linguistic and cultural level, as the old native Irish culture that was largely oral, delighted in performance and improvisation and implied an audience, gave way after the famine to the weight and authority of a written tradition of verse, prose and drama in English, a language that was cosmopolitan and concrete.

This submerged population group, passively existing as subject matter, was suddenly charged with potential for many Irish writers by the electrifying political changes occurring in the second decade of the twentieth century. As writers are frequently attracted by the spontaneous release of energy generated in a revolutionary situation, it was inevitable that the events of Easter 1916, the result of a volatile combination of poetical patriotism and slum socialism, should capture the imagination of young men such as O'Connor, O'Faolain and O'Flaherty. But as even Mao Tse Tung discovered, the lava flow of revolution has an innate tendency to thicken and grow sluggish as new institutions crystallize out dedicated to harnessing, channelling and finally inhibiting until the next eruption, the release of energy. As Frank O'Connor was later to write of the civil war period — « What neither group saw was that every word we said, every act we committed, was a destruction of the improvisation and what we were bringing about was a new establishment of Church and State in which imagination would play no part, and young men and women would emigrate to the ends of the earth, not because the country was poor, but because it was mediocre » (2).

So Ireland's young writers found themselves bewildered onlookers as the curtain rose on the new State and out from the protection of the wings marched, in place of the noble army of martyrs, warriors, musicians and peasants of the dream, — a procession of small farmers and smaller business-men, seminarians and civil servants, gombeen men and party hacks, censors, sneerers and begrudgers, bearing like unwise men from the west their gifts of bureaucracy, hypocrisy and orthodoxy. Little enough, it turned out, had really changed. A hundred years previously Maria Edgeworth had used the short narrative to demonstrate with prophetic irony in *Castle Rackrent* that the rise of the Quirkes had little connection with the liberation of the masses. In the process of achieving power Jason Quirke becomes the rackrent of the new dispensation. The novelist John Broderick trenchantly underlines the relevance of this fable in a recent review. Commenting upon the difference between revolution and rebellion he says : « Most of the patriot politicians were content with the latter : more than willing to take over existing institutions, rather than change them. As a result, all that happened was that the country ended up with new backsides in the old saddles ; and most of them could not even ride » (3). However, intelligent dissent was now heard from within the ranks of those whose loyalty to Ireland could not be impugned. One of the tools used by these revolutionaries turned writers to gauge the spiritual well-being of the State they had helped to create was the short story form, and among the classic indicators common to writers of integrity was the question of the encouragement or inhibition by community pressures of the imaginative life of the individual.

EXEMPLUM

Frank O'Connor refers in the introduction to both his collection of Modern Irish short stories and to *The Lonely Voice* to the preference shown by folk storytellers such as Timothy Buckley, The Tailor of Gougane Bara, for « marvels ». He rightly regards this as symptomatic of a difference of emphasis between the oral and written forms of storytelling. The significance of incident for its own sake to the traditional teller of tales, the first requirement of whose art is to engage and hold the attention of an easily distracted audience, is clear. Indeed there is a tendency for such stories to remain at the level of anecdote as sometimes happened in the tailor's own pieces.

However, O'Connor's attempts to shake off the idea of an audience entirely are disingenuous and probably not unconnected with the childhood desire, born of embarrassment, to disown the shabby disreputable figure of his paternal grandmother, who represented aspects of Irish peasant life unpalatable to his adolescent pride. The miseries of shame caused by her appearance and eating habits are stingingly real as recounted in *An Only Child* (4). Yet he remembered also her repertoire of intricate Gaelic poetry and when he came to write the story in which she is the central figure (« The Long Road to Ummera »), he allowed the ancestral vitality, almost smothered in her shrivelled old form, to triumph over the middle class pretence of her grocer son. His world with its thriving business, little house in Sunday's Well, carpets, china and chiming clocks, is no match for the simple magic of the words she forces him to repeat over her coffin — « Neighbours, this is Abby, Batty Heige's daughter, that kept her promise to ye at the end of all » (5). In this story O'Connor as artist shows an intuitive understanding of the audience within an audience, a concept also beautifully handled by Somerville and Ross in « Lisheen Races Second Hand », a small masterpiece which O'Connor was prevented by critical rigidity from valuing accurately.

Regardless of theorizing, any story is dead unless it has at least a potential audience of some kind. Despite the fact that different criteria may be applied in judging a story by a listening rather than a reading public, yet however the balance of emphasis between the basic elements of the aesthetic equation may shift, the elements themselves remain the same — artist, material and audience. The example of a brief analysis of three stories may help to demonstrate the nature of this balance, its relationship to the transition from an oral to a written culture and the significance of these factors for our examination of the theme of imaginative response. I have deliberately selected three stories in which the crucial narrative incident is the same, the striking of a bargain. The stories represent three distinct stages in the development of the form.

The first example is by Padraic O'Conaire, a travelling storyteller, born in Galway in 1882 and so curiously an exact contemporary of James Joyce. The story « My Little Black Ass » (6), familiar to generations of Irish school children as an example of limpid Irish prose, is a good representative of a story very close in feeling to the oral tradition. O'Conaire tells with simple humour how he came to possess the little black donkey which became his constant travelling companion on the roads of

Ireland. Greatly taken with the appearance of the beast when he first sees it at a fair in Kinvara, he makes an offer of one pound for him to his tinker owners. They respond in the manner of their kind with exaggerated praise of the donkey's looks, intelligence and personality, finally agreeing to a price of « a pound and sixpence for each of the children ». Once this is settled on, tinker children miraculously materialize from everywhere and nowhere. The author extracts himself from the crowd with the donkey, whose stubbornness he overcomes by a ruse.

The primacy of incident in itself here suggests anecdote. Concentration is focussed on the personality of the storyteller, and the imaginative element lies in his skill in unfolding the tale and presenting humorously his ability to stand his ground in a battle of wits with first the tinkers and secondly the donkey itself. There is no attempt to refine the secondary impact of narrative through an extended development of imagery.

The second example — Seumas O'Kelly's « The Can with the Diamond Notch » (7) — employs an almost identical incident at its narrative focus. Festus Clasby, a prosperous merchant, is cheated by tinkers in a haggling match over a tin can. This time, however, although obviously close to traditional oral sources, the story is conceived primarily as a piece of *writing*. Imagery and incident are of equal importance. Clasby himself is, for example, surrounded by words denoting a devotion to the values of the market place — accounts, figures, mortgage, credit, profit, financial, price, business, shop, counter, security, debtors, purchases, insurance policy, cheaply, commercial, merchandise, etc... The meaning of the story is not entirely contained in the action described, but is revealed in the suggestive power of a series of images whose deliberate structuring would probably be beyond the power of any spontaneous performance. The mood is reflective rather than picaresque.

The tinker Mac an Ward (whose name is Irish for son of the poet) solicits a response from Clasby to the brightness of the can with the persuasive rhetoric of the poet. Clasby, however, sees the article in a utilitarian rather than an aesthetic light. The opening section of the story has shown us Clasby as a man representative of a newly emerging native bourgeoisie whose values are bounded by notions of commerce and respectability. The conflict is therefore not just between himself and the tinkers over a tin can, but between two opposed views of life, one shrewd, calculating and narrow, the other jubilant, spontaneous and poetic. It is an opposition reflected in Herbert's lines

« A man that looks on glasse
On it may stay his eye ;
Or if he pleaseth, through it passe
And then the heav'n espie ».

(« The Elixer »).

Clasby, looking on glass, will always see a window rather than a view. His ultimate defeat is at the hands of the rich possibilities of life which he denies, rather than at the itchy fingers of Mac an Ward's tribe. Before ever he met the tinker we noted that his conversation was merely the platitudinous accompaniment to a business deal ; the trust placed in him was « technical », he was a « human casket », and even his respectability a dark illusion to be dispelled by the penetrating gleam of eloquent roguery. He has cheated himself by shrivelling to the measure of conventionality for the sake of his business ; the swindle of the can with the diamond notch is only an external confirmation of his spiritual poverty.

Mary Lavin's « Frail Vessel » (8) represents a further sophistication of this idea. The incident in terms of the actual striking of the bargain (in this case a related series of bargains) has receded in importance, as subtlety of language comes into its own. There is no secondary audience within the story. What the suggestive power of the words discloses is a complex opposition of attitudes. Meaning radiates from but is not confined to or explainable in terms of incident or anecdote. Information comes to us filtered through the consciousness of one of the central characters — Bedelia. The action takes place during the year following her mother's death, a year which sees both her own marriage and that of her sister Liddy.

Mary Lavin explores the contrasting philosophies of life of the two sisters in terms of their attitudes to their respective marriages.

Bedelia's viewpoint, that marriage is a practical rather than a romantic expedient, finds expression through a vocabulary whose utilitarianism and narrowness of range suggest a constriction similar to that revealed in O'Kelly's Festus Clasby. In the first two paragraphs of the story she sees herself as having placed her

sister under an obligation, a favourite game of Bedelia types in
Lavin's work. « Wasn't it partly for her sake that she and Daniel
had gone on with the arrangements... », indicates the consonance
of her outlook with that of the community, « people knew that
was the reason », and prophetically characterizes her marriage as
« an immediate formal settlement » (9). Money is power to
Bedelia, her values are all commercial, and so she is caught
unawares by the romance that develops between her sister and
Alphonsus O'Brien, a down-at-heel solicitor. She tellingly
misinterprets the growing familiarity of Liddy and O'Brien and
keeps Liddy's attempts at sisterly contact at bay by a fusillade of
financial imagery — « No rent, compensate, loss, store space,
question of money, standard of living, your little contribution,
keeping accounts » (10), — the machine-like rattle of the words
riddles the tentative approach as effectively as bullets. At the end
of the story, having bargained Alphonsus O'Brien out of Liddy's
life only to discover that she, like herself, is pregnant, and
therefore useless as an unpaid skivvy Bedelia reveals her true
nature, screaming at her sister that she will never see her
husband again. Liddy's whispered reply « even so » is « inexplicable » indeed, for where could such a phrase be entered in the
neatly balanced account books of a life like Bedelia's.

The story is powerful because it is subtly drawn. Bedelia is not
a monster, rather a figure of pathos. Judged conventionally her
actions are justifiable, while Liddy could be regarded as irres-
ponsible. But Liddy was too inwardly alive to be trapped by
convention. She responds to the possibility of romance presented
by even so unlikely a figure as Alphonsus O'Brien, and her
response reveals to Bedelia a dimension of experience from which
she is excluded. As in O'Kelly's story it is the materialist who is
discomfited with in this case the added torment of being
tantalizingly conscious of a warm, pliant world of human
relationship to which the frozen heart has no access.

SURVEY

We begin this whirlwind tour of the Anglo-Irish short story
with a look at the work of George Moore, James Joyce and
Somerville and Ross, whom I have grouped together because
they were the first writers of the twentieth century to achieve
distinction in the form. I take the unpopular position of de-

precating the posthumous reflation of Moore's reputation as a short story writer. His stories seem to me a string of highly artificial pearls despite the fact that they have been gobbled down by some commentators with the uncritical relish of real swine. There is always about him a touch of the grand seigneur — the dilettante of his country's social and economic problems. His tone moreover is unflaggingly patronizing and although he usually manages to confine this to artistic and intellectual rather than overtly social attitudes, one is left with an unpleasant suspicion that his brutish description of « Mickey Moran » as a representative Irish peasant in « Parnell and His Island » (11) betrays his real position in the matter.

He does, it is true, essay an analysis of those forces in society tending to stunt the development of the imaginative life of the individual, but he is too gross, too directly polemical and too lacking in restraint for the impact of much of his work to survive the changes in Irish society that have rendered the greater part of his attack redundant. His fault is one of much nineteenth century writing, that of suspending the dramatization of an action in order to sermonize, although in Moore's case the « sermons » are as likely to demonstrate his own cosmopolitan cleverness as the profundity of his insight into the lives of his contemporaries. The writing has been compared to that of James Joyce, and indeed they do share certain targets, but the mood in Joyce to which Moore is closest is not the oblique artistry of any of the published works, but rather the shapeless frontal fury of Stephen Hero.

In the first story of The Untilled Field (12), « In the Clay », a sculptor shakes the dust of Ireland off his feet when a nude statue he has created is smashed at the indirect instigation of a philistine priest. Unfortunately the obvious symbolism is matched by an equally simplistic declamatory style. Other inhabitants of the untilled field, such as Julia Cahill and Ned Carmody, also scrape its mud off their boots in later stories before heading off to America or the continent in search of freedom, away from the interference of the ubiquitous clergy. The theme is as impeccable as its treatment is lamentable. Another volume of stories, Celibate Lives, apparently replete with subjects sympathetic to our analysis, proves on examination to be merely a literary confection, the product of Moore's mature spinsterhood. Despite references on the dust jacket of its latest edition to 'the avant garde` and `authenticity`, and to the inclusion of one story about an Edwardian drop-out and another about two female transvestites, gentle readers need not agitate themselves. It is as we discover all too soon just that nice Mr. Moore being deliciously wicked. For all his continental airs, Moore as a storyteller is a provincial.

« Provincials » in fact was the name James Joyce intended giving to a sequel to *Dubliners* perhaps in emulation of Moore (13). On the whole, however, Joyce did not care for *The Untilled Field* which he read while working on his own volume of stories (14) and would probably have been incensed at the suggestions now current that he was heavily influenced by Moore's work in the genre. One hesitates to attempt a thumbnail sketch of a work of complex meaning like *Dubliners* (15), nevertheless even such a cursory glance as space permits shows that in his « chapter of the moral history » (16) of Ireland, Joyce is concerned with a variation on our theme, and like Moore comes to see social and religious structures in Ireland as involved in a relationship of parasitic symbiosis with the individual. The citizens of his fictional city are trapped, their imaginative faculties paralysed by scrupulous religiosity (« The Sisters »), filial duty (« Eveline ») or the adjustments of personal attitude required to hold down even a menial job (« Counterparts », « The Boarding House »), looking forever over their individual shoulders to see « what *they* would say » once a back was turned. The « style of scrupulous meanness » (17) acts like a surgical instrument peeling away layers of adipose tissue to lay bare a language system so drained and weary that it can no longer express the sharpness of personally experienced reality. Even the principle of beauty is enervated and unreal. Eliza's statement that the dead priest makes « a beautiful corpse » contrasts strangely with the clearer observation of the boy in the first story — « There he lay, solemn and copious, vested as for the altar, his hands loosely retaining a chalice. His face was very truculent, grey and massive with black cavernous nostrils and circled by a scanty white fur » (18) — while in the final story Mrs Malin's characterization of everything from scenery to fish as being also « beautiful » suggests a similar anaesthetization of response.

The world of Somerville and Ross's R.M. stories could hardly provide a more startling contrast to the work of Joyce. Nevertheless he himself would probably not grudge these two daughters of the Big House their niche in literary history, if only for the deliberateness of their art and the precise way in which they calculate the effect of each word on the general texture of their prose. There is, moreover, a striking similarity between humourless English condescension as portrayed in Somerville and Ross characters such as Leigh Kelway (« Lisheen Races Second Hand ») (19) and Maxwell Bruce (« The Last Day of Shraft ») (20), and Joyce's later presentation of Haines in *Ulysses*. The « Protestant Ladies » are unfortunate however in that their reputation has been stranded by historical accident ; for while the ethos of their world was firmly established, they were the immediate predecessors of, and are often judged in the company of writers who saw the exploration of the question of Irish National identity as among the main functions of the new literature, O'Connor, O'Faolain and O'Flaherty. As a consequence, a combination of literary pomposity and national sentiment has obscured the proper evaluation of their work, and made even so sensitive a critic as Frank O'Connor apologize for having been guilty of « rereading the Irish R.M. off and on for forty years for the mere pleasure of it » (21).

Indeed, with regard to the general practice of literary criticism as a trade, I have memories, pleasing in retrospect, of a slightly pretentious literary meeting in Dublin, at which in response to some timid query from my schoolboy self the late Brendan Behan opined that « the critic is like a eunuch in a harem. He sees the job done every night but he can't do it himself ». One of the first of these eunuchoid commentators to carp at the writing of Somerville and Ross was Ernest Boyd (22). Boyd initiated the still continuing attempts to divert critical attention away from the genuine achievement of the R.M. Stories into the consideration of something regarded as more « serious » i.e. *The Real Charlotte*, a book of such unreadable though doubtless « worthy » dullness that only a highly specialized variety of bookworm could bore its way into the soggy interior. It remains the prey of such insects and is now thoroughly riddled with evidences of their passage, despite the fact that it is by no means so accurate, complete or convincing an account of protestant, Anglo-Irish life as, for example, Leland Bardwell's recent *Girl on a Bicycle* (23).

The R.M. stories are the literary equivalent of sporting prints. Like Jane Austen, the authors recognized and indeed made a virtue of their limitations. It is canvas rather than viewpoint that

is foreshortened. Accusations of a patronizing tone or of stage
Irishry are ludicrously wide of the mark and a comparison of the
treatment of Irish court procedures in, for example, Seumas
O'Kelly's « The Fairy Bush » (from a leprechanaiocht of pish-
roguery and peasant cunning entitled « The Leprechaun of
Kilmeen »), Frank O'Connor's « Legal Aid », and Somerville and
Ross's « The Boat's Share » will indicate quite clearly that had
the authors of the R.M. stories been Edith *O'Kelly* and Martin
*O'Connor* such imputations against them would never have arisen.

The R.M. himself represents the rational world defeated by the
humorous imaginative anarchy of the Gaelic mind. He admi-
nisters a British legal system that had descended upon the native
Irish in a manner akin to the colonial processes described by
Conrad in *Heart of Darkness* — « They were called criminals, and
the outraged law, like the bursting shells, had come to them, an
insoluble mystery from the sea » (24).

However, the Irish peasantry of Somerville and Ross live
undefeated in their vitality of language, and know well how to
turn the « mysteries » of conventional expectation to their own
advantage —

a wrathful English voice asked how much longer the train was
going to wait. The station-master, who was at the moment
engrossed in conversation with the guard and a man who was
carrying a long parcel wrapped in newspaper, looked round,
and said gravely :
« Well now, that's a mystery! »
The man with the parcel turned away, and convulsively
studied a poster. The guard put his hand over his mouth.
The voice, still more wrathfully, demanded the earliest hour
at which its owner could get to Belfast.
« Ye'll be asking me next when I take me breakfast »,
replied the station-master, without haste or palpable annoyance.
The window went up again with a bang... (25)

It is clear from such stories as « The Last Day of Shraft » (26)
that Somerville and Ross recognized and sympathized with the
techniques of subterranean survival adopted by Irish folk culture.
There is, moreover, in this story an accuracy of observation, a
Breughelesque realism of detail, so that although we are looking

inside a nineteenth century Irish peasant cabin, what we see are universal human types in a universal human situation. The description of the singing of « Ned (sic) Flaherty's Drake » is a model of artistic economy. The relationship between the rival poets is deftly and dramatically presented and what is in fact a genuine folk ballad introduced in what anyone who has attended oiche cheoil or chéilí will recognize as a perfectly realized atmosphere. The writers moreover show themselves aware of a complex inter-relationship between performers and audience, with the Englishman, Maxwell, playing a crucial though passive and easily manipulated role as point of reference.

A similar depiction of the tweedy dabblings of British officialdom in the Gaelic way of life is given in « Lisheen Races Second Hand » (27). Leigh Kelway, private secretary to Lord Waterbury, is under the impression that he can come to grips with Irish reality, « master the brogue » and embody his insights in a novel after one brief official visit. We find him lodged, by a series of mishaps, in a roadside cottage bulging with returning race-goers, who display a native skill in the art of narrative that his projected novel would do well to equal. Slipper's performance as a storyteller delights an audience of varying degrees of sophistication, the least aware member of which is actually Kelway himself. The rest of the gathering observe with ironic amusement as the magic of Slipper's narrative gradually uncoils the pukka figure of the Englishman from his reserve, like a python at the mercy of a Hindu snake-charmer's rhythmic wiles. At the crisis, the stiff upper lip bristles, then softens to an inane droop as the premises of his unimaginative prosaic world are swept away by the force of a celtic combination of reality and fantasy. In Slipper's skill at weaving yarns, as in the originality and freshness of speech of a series of matriarchs like Mrs Cadogan, who deserve to take their places with the Slipslops, Malaprops, and Bessie Burgesses of literature, Somerville and Ross reveal to us an imaginative vitality that, regardless of social distinctions, mark these peasant characters as the human superiors of all such as Leigh Kelway.

Slipper and his storytelling would find a natural welcome in the world of my next group of writers who came themselves from « authentic » peasant stock — Padraic O'Conaire, Seumas O'Kelly and Liam O'Flaherty. Written in Irish in the original, O'Conaire's work is relevant to us mainly as an example of the art of the seanachai, but stories such as « Put to the Rack » (28) and « Little Marcus's Nora » (29) are worth pausing over for themselves, for they show how broad was the scope and sympathy of such a craftsman, and how divorced from reality the narrow puritanism of the pseudo-celts of the Playboy riots. « Put to the Rack » deals with the problem of sexual identity as experienced by a young girl sold into legal concubinage by her father. She finds the physical intimacy of marriage with an older and uncouth man so gross that she deserts him, only to return when she discovers herself pregnant. She dies in childbirth, and the narrator expresses contempt for the husband's callous pleasure at the birth of his son.

« Little Marcus's Nora » is a story unfortunately symptomatic of the fate of many inexperienced country girls. Nora, daughter of man who has improved himself and subsequently hung the weight of his respectability round his children's necks, is seduced by a young college student, and finally emigrates to London where she winds up on the streets. After some years of this life she chances across her erstwhile lover outside a theatre. O'Conaire's subtlety as a storyteller manifests itself in Nora's desperate avoidance of what could have been a richly sentimental meeting. This incident shocks her into returning to Ireland where the proceeds of her streetwalking, regularly sent home, have ironically increased the family's prestige in the community. However, her London habits have become engrained and when she gets drunk at the local pattern, her father exports her back to England. It is remarkable how O'Conaire skirts the pitfalls of moralizing on the one hand, and sentimentalizing on the other in both these stories, where the false values of a rural society are seen as first alienating and then destroying vital young shoots of life.

The atmosphere of Seumas O'Kelly's « The Weaver's Grave » (30) is less representational than that of O'Conaire's tales, its truths poetic and symbolic rather than social, yet it too deals with matter pertinent to our enquiry. The subject is close to the universal « why » of E.M. Forster's *A Room with a View*, and for O'Kelly, as for old Mr. Emmerson in that novel, « By the side of the everlasting Why there is a Yes, a transitory Yes if you like, but a Yes » (31), O'Kelly's treatment is on the whole the more successful, relying for its resolution upon the acceptance by the central characters of a world in which the only reality is sub-

jective and imaginative, whereas Forster's final puny harmony
— a domestic vignette of Lucy darning George's socks — fails
totally to balance the cataclysmic question of the opening
chapters. Moreover, while in Forster the prevailing mood of social
comedy is periodically fractured by the irruption of unabsorbed
globules of symbolism, O'Kelly employs a stylistically pleasing
consistence of tone and imagery.

The subsidiary characters of « The Weaver's Grave » are
stylized, almost emblematic figures. Meehaul Lynskey, the
nail-maker, has a chinkling ring to his name, a warped body,
small sharp eyes and the spiritual horizons of a nail-making
machine. Cahir Bowes, heavy and stony as his name and
occupation, has keen grey eyes, glint-like as the mountains of
stone he has broken, and a view of life also constricted by his
former occupation. The repetitious blows of age have reduced
these two old men to ciphers, but years alone cannot dim Malachi
Roohan whose spirit of nihilism, wonderful but terrible in its
honesty, blasts away cant, caution and pretence —

One flash of the eyelids and everything in this world is gone...
   « The world is only a dream, and a dream is nothing at all !
We all want to waken up out of the great nothingness of this
world ».
   « And, please God, we will », said Nan.
   « You can tell all the world from me », said the cooper,
« that it won't ».
   « And why won't we, Father ? »
   « Because », said the old man, « we ourselves are the dream.
When we're over the dream is over with us. That's why » (32).

The bleakness of the old man's prophecy seems to operate
subliminally on the widow, wakening her to experience like a
frosty disintegration of the soil that allows new growth. The fiery
beauty of the evening star may call forth only paltriness from the
withered heart of Meehaul Lynskey, but the widow has already
begun to personalize the human beauty of one of the twin
gravediggers. Their handsomeness had earlier seemed dulled by
its repetition, but now the star shines like a love token over the
head of the man she has silently chosen. By the end of the story
even the digging of a grave has taken on a quality of youth and
joy, as the widow responds to the lilt of human love, passionate
but transitory — 'The earth sang up out of the ground, dark and

rich in colour, gleaming like gold in the deepening twilight of the place (33).

The earth of O'Flaherty's Western Isles is neither so dark nor so rich, and love's bloom in that barren soil is but the span of a day as we see in « Spring Sowing » (34). The grinding toil of the newly weds' relationship with the elements permits little in the way of self realization. One brief spark of warmth struck from human passion thaws them into momentary individuality before this too is snuffed out and they return to anonymous peasant-hood. Of course it is not only elemental forces that conspire against the development of the individual response. « The Fairy Goose » (35), one of O'Flaherty's best stories, bears an allegorical message to fairy geese and white blackbirds of all kinds as to how society and its structures may deal with them. The goose acts as a catalyst, its oddities releasing latent psychic energies in the small village community. It becomes the focus of a struggle for authority between two rival kinds of magic, the ritual anathe-matizing of the priest and the druid charms of Mary Wiggins, until, a very figure of the rejected artist in its Wildean elegance and refusal to concede to the claims of natural goosehood, its neck is wrung and its innocence trampled by the muddy boots of village louts.

Daniel Corkery, a man of cultivated taste and the mentor of O'Faolain and O'Connor, can seem limited and artificial if contrasted with the earthy vigour of such writing. (Compare, for example, « The Spancelled » with O'Kelly's « Weaver's Grave »). This feeling of narrowness is reinforced by many of the stories of *A Munster Twilight*, his best known collection, whose title suggests a provincial variation of what Joyce called « The Cultic Twalette ». He had, furthermore, a penchant for Irish Gothick, and his attempts to create a suitably twilit ambience call to mind opera or melodrama — the curtains part to disclose the last rays of the sun as they strike romantically the noble ruins of a deserted abbey. — Is the stage set for Benedict, Boucicault, Corkery perhaps ? Paradoxically enough, of the two best stories in the book, one is about an opera company, the other is an eighteenth century romance.

In « The Breath of Life » (36), Ignatius O'Byrne, a retired violinist is resurrected from the back street of a provincial town to play with the orchestra of a visiting opera company. An individualist not only in his intuitive approach to music, but also in his faulty execution, his flat playing brings him into conflict with the structure of the orchestra until, despite the cover provided by the narrator's musicianship, he is detected and dismissed by the conductor. When the spirit of poetic justice strikes this man down with rheumatism disaster threatens, till Ignatius seizes the baton and with some inspired gesture unlocks all the hidden richness of the orchestra. Nevertheless, when the opera company passes on to new engagements the old violinist is left behind — the orchestra is a commercial outfit and inspiration is a dangerously undependable commodity.

Almost a prose version of the Aisling, « Solace » (37) is a powerful depiction of poetic nobility rising beyond the restrictions of social and historical circumstances. The poet, Eoghan Mor O Donovan, feels his little world of toil well lost in the gaining of a poem that trancends and immortalizes the sufferings of himself, his family and his race. His ecstasy of creation seems to echo Horace's — « Exegi monumentum aere perennius » — and he literally and improvidently kills his fatted calf to provide feasting in celebration of his art. In a coda we are provided with the perspective of the master race, with a view of the poet's hosting from an « enlightened » English traveller. He pokes among the cinders of a culture he cannot understand, lamenting the impracticality of the Irish while we who have witnessed the joy of an artist's refusal to be merely a peon, recall the warmth and brave flame of the Bardic fire. (I have not located an exact original for this passage, but it is not entirely unlike a description of the 18c. English traveller, Young (38), which remarks the vivacity, eloquence and love of society of the « common Irish », together with their addiction to hurling (« the cricket of savages » !) and sums us all up as being « hard drinkers and quarrelsome ; great liars, but civil and submissive »).

Even in summary these two stories epitomize the struggle of the creative mind to escape the constraints of conventional response. Corkery is of course also of consequence to us in providing a convenient bridge to his two most famous protégés, who while offering interesting possibilities of contrast and comparison — O'Connor intuitive and discursive where O'Faolain is intellectual and formal — continue with the treatment of this subject in their different ways.

O'Connor's celebrated series of childhood stories deals with the friction between a child and adult institutions which he does not fully comprehend and of which he becomes an unconscious infant parody. « My Oedipus Complex » (39) for example sees the child defining his need for self expression against the formal relationship of marriage, while in « The Drunkard » (40) Larry acts in ironic mimesis of his father's folly, and in « The Idealist » (41) he escapes from the conformist pressures of school into an imaginative world in the invisible presence of first Etonian « toffs » and later Western desperadoes. The ironies become deeper, almost Swiftian, when O'Connor is dealing with the destruction wrought by ideals elevated to the level of rigid orthodoxy in the « mature » world. In « Freedom » (42) and « Guests of the Nation » (43) he expresses shock and disgust at the denial of human qualities for the sake of an abstract principle. As he says in *An Only Child* — « I could be obstinate enough when it came to the killing of unarmed soldiers and girls because this was a basic violation of the imaginative concept of life » (44).

Like Shaw in *John Bull's Other Island* (45), O'Connor shows himself in « The Ugly Duckling » (46) to be aware of the destructive unreality of living too exclusively in the realm of imagination. Nevertheless, it seems safe in the light of the evidence both of his fiction and of his autobiographies to conclude that his turning finally from poetry to storytelling in « celebration of those who for me represented all I should ever know of God », is related to his own response to « the imaginative concept of life ».

O'Faolain's view of the individual as opposed to the collective response in the civil war period is similar to O'Connor's, going even so far as to balance in « The Patriot » (47) the narrow political passion of a Corkery-like orator, Bradley, against the personal fulfilment of the narrator and his bride. However, the most interesting recurrence of the theme of imaginative response is in « Midsummer Night Madness ». The narrator, who is presented from the start as a man sensitive to beauty in nature, is sent on an intelligence mission by the I.R.A. to investigate the inactivity of a local battalion. Its commandant, Stevey Long, has established headquarters in the house of an Anglo-Irish roué — Henn, whose exploits were among the legends of the narrator's childhood. Whatever about the weapons of war, Long has plied the weapons of peace and love not wisely but too well, with the result that old Henn's half tinker servant, Gypsy, has become pregnant. Henn is forced into what he regards as a morganatic marriage to conceal this disreputable fact.

Such a bald statement of the narrative dealing only in action omits a very remarkable factor, the subterranean action of a group of images of the kind described in the opening of this essay as a characteristic indicator of the presence of imaginative life, in attracting the narrator across the boundaries of prejudice and revolutionary commitment, until finally and indeed remarkably he is united in feeling not with his military ally Stevey, but with his traditional enemy, old Henn. And the reason ? Quite simply, these two characters alone share in the story something deeper, more permanent, than divisions of class, ideology or age, — the ability to respond joyously, imaginatively to the experiences of life.

Just as the narrator responds to the summer evening in the opening lines, so old Henn reaches out to the beauty of women whose breasts are « like tulips », an epicurean refinement lost on Long to whom it is all just a question of « great titties ». The conflict between the celebrators of life, and its prudent despoilers, is succinctly drawn in a small scene where Stevey interrupts a discussion of fishing prospects between Gypsy and the old man.

(Stevey's) voice was rough and coarse beside the rich voice of the girl and the cultured voice of the old man.

« Leppin' ? Rise ? Rise how are you ! That was me spittin' when she wasn't looking ».

« Oh, there was a rise » she cried. « I saw their silver bellies shining as they leaped ».

« Ooh » mocked Stevey. « Bellies ! Naughty word ! Ooh ! » (48) (which is fairly ironic, considering the effect his 'leppin' and 'risin' have had on her 'belly').

When one remembers how close O'Faolain was to his own republican involvement when he wrote this story, there is an astonishing integrity about his presentation of the relationships between revolutionary and aristocrat. In later stories analyzing the censorious small-mindedness of the new Free State, O'Faolain maintains this stance. Moreover, the tone is ultimately optimistic as well as comic, and the possibility of a real and courageous stand for artistic and personal freedom shines beyond even the all too human figure of « an old master » like John Aloysius O'Sullivan.

One of the subjects dealt with by both O'Connor (in « The Paragon » (49)) and O'Faolain (in « Up the Bare Stairs » (50)) is the burden of obligation placed on children by their parents' sacrifices, so that they are expected to fulfil, not their own potentialities, but the ambitions and social aspirations of an older generation. In Mary Lavin's world, where Mother Ireland has abandoned her harp for a huster's shop, this facet of Irish, indeed human life, is examined in a remarkable story called « The Widow's Son » (51). This is a tale with two endings ; but both are cul de sacs and it is clearly implied that whatever action the widow takes, and whether her son lives or dies, she has in practice lost him anyway, not through mere physical accident but through the gradual hardening of her own emotional arteries.

Perhaps more representative of Mary Lavin's art are the two stories « Posy » (52) and « The Will » (53). Either could be taken as a perfect illustration of the title of my essay. In both, a central character whose joyful accord with nature is mirrored in the imagery of freshness and organic growth, comes into conflict with the unyielding structure of conventional social attitudes, yet manages to keep the flag (in Posy's case a bright red scarf, and in Lally's a jaunty blue feather) defiantly flying. Most significant of all perhaps, in both stories the clouds part momentarily and the claustrophobic atmosphere of respectability and repression is illuminated by a shaft of imaginative spontaneity whose rays can reach into even the dusty corners of Daniel's heart — « And if he never saw the upper sunlit air, nor ever now would see it, by the thrust of her flight, he knew that somewhere the sun shone » (54).

CONCLUSION

In summary — Ireland's historical evolution produced a « submerged population group » whose culture cherished imagination, spontaneity and performance, and which learnt to value the spirit of independence in a 700 year battle with an alien way of life. Thus the struggle of the imagination against the constraints of rationality, respectability and authority became both a source and a theme of much Anglo-Irish literature and in particular of the form closest to the oral folk tradition, the short story. Moore rails against narrow clericalism stifling the personal impulse ; Joyce presents the citizens of Dublin as victims of a suburban paralysis of the spirit ; Somerville and Ross celebrate secret sources of vitality in the folk artistry of the Irish peasant ; O'Conaire views with compassion the quest for sexual identity in rural Ireland. O'Kelly sees subjective reality as more powerful, even more permanent than the material world ; O'Flaherty shows us the herd instinct at work linking man and animal in brute opposition to uniqueness ; for Corkery the joy of artistic creation conquers circumstance ; in both O'Faolain and O'Connor imagination and sensitivity throw a humane bridge over otherwise impassable chasms ; and in Mary Lavin the clear song of a bird has occasionally the power to drown the shrill note of the cash register. All of these writers reveal to us, in their different ways, the individual consciousness awakening and defining itself against the traditions and assumptions of society.

Stephen Dedalus tells us that « when the soul of man is born in this country there are nets flung at it to hold it back from flight » (55). In the Anglo-Irish short story we see not only the threatening mesh of the nets, but also occasionally a flash of wings marking the triumphant sunward flight of the soul.

# NOTES

1. Frank O'Connor : *The Lonely Voice*, Papermac, p. 18.

2. Frank O'Connor : *An Only Child*, London, Macmillan, 1965, p. 210.

3. John Broderick : « Bards and Bullets » in *Irish Times*, December 10, 1977.

4. Frank O'Connor : *An Only Child*, pp. 19-20.

5. Frank O'Connor : « The Long Road to Ummera » in *The Stories of Frank O'Connor*, Hamish Hamilton, 1965, p. 137.

6. Padraic O'Conaire : « My Little Black Ass » in *Field and Fair*, tr. Cormac Breathnach, Mercier, 1966.

7. Seumas O'Kelly : « The Can with the Diamond Notch » in *Irish Short Stories*, Mercier Press, n.d.

8. Mary Lavin : « Frail Vessel » in *The Stories of Mary Lavin*, Constable, 1964.

9. Lavin : *op. cit.*, p. 1.

10. Lavin : *op. cit.*, p. 9.

11. George Moore : *Parnell and his Island*.

12. George Moore : *The Untilled Field*, T. Fisher Unwin, 1903.

13. James Joyce, letter to Stanislaus Joyce, 12 July, 1905, in *Selected Letters*, ed. Richard Ellman, Faber, 1975, p. 63.

14. *Ibid.*, p. 44.

15. James Joyce : *Dubliners*, Penguin, 1973.

16. James Joyce : *Selected Letters*, p. 83.

17. *Ibid.*, p. 83.

18. James Joyce : *Dubliners*.

19. Somerville and Ross : *Experiences of an Irish R.M.*, Everyman Library, London, Dent ; New York, Dutton, 1969.

20. *Ibid.*

21. Frank O'Connor : *The Lonely Voice*, pp. 34-35.

22. Ernest Boyd : *Ireland's Literary Renaissance*, Dublin, Allen Figgis, 1968, pp. 385-386.

23. Leland Bardwell : *Girl on a Bicycle*, Dublin, Irish Writers Cooperative, 1977.

24. Joseph Conrad : *Heart of Darkness*, Penguin, 1976, pp. 22-3.

25. Somerville and Ross : *op. cit.*, p. 207.

26. *Ibid.*, p. 260.

27. *Ibid.*, p. 56.

28. Padraic O'Conaire : *The Woman at the Window*, Mercier Press, 1966.

29. *Ibid.*

30. Seumas O'Kelly : *The Weaver's Grave*, Dublin, Allen Figgis, 1965.

31. E.M. Forster : *A Room with a View*, Penguin, 1976, p. 32.

32. O'Kelly, *op. cit.*, pp. 50-51.

33. *Ibid.*, p. 75.

34. Liam O'Flaherty : *The Short Stories of Liam O'Flaherty*, Four Square, 1966.

35. *Ibid.*

36. Daniel Corkery : *A Munster Twilight*, Mercier, 1967.

37. *Ibid.*

38. Arthur Young : *A Tour in Ireland 1776-1779*, ed. A.W. Hutton, Irish University Press, 1970, pp. 146-7.

39. Frank O'Connor : *The Stories of Frank O'Connor*, London, Hamish Halmiton, 1965.

40. *Ibid.*
41. *Ibid.*
42. *Ibid.*
43. Frank O'Connor : *Modern Irish Short Stories*, ed. Frank O'Connor, World Classics, 1968.
44. Frank O'Connor : *An Only Child*, p. 240.
45. Bernard Shaw : *John Bull's Other Island*, Constable, 1964, p. 85.
46. Frank O'Connor : *My Oedipus Complex and Other Stories*, Penguin, 1967.
47. Sean O'Faolain : *The Finest Stories of Sean O'Faolain*, Bantam Classics, 1965.
48. *Ibid.*, pp. 17-8.
49. Frank O'Connor : *My Oedipus Complex and Other Stories*.
50. Sean O'Faolain : *The Finest Stories of Sean O'Faolain*.
51. Mary Lavin : *The Stories of Mary Lavin*.
52. *Ibid.*
53. *Ibid.*
54. *Ibid.*
55. James Joyce : *A Portrait of the Artist*, Penguin, 1968, p. 203.

# FIRST IMPRESSIONS : 1968-78

## Maurice HARMON

On April 27, 1968 the *Irish Press* began a weekly page devoted to Irish writing. It was comprised of a short story, or an extract from a novel, and some poems. Writers throughout the country took advantage of this opportunity to have their work featured in a national newspaper, but it was the young and emergent writer who benefited most. Seán O'Faoláin could win first prize in international competitions for the best short story of the year ; Mary Lavin and Benedict Kiely could publish in the *New Yorker* ; Terence de Vere White, William Trevor, Bryan Mac-Mahon, Edna O'Brien and John McGahern, because of their reputations as novelists, could always interest editors and publishers in their short stories. But for the emergent writer the *Irish Press* provided a considerable home readership, recognition where it was most important, a regular outlet, and the stimulus of publication. The success of this revolution may be measured in part by the number of anthologies that have already been published :

*New Irish Writing 1*, edited by David Marcus, Dublin, Dolmen Press (1970).
*Best Irish Short Stories*, edited by David Marcus, London, Paul Elek (1976).
*New Irish Writing*, edited by David Marcus, London, Quartet Books (1976).

*Paddy No More. Modern Irish Short Stories*, Nantucket, Longship Press (1977). Dublin, Wolfhound Press (1978).

*Best Irish Short Stories 2*, edited by David Marcus, London, Paul Elek (1977).

In the above list all but the first are comprised of short stories, all by writers who have had their work featured in the *Irish Press*. In the following list of individual collections of short stories, only Bernard McLaverty is not associated with this newspaper :

Neil Jordan. *Night in Tunisia*, Dublin, Irish Writers' Cooperative (1976).

Maeve Kelly. *A Life of Her Own*, Dublin, Poolbeg Press (1976).

Gillman Noonan. *A Sexual Relationship*, Dublin, Poolbeg Press (1976).

John Feeney. *Mao Dies*, Dublin, Egotist Press (1977).

Maura Treacy. *Sixpence in Her Shoe*, Dublin, Poolbeg Press (1977).

Brian Power. *A Land Not Sown*, Dublin, Egotist Press (1977).

Bernard McLaverty, *Secrets*, Belfast, Blackstaff Press (1977).

In one imaginative gesture, Tim Pat Coogan, editor of the *Irish Press*, and his dedicated literary editor, David Marcus, changed the conditions within which the young writer works. The contrast with the 'fifties and 'sixties is remarkable. At that time writers who had a collection of stories ready for publication were told to write a novel or two first ; then their book of stories might be considered. The appearance of the literary page also helped to make up for the decline of literary magazines in Ireland and the decrease in the number of journals abroad to which the aspiring writer might send his work.

It is of course too soon to assess the new writers. It would be as difficult and hazardous to judge their work now as it would have been to have judged Seán O'Faoláin's in 1930, even before he had published *Midsummer Night Madness*, or to have predicted the development of James Joyce after he had written a few stories for a Dublin newspaper. But it may be useful in the context of the other essays in this collection, several of which examine the work of established writers, to give a report on what seems to be happening in the short story, admitting readily that the comments are necessarily tentative and based on insufficient evidence.

A few general observations may be made. The new writers are on the whole not experimentalists in terms of form or of narrative techniques, indeed less so than some of the contemporary novelists. The classic form of the short story, as practised by Mary Lavin, Frank O'Connor, Liam O'Flaherty and Seán O'Faoláin, is still the accepted mode. This involves a chronological nârrative, with minimal characterisation, careful attention to setting, one or two incidents, a taut control of tone and development, and the general sense of all the ingredients moving towards a moment of insight. Not all the new writers have this sort of ideal in mind, nor are they restricted by these conventions, but their innovations are not radical and are found mainly in the work of two writers, Neil Jordan and Desmond Hogan.

Nor are the new writers much concerned with revolutionary nationalism, which stemmed in the past from the personal involvement of writers in the revolutionary movement. James Plunkett could still treat this subject in *The Trusting and the Maimed* (1955) and it surfaced in Seán O'Faoláin's *I Remember !* *I Remember !* (1959), but the recent violence in Northern Ireland has not exerted the same fascination. Benedict Kiely's long short story *Proxopera* (1977) is a complex imaginative response to that violence, but there is no ambiguity in its tone of love for a region and a landscape so cruelly violated by evil figures. The cause that never dies has in fact withered in the past ten years and has little appeal to the literary imagination ; the gunman lacks the mystique of nationalism, the myth of heroism, or the sanction of tradition. When the violence in Northern Ireland appears in the contemporary story, it does so as context and background, and as something to get away from. John Morrow alone seems able to present it with a healthy black humour.

In « Generations Apart : 1925-1975 » (in *The Irish Novel in Our Time*, edited by Patrick Rafroidi and M. Harmon), I discussed the changing conditions of Irish writing in the last fifty years ; it would be superfluous to go over that material again. What we all know is that Irish society has become less restrictive and more tolerant in recent years ; the writer suffers less from either official or private censorship. The kind of hostile reaction that greeted Edna O'Brien and John McGahern has not been as vocal in the 'seventies. Issues which were once taboo are now freely discussed on radio and television, in magazines and in newspapers. It is hardly necessary to stress that Irish society is more open and more tolerant. The literature reflects these changes in its expanded range of subject matter and in its treatment of human relationships. Since society itself has become less restrictive, the old issue of individual and society has virtually disappeared. The view of the individual as social victim is no longer dominant. Similarly the influence of the Catholic Church is less direct ; the issues of personal guilt and the problems of the Catholic conscience have decreased in importance as subject matter. Writers treat sexual relationships, for example, with a new freedom and the problems of mixed marriages in a manner that has more comedy in it than guilt or suffering. Ironically, the absence of pressure from church and state leaves the writer with less definable objects for attack. Take away the habitual enemies and you deprive a man of those very forces against which he could measure his individuality and discover his identity. Up to the publication of the *The Dark*, the dominant images in the formation of the adolescent imagination were linked closely to church teaching and practice. The assertion of self-reliant manhood, or the affirmation of the freedom of the imagination often involved breaking free of definable shaping forces. The struggle now is not with laws of church and state or with social conformity, but with personal relationships and through individual powers of perception and understanding. The inner life is now the arena in which the self faces its choices and comes to terms with its own humanity. Not that social pressures are no longer a force, or that the Catholic conscience has died, or that political issues are without weight, but their influence is felt, measured and determined within the individual and are manifested through other individuals. The former conflict of man against society, or man against Church, has been replaced by a fluid drama of human interaction and the nuances of the individual's inner life.

There is much less reference now to the rural scene. In the post-revolutionary generation urban life was regarded as alien, something that the writers and their families had little experience of. Instinctively, and by family tradition, they wrote about the rural roots from which most urban families had come and with which they retained close connections. The sense of the east-west, or urban-rural, division was strong and writers tended to romanticise the country way of life, specially if it was beyond the Shannon, or in West Cork, Kerry, or Donegal. Some of the best stories in the post-revolutionary period — « The Long Road to Ummera », « Uprooted », « Galway Bay » — have this theme in common. Writers tended to transform reality, by making the countryside seem more representative than it actually was, as Frank O'Connor did in « Peasants », « In the Train » and « The Majesty of the Law ». In these he built into the narrative a sense of instinctive loyalty to old values. The western peasants in « In the Train », for example, refuse to cooperate with the legal system in Dublin ; instead they operate an older form of punish-ment : they will not inform on the woman who killed her husband (that would be to give way to the mode of justice brought in by invaders), but they will boycott her, driving her from their community. The old man in « The Majesty of the Law » gestures to the landscape and speaks mysteriously of the knowledge that has been lost. Over and over in such stories the tendency is to dilate reality, to see a glory in the skies, to lament the passing of former greatness. There are several examples : the ending of « Uprooted », the burial of the old cobbler-storyteller in « The Silence of the Valley », the heroic islander in « Galway Bay », making his last journey to the mainland fair. Writers now see the country way of life in realistic terms. Their point of view has more in common with Patrick Kavanagh's portrayal of the sub-culture of the small farm than with Frank O'Connor's Yeatsian notion of the peasant as repository of tradition.

Maeve Kelly's « The Last Campaign » is a story about the disappointments and setbacks of life on the farm. It is dense with the detail of daily life, the chores, the sparse conversations. Martha and Joe suffer yet another calamity, when their herd is condemned, but what the story really conveys is their tough and generous humanity. They work hard, they suffer successive losses, their marriage is barren, but they are fertile in love, in courage, in humour, in the ability to pull together and fight back against misfortune. The contrast with Liam O'Flaherty's « Spring Sowing », that delicate, romantic account of the young couple making their first potato sowing is striking, but some of the same human lessons are there, although made without O'Flaherty's mystique of the land. In the process Maeve Kelly reveals the characters of the two people, the man more taciturn, the woman with a more active mind. The story's resonance is achieved through these portraits, for what they tell us about two people, not by what they evoke of old faiths.

Maeve Kelly's stories are in the tradition of Mary Lavin's studies of rural and middle-class life. While she lacks the older woman's depth of vision, she resembles her in the warm humanity that she brings to her stories. In « Day at the Sea » two brothers return to the Clare coast from which their old mother had come in the remote past. The boys have married the land, they give their energies to it in unrelenting and orderly toil. At her request « they go west to a different landscape, to a place of primeval memories », where the younger brother wallows for a day in his soul's ecstasy.

Indeed one of the pleasures of reading the new writers is this quality of warm humanity that many of them have. Bernard McLaverty writes with quiet humour and compassion, and above all with a strict concern for craft. « Between Two Shores » is a simple story in essence and develops with deceptive ease. It is an account of an Irishman returning to visit his wife and family. He remembers his loneliness in London, his affair with a nurse, and thinks of his wife waiting eagerly for him. His secret is the syphilis that he has contracted in London and which he has left untreated. « St. Paul Could Hit the Nail on the Head » is an obliquely humorous account of a hardpressed Catholic wife married to a Protestant. Despite the likely consequences, she makes a room available in her home for the lonely priest who comes to visit her in the city. The humour implicit in this story resembles the situation of the wife in Emma Cooke's « Family Occasion ». She has married a Catholic and finds her visits to her Protestant family with an increasingly large brood of children dismayingly difficult, but ultimately comic.

Maura Treacy's characters have an active inner life in which they imagine things happening, projecting and acting out their fears and phantasies, as Nally does in « The Weight of the World ». For the most part, her stories are low-keyed, psychological vignettes about human relationships. In a gentle, reflective manner, she treats of loneliness, dissatisfaction, longing for improved conditions. Her characters watch and wait ; they hope for change, as does Delia in « An Old Story », but there is really little change. Delia, for example, dreams of women with a home, with children, with a husband who will take them for a drive on a Sunday. When she does marry, her husband goes fishing on a Sunday, as he has always done. What else should she have expected ?

Brian Power's stories focus on two separate but overlapping worlds — the inner-city and the presbytery. The former has its ugly face, of crime, vandalism and deceit ; its inhabitants are victims of impoverishment and social deprivation. Power depicts the ugliness in its own idiom and life-style but reveals within it the mysterious operation of goodness. No man is totally bad ; within him stir memories of home or of acts of kindness, stirrings of conscience that rise to the surface of his life. The world of the priests is more middle-class, but gullible to the con-men from the inner-city, for here too a generous humanity triumphs. In « Requiem », an old priest, somewhat outdated by the changes introduced by Vatican Two, pays his last respects to his faithful sacristan, feels the nudges of mortality, but is still able to cope with fresh young curates who do not know their place.

In some ways it is easier to illustrate the changed attitudes towards traditional values by examining a number of stories that incorporate the more permissive aspects of Irish society in the 'seventies. Gillman Noonan's « God and Ye Olde Curiosity Shop » turns the traditional portrait of Irish mother and son upside down. The first person narrator had what he calls an « agnostic and liberal upbringing in the obscurantist forties and fifties », an opening sentence that alerts us to the deliberate aim of this story to place imaginative landmines under sacred cows. His mother, a ravishing, liberated widow, is an agnostic and freethinker. At first he adores her, as does everyone else. She is a doting mamma, even to the point of encouraging and facilitating his love-affairs as soon as he is able to have them. So what more could a boy want ? The twist comes, when he grows to hate his mother for the very things that make her so acceptable in the first place : her liberal morals and the civilised veneer that she has created for both of them. He is a Stephen Dedalus without the nets. Not having God thrust upon him in boyhood, he has to find Him for himself, which he does : he rejects his mother's hedonism and becomes a Church of Ireland minister.

There is much more to the story than can be suggested here, but clearly we are a long way from conventional images of mother machree. Seán O'Faoláin did some of this debunking towards the

end of *Stories* (1958), in « Childybawn », « Unholy Living and
Half Dying » and « Lovers of the Lake ». His aim was to show
that beneath the agnosticism of the modern Irishman lies a deep
layer of pious Catholicism. Noonan's character overcomes his
mother's influence by turning religious, or, more exactly and
more ironically, by finding a form of Christianity not too different
from what he had found in the antique shop run by his mother.
In his view the Church of Ireland has an old-fashioned, antique
look about it ; it therefore suits his dilettantish character.

Gillman Noonan is interested also in what binds men and
women to each other. Opposed to sentimental notions about love,
marriage and living happily ever after, he is fascinated by the
inexplicable oneness of some couples, whose relationships persist,
when young love has long passed, or when sex has become routine.
Something else is there — acceptance, defeat, consideration, a
realisation of the pitiful human condition — any number of
possible explanations suggest themselves to him. And it is this
something that he would have us see, sometimes harshly, as in
« Between the Cells », sometimes gently, as in « Money for the
Town », sometimes more complexly, as in « Shamrocks », in
which the Irish wife exiled in Germany sees beyond « the trite
acceptance in for better or worse ». The title story of his
collection is a satirical send-up of the conventional male role of
cunning pursuit of the female object. Here the Irish Romeo is
matched against the teutonic Helga, who has herself programmed
to find a sex partner for every other month, which is when she
can conceive. Sean (what else can he be called ?) is put off his
stroke by such calculation, so unexpected, he thinks, in a
woman ; he does not see it as a mirror image of his own
« carefully cultivated manner ».

More sacred cows sink to their knees in Sean MacMathuna's
exuberant story « A Straight Run down to Kilcash ». The setting
is that traditional one — the boarding school run by religious,
but the expected traumas of conscience are not present. The « I »
narrator is not like Stephen Dedalus, or the girls in Kate
O'Brien's *Land of Spices*. He has an eye for the servant girls in
the school and without much ado about anything has an affair
with one of them every other night in a little room lined with
chamber pots. Naturally, these nocturnal activities have their
effect on the playing field, where he fails repeatedly to shoot the
ball between the posts. When the priests finally shine a torch on

the naked bodies on the closet floor, none of the conventional guilt and shame comes over him. Instead he wants to know which of them held the torch, for as he says accusingly and tellingly, the light lingered more on the girl than on himself. When he is « rusticated » — not expelled as would have been the case in the past — his father comes to collect him, not as the outraged parent, but as one man to another, anxious to hear the details : « What was she like, son ? »

Denis has proved himself : he's a chip of the old block, can inherit the farm, marry the girl next door and live happily ever after, or as his father memorably phrases it — it's a straight run down to Kilcash, that being the family graveyard and a straight run down to it being the « local euphemism for a happy life ». His escapade with the girl has led him into this trap, but there is justice in it, as the story slyly shows.

Sean MacMathuna writes with comic skill and intelligence, quite happy to « send up » traditional literary notions of Irish education, the so-called power of priests in boarding schools, and the conventional view of the puritanical Irish parent. The echoes of Stephen Dedalus at Clongowes may be coincidental, but the story does not suffer as a result. And the portrait of the rogue of a farmer, a rip-off artist of the 'seventies is masterly. Patrick Kavanagh's tormented Patrick Maguire is a long way from this « hoor », who gleefully declares that Ireland is « a paradise for farmers » and that there are « grants for pissing crooked ».

When Denis goes to bed, the old iconography on the walls has a banal quality : « Mary Magdalen holding a chalice, the Little Flower with a little flower, and a huge Sacred Heart bearing the inscription that John and Eileen Stack were enrolled in the League of Eternal Prayer ». He cannot sleep and in ironic deflation his thoughts drift outward — to his father boasting of sexual exploits in the local pub, to his mother's dried-up body tending the cooker, to the life he has settled for and been saddled with.

Frank sexuality is a feature of the new writing, although it is not excessive. Some writers have a harsh vision that resembles that of Patrick Boyle. Gillman Noonan's « Between the Cells » is a confessional account of a sordid and unhappy relationship : a husband and wife estranged, the wife in hospital, the husband's girl friend pregnant. Trying to raise money for an abortion, he feels debased, yet his love for his wife endures, as though they were « outcasts of some kind full of a mixture of damnation and sainthood, people who will only find themselves in a new dimension of growth that stemmed from beneath layers of decay and disease. Yet some all-acceptance is there already, however tentative ».

John Feeney's characters are isolated — from home, from loved ones — in a hostile world of institutions, urban ugliness and debased values. They suffer in an alien environment, like the girl in « Dirty, Dirty » ; they inhabit a private mental world that their colleagues will not even try to understand, like the priest in « Mao Dies ». Feeney's stories sometimes rely on a drastic bringing together of the strange and the familiar, the outlandish and the conventional. In « Scourge of the Reds » he formulates a drastic juxtaposition of the personal and the cataclysmic through the figure of Fr. Flood, whose personal sexual torment is related through images of plague to the advance of the menace of Communism. Michael Foley's comic imagination, on the other hand, can mock the crudities of human behaviour and can bring the ugly and the beautiful into challenging contact.

One of the best shaped stories, with a strong sensual emphasis, is Clare Boylan's « Not a Recommended Hobby for a House-wife », a witty account of the annual get-together of a few « old girls », who pity Maria because she seems to have gone to seed. At the end, however, her lover enters and sweeps her off in a radiant expression of fulfilled sexuality. Another point of view is found in John McArdle's « The Warmth and the Wine ». Here the Irishman abroad is faced with what Austin Clarke used to call « the bright temptation » in the figure of a beautiful, sensual, liberated girl, with whom he spends a delightful evening in a restaurant and who expects that their rapport will lead to love-making. But even when she does manage to share his bed, he remains faithful to his wife. Is he to be admired for such loyalty ? Is he to be condemned for being so hard on the Dutch girl ? O'Faoláin and O'Connor also treated this problem and also used the device of bringing products of two cultures together for purposes of contrast and judgment. O'Connor used to imply that sexual freedom was acceptable in another country, but not at home. O'Faoláin in his later work outgrew such inhibiting dichotomies and wrote of loves that know no national boundaries, as in « The Faithless Wife » and « Foreign Affairs ».

The effects of the more liberal environment in Ireland today are seen in many of these stories with a sexual theme. Kate O'Brien's *Land of Spices* was banned for a one sentence reference to homosexuality. Desmond Hogan's « A Poet and an Englishman » has homosexuality as one of its main issues. In this story Peader and his wife, Sandra, go to Kerry, where he has been raised by a man called Michael. The journey brings back boyhood associations, in particular memories of Michael, who had minded and seduced him. Those memories, becoming stronger as the couple drive closer to the town, create a silence between them, an estrangement. In an act of exorcism Peader makes love to a boy he meets in the town, reenacting his own affair with the older man, then seeks Sandra, who has fled when she discovers them together. The story handles a complex and delicate emotional situation and this emphasis on personal relationships is characteristic of the contemporary story in Ireland.

Another characteristic is a concentration on ordinary things. In Michael Foley's « The Stranger », the visitor's sentiments are seen to be unusual : « He spoke of the beauty of ordinary things, how in the rush and bustle of our lives we tend to undervalue all that is most precious ». Not that human awareness can be changed forever ; the story is careful to suggest that one man's words or one man's example cannot do that, but Michael Foley's work, like Dermot Healy's is intensely sensitive to the real world. This world, Healy says in « Jude and his Mother » is « contained with the maximum of pleasure on the shiny surface of a penny piece ». Any reality, he declares, is only appraised by its followers. In « The Island and the Calves », he concentrates on the phenomena of the visible and the audible, writing of one of its characters — « at last he had authenticated the outside world, and each part was now sustained by itself and no longer needed a deity nor an interpreter ». The gravity of the relationships between perceiver and object recurs in these writers. Here the whole story affirms an appreciation of the ordinary in the intensity of its imagined details, and in its counterpointing of the natural setting against the ritual of the Mass. Nature is the song of songs.

Some of Juanita Casey's stories are almost entirely descriptive ; their movements follow and reflect the associations of an individual mind, so that her work is attentive to myriad, shifting perceptions, to radiantly accurate description, as when the boy comes upon the dead peacock in « The Well », or the menacing zebra : « the flaring bands on its body shook and rippled... it had an intensity, a feline, white-hot fire behind the bars of its painted hide ».

In Gillman Noonan and Neil Jordan we find new images in the Irish imagination ; the techniques emphasise the swirl of objects, broken figures, images, a dance of phenomena, what Noonan calls in « Artifacts » « the drift of senseless forms ». Jordan concentrates on the reality outside of and around his characters. All the people in *Night in Tunisia* are, he says, « trying to break out of their personalities ». The actions that they engage in break down barriers either « to destroy their separateness, or redefine their personalities ». His characters are shaken out of their routines : Reg in « The Old Fashioned Lift » by the intrusion of the new cleaning girl ; the civil servant is drawn away from his office by the girl in the orange blouse in « A Bus, A Bridge, A Beach ». The Woman in « Skin » responds to an inner urge and goes to the seaside ; the boy in « A Love » separates finally from the older woman ; the boy in « Night in Tunisia » comes of age.

Jordan treats character in what he calls an « elemental way... getting behind the social persona to the more basic constituents ». He projects people in settings, as though his imagination conceived them in cinematic terms, figures within settings, against changing shapes, within different perspectives. The man in « A Bus, A Bridge, A Beach », where the title indicates Jordan's vision, « filled his day with events... and each event gave rise to several more events and so on, in infinite series ».

One of his main interests is the relationships between generations. His heroes are often adolescent boys, who tend to be self-absorbed, to be adrift in a flux of anxiety, to feel the precariousness of existence and the fragility of relationships. Stories are told from their limited perspectives. The boy in « A Love » lacks historical perspectives. While he can register the objective reality of De Valera's funeral, he cannot measure the importance of the man or the significance of his passing. The dead leader is remote, his power not defined : « his angular face and his thirties collar and his fist raised in a gesture of defiance towards something out there, beyond the rim of brown photograph, never defined ».

Three generations overlap in the story — De Valera's, the older woman's, the boy's — and from this conjunction of ages, values, attitudes comes a failure of understanding that reveals and contains feelings of longing, love and limited sympathy. Between the boy and the woman, love is less a sharing of feeling, as a « secret », a « desecration », an offensive act against each other and against objects, figures, forces outside of them :

> I remembered the nights lying in your old creaking bed that looked out on the sea, our movements like a great secret between us, silent, shocking movements, our silence a guard against my father who had the room down below, our love-making a quiet desecration of the holiday town, of the church at the top of the hill, of the couples you fed so properly at mealtimes, of my embarrassed adolescence, the guilt you tried to banish in me, the country, the place, the thing you tried to hit at through me you taught me to hit through you. And all the time for me there was my father lying underneath, cold most likely, and awake and I wanted him to hear the beast I was creating with you, I wanted him to hear it scratching, creaking through to him from above, for your body was like the woman he must have loved to have me...

Such love is not free in itself, nor of the past, nor of the psychic urges that motivate it. The relationship is fraught with compulsions that bring the boy and the woman together and drive them apart. When they travel westward to sources and hoped-for explanations, their lovemaking, accompanied by that past complication of woman, boy, father confirms that their love is finished. When she goes to take the waters at Lisdoonvarna, he, uncomprehending to the end, does not know whether this means to drink them or to bathe in them.

Already in this story the momentum is to transcend occasion and setting ; the interest on memorable, evocative, or definable moments leads away from specific place and event, even though it tethers itself securely to them. In the title story, another account of adolescence in search of self, in search of love, in ambiguous relationship with the father, the circumstances of place are also well-realised, but they are drawn into the story, made part of its imaginal design, to which they give metaphorical richness. Everything in the story, place, incident, dialogue, description, becomes evocative of the time and state of adolescence. The story is rich in implication and suggestion ; it creates atmosphere, feelings of time and place, moods, fleeting relationships. Its movement is neither consecutive nor chronological, but fluid, wave-like, resonant, always evocative of more than appears in any one passage. The boy's reflections on the sea might be applied to it :

> The sea had the movement of cloth but the texture of glass. It flowed and undulated, but shone hard and bright. He thought of cloth and glass and how to mix them. A cloth made of glass fibre or a million woven mirrors. He saw that the light of twilight was repeated or reversed at early morning.

Against the background of long summer days, seaside, games of tennis, aimless hours, Jordan portrays the relationship of the boy with his father, a musician. Knowing the boy's potential, the father would like to teach him to play well, but the son, rejecting him, defiantly tinkles out rubbishy tunes on the piano. The relationship is at once particular and symptomatic : on the one side, the loving urge to transmit knowledge, on the other, the involuntary urge to rebel. Above and beyond both man and boy is the sound of Charley Parker's playing of « Night in Tunisia », a catalyst that brings the boy out of his adolescent inertia ; in that scale of values, differences are diminished :

> The notes soared and fell, dispelling the world around him, tracing a series of arcs that seemed to point to a place, or if not a place, a state of mind... He decided it was a place you were always in, yet always trying to reach, you walked towards all the time and yet never got there, as it was always beside you.

The music is expressive both of adolescent need and of adult aspiration and the understanding that comes to both. It is also an analogy for the style of the story and what it seeks to evoke in words.

It could be said that Jordan's work subsumes the emphases and conditions already noted in his contemporaries : the avoidance of nationalism, the indifference to social and religious concerns and the unembarrassed treatment of sexual matters. He is different from the others in his view of character, in his affinity with overseas writers, like Borges and South American writers, above all in his style ; the evidence is that an individual talent is finding itself slowly but surely. While it would be premature to predict the likely directions of these new writers or to compare them at length with their predecessors, the evidence is that the revolution begun by David Marcus in 1968 has been steadily gaining ground and that we can anticipate the emergence within the next ten years of a number of good writers.

# IRISH SHORT STORY WRITERS

# WILLIAM CARLETON
## AS A SHORT-STORY WRITER

### André BOUÉ

When the first series of Carleton's *Traits and Stories of the Irish Peasantry* came out in 1830, it met with instant and remarkable success. Discerning critics enthusiastically praised its unprecedented realism. In those two small volumes, an unknown world was revealed to a wide English-speaking public. Three years later, the second series of what was to be Carleton's masterpiece won him general applause. Though his somewhat unfair treatment of priests was censured in Catholic circles, he was unanimously acknowledged as the best delineator of the life and manners of the Irish people.

Carleton's originality lay in the extreme vividness of his portraiture. This resulted from an intimate knowledge of his subject served by uncommon descriptive powers. When he entered the literary scene, a few other writers had recently brought Irish life into fiction. He joined the pioneers of the new Irish literature in English, definitely national in character, that had begun to develop at the turn of the century. Those half-forgotten authors, whose art is often imperfect, are historically important because the social types and modes of life which they described were swept away by the Great Famine. All drew on personal experience or accounts received from the preceding generation. Each kept, if not to the prejudices, at least to the outlook of his class. For that reason, Carleton's contemporaries could give but a limited or distorted image of the mass of the people. Maria Edgeworth and Lady Morgan looked upon Irish peasants with undeniable sympathy, but from a hazy distance. Lever and Lover were too often inclined to caricature them in order to amuse their readers. Griffin and the Banim brothers, being of Celtic stock, born in Catholic families, had closer contacts with them and portrayed them more faithfully. But of all these writers, Carleton alone was bred among the peasantry and witnessed the circumstances of their private lives to which no foreign observer was admitted. The class in which he grew up owes its right place in literature to his uncouth genius.

The son of a humble Catholic farmer, he was born in 1794 in the parish of Clogher, Co. Tyrone, and received his early education at various hedge schools (1). Much of what he learnt from his parents during this period was to be useful to him as a writer. His father, a genuine *senachie* (2) endowed with a rich memory, made him familiar with local legends, tales, customs, traditions and superstitions. His mother, whose sweet voice used to attract crowds at wakes, dances, and all festive occasions, awakened his interest in ancient Irish music (3). Intended for the priesthood, he studied classics for two years, but for some obscure reason had to renounce his ambition. There is every indication that this failure was a sore disappointment to him and determined both his career and his anti catholicism. Back in his native place, he lived in idleness until his relatives grew weary of supporting him. Then he started on a wandering journey to Dublin where he arrived in or about 1819. After a period of wretched poverty, he made his way into Protestant circles. In 1827, he met the Rev. Caesar Otway, well-known author of topographical works and editor of the *Christian Examiner*, a religious magazine then conducting a violent campaign against Catholic Emancipation. The proselytizer at once perceived that Carleton's precise knowledge of Irish peasant life could serve his propaganda and invited him to make his literary début under his direction.

Most of Carleton's contributions to the *Christian Examiner* were melodramatic sketches containing little more than venomous attacks on the Catholic Church. Yet four of them, in which instinctive realism got the better of polemics, showed where his power lay. Later they were rightly included in *Traits and Stories*. His first production, « A Pilgrimage to Patrick's Purgatory » (1828), which in a revised form became « The Lough Derg Pilgrim », was a vivid though biased account of the pilgrimage he had himself made in his youth. The wry humour of « The Station » (1829) exposed the materialism of Catholic priests. « The Lianhan Shee » (1830) recorded a curious local superstition. « Dennis O'Shaughnessy Going to Maynooth » was largely autobiographical, its hero being no other than a young peasant aspiring to the priesthood. Its publication began in 1831 but was soon interrupted, apparently because Carleton's picture, based on loving memory, was too truthful and sympathetic to suit his employer's purpose. However that may be, their collaboration came to an abrupt end and was never renewed.

Carleton had soon realized that the distorted portrayal of Irish life which Otway required of him was unworthy of his talent. So, while he continued to write out of necessity, therefore too often indiscriminately, for the *Christian Examiner* and other magazines, he made it his ambition to give a faithful and complete picture of the life and manners of his countrymen, perhaps with a view to emulating what Walter Scott had done for Scotland. His best productions, only a few of them already published in periodicals, made up his *Traits and Stories* (4). This Brueghel-like representation of the scenes of his youth established his fame. Hardly less excellent were the shorter pieces published in 1845 as *Tales and Sketches* (5). Most of these had appeared in 1840-41 in the short-lived *Irish Penny Journal*. Characteristically, Carleton considered them almost as scientific contributions, so proud was he to display his unrivalled knowledge of popular life in a serious paper mainly dealing with archaeology and folklore (6). As he was all his life an impecunious and, though apt to work by fits and starts, a prolific writer, he maintained a sporadic flow of stories in the same realistic vein even if they were mostly of inferior quality. He also made it a point to prove that his capacity was not limited to the short story. His first novel, *Fardorougha the Miser* (1837) was an immediate and lasting success. Those that followed were often lengthy or melodramatic, or both, and at times overburdened with polemics. Never could he surpass the tales and descriptive sketches which had made his name.

Many an author draws the material of his first writings from actual experience, in particular from recollections of his youth, this period of life being generally richer in emotion than mature age. Sooner or later, as his stock of memories is running out, he must resort more and more to invention or, in his search for new subjects, enlarge his information by travel, social intercourse or documentation. Though Carleton obviously felt the need of this regeneration, he could never achieve it. The steadily decreasing quality of his later work has no other cause. With him, mastery instead of apprenticeship is characterized by the predominance of memory.

His imagination, though remarkably alert, was more repro-ductive than creative. A swarming life fills his pages, but scenes, plots and characters are little more than kaleidoscopic reflections of the reality which he has actually seen. It follows from this that he is at his best when he concentrates on description or em-broiders upon real incidents or traditional tales. As the auto-biographical fragment he left when he died confirms, his almost unique source was the relatively short portion of his life he spent in Tyrone. But what inspires this close relation of his work to past experience is much less duration than affective intensity. He longs to re-create and perpetuate the happy days of his ado-lescence, so that his vision is inevitably subjective. His ever-present personality manifests itself in the recurrence of themes and situations as well as in digressions or veiled confidences. Yet autobiography remains accessory in his fiction. Even when he models some of his characters on his past self, as it is obviously the case with Dennis O'Shaughnessy or Jemmy M'Evoy, the pathetic hero of « The Poor Scholar », he does not primarily aim at drawing a portrait of himself. No doubt he avails himself of the opportunity for paying off a few old scores with priests and schoolmasters, but he never ceases emphasizing typical rather than personal traits, because even then his subject remains the whole rural community.

The panoramic view he wants to present to his readers he builds up by accumulation. Each particular subject he selects is suggested by some remembered individual, event or narrative, and developed so as to illustrate some characteristic aspect of Irish life. Each of his stories, however funny or moving, is deliberately descriptive and furnished with a great wealth of detail. In *Traits and Stories*, among other topics, he deals with marriage in « Shane Fadh's Wedding » and « Phelim O'Toole's Courtship », death in « Larry M'Farland's Wake » and « The Party Fight and Funeral », education in « The Hedge School » and « The Poor Scholar », religion in « The Station » and « The Lough Derg Pilgrim », superstition in « The Donagh » and « The Lianhan Shee », secret societies in « Wildgoose Lodge ». In *Tales and Sketches*, we find a gallery of lifelike portraits of typical individuals such as the fiddler, the dancing-master, the matchmaker or the *senachie*. Other stories in the same book refer to popular manners and customs, the wide-spread belief in fairies and apparitions (« The Fate of Frank M'Kenna », « Frank Martin and the Fairies »), the traditional spinning contests between unmarried females (« The Rivals Kempers »), the illicit distillation of whiskey (« Bob Pentland, or the Gauger Outwitted », « Condy Cullen, or the Exciseman Defeated »). In his exhaustive exploitation of memory, Carleton follows no preconceived plan. Themes once briefly mentioned are often taken up and developed elsewhere, so that his stories are closely linked and even seem to spring from one another. A good example of this is « Shane Fadh's Wedding », based on his recollections of the marriage of his brother John. All the minor elements here form the substance of other tales. We find the preliminary courting and negotiation in « Phelim O'Toole's Courtship », the funeral rites in « Larry M'Farland's Wake », the runaway match in « Alley Sheridan » (7), and abduction by force in « The Fair of Emyvale » (8).

However primitive this patchwork technique may seem, it goes far towards creating the illusion of life, and the precious counterpart of its disorder is constant variety. Carleton was a spontaneous writer who took little care of form. His education was defective and the only models he had when he started writing were the traditional tales handed down by his father and some desultory reading. Though indolent by nature, he wrote quickly, without adequate revision, because he was always hard pressed by need. Besides, he had a utilitarian notion of literature. Not only was he proud of the documentary value of his writings, but he was bent on expressing his views on the social and political problems of his time. For all these reasons, he made no sustained effort to improve on the model of amorphous narrative he had received from tradition, and it would be vain to look in him for the artistic sophistication of the modern short story.

Curiously enough, he made his closest approach to it, apparently by pure instinct, in « Wildgoose Lodge », one of his early productions. The tale is based on an actual agrarian outrage, the midnight burning by Ribbonmen of a farmer's house and its inmates (9). In the abrupt beginning, he exceptionally discards the once-upon-a-time convention of folk tradition. Attention is focused throughout on the narrator's emotions. The mysterious summons he receives, the anxiety and misgivings he feels, the cold darkness of the rainy winter night, the late meeting of the conspirators in the lonely chapel, the diabolical cruelty of the leader, gradually create suspense and quite naturally lead to the horror of the final scene. A strong impression of truth is here artistically produced by suggestiveness of detail, rapidity of action and relative terseness of style. But such compression is rare in Carleton.

He is reported to have said of his characters, as he wished to insist on their veracity : « I found them, and only gave them a linked embodiment » (10). What matters to him is fact, rather than arrangement or causality. He takes little interest in the aesthetic aspect of literary composition because, insofar as he does not write for money, his aim is either descriptive, moral or polemical. No doubt he wants to entertain his readers, to provoke their mirth, their pity or their indignation, but his ultimate purpose is to instruct them, and to achieve it, he prefers explicitness to suggestion and applies himself to the retailing of incidents rather than to the creation of mood. Fiction to him is chiefly the means of dealing attractively with actual truth. Consequently, he gives little autonomy to the imaginary world he invents. Characters born of his fancy are rarely brought together with a view to an objective study of their reactions and development, but are as a rule strictly guided along a predetermined course. He is thus led to sacrifice the plots of his novels as well as the simpler but all the more delicately balanced anecdotal basis of his stories, making them, not carefully elaborated aesthetic constructions, but mere supports for his subjects.

The perfect verisimilitude of characters and situations drawn from life cannot fully redeem the faulty structure and lack of unity of some of his best stories. « The Hedge School », he tells us, is based on fact : crafty peasants, having failed to engage a schoolmaster for their children, resolve to abduct one from a neighbouring village. They make him drunk, carry him in a sack, and eventually persuade him to stay with them. Such might have been the substance of a well-balanced and lively tale. But Carleton, in a lengthy prologue, recalls the origins of the hedge schools, discusses their curriculum, the training and ability of their teachers. Then he overstretches his action by adding to it a series of well-managed but ill-connected scenes in which he minutely describes the building of the school-house, the activity in the class-room and the social status of the master. And on to this he tags an incongruous conclusion, in order to remind us that hedge schoolmasters were sometimes active members of the rural secret societies. The jolly pedagogue unexpectedly and most improbably turns out to be a dangerous terrorist. Too many of Carleton's stories are thus encumbered with superfluous matter. Unconcerned with literary technique, he pours out the rich flow of his memories into his pages. Yet he always holds his reader's attention. The artistic imperfections of his work never obliterate its peculiar charm.

His humour, to which his prose largely owes its distinctive flavour, is fundamentally that of the country-people among whom he lived. It is at once rude, exuberant and serious. It is eminently national, since its main elements, fantasy, the macabre and verbal play, are characteristic of the Gaelic tradition and obviously derived from it (11). Carleton's broad comedy cannot be assimilated to the burlesque of Lever and Lover, as it is mostly a subtle parody of the current representation of his countrymen in literature. Irony is hardly veiled in the story of Phil Purcel who goes to England to sell his pigs at twice their value and even succeeds in selling his last one many times because each night they sleep and escape together. The feigned stupidity of the cunning Connaught peasant deceives English buyers by flattering their false notions. They look upon him with contempt because he plays his part to perfection (12). Long before G.B. Shaw, Carleton made fun of the myth of the Stage Irishman. Phil Purcel is the ancestor of Tim Haffigan (13). Larry O'Toole laughs so heartily at his son's pranks that he falls from his stool (14). Phaddy tumbles down his chimney while sweeping it (15). Carleton freely indulges in farce, but never makes it humiliating for the Irish, never makes it suggestive of social or racial inferiority. However brutal his polemics, however dogmatic his moral preaching may be, his amused perception of human oddities is always indulgent. Far better than his contemporaries, he has expressed the singular mixture of mirth and melancholy which distinguishes the Irish character. There is great psychological insight in the long rambling monologue of Peter Connell when the poor man, utterly distracted by the death of his wife, evokes her memory in a medley of tears, funny stories and popular songs (16). Carleton does not coolly use comic devices to raise a mechanical laugh, but puts all his heart in his jokes. Laughter with him is often on the verge of tears, as it is among simple folk.

His rugged style itself paradoxically contributes to his excellence, because it is quite appropriate to his subject-matter. The naturalness of his dialogue is all the more striking as it includes a skilful representation of dialect. His picturesque imagery illustrates the vividness of popular imagination.

Carleton's untrammelled art is that of the peasant story-teller. An acute observer of his countrymen, he was also one of them, their representative and their mouthpiece. As such, he stands unrivalled in Irish literature. His lack of discipline, his bent for polemics, the limited scope of his observation, are less apparent or less prejudicial in his stories than in his novels. In these stories, his deep understanding of human nature, his dramatic gift, his humour and pathos, appear in their full maturity. In them, he realized his ambition to be the historian of his people.

# NOTES

1. Hedge schools were originally so-called from the fact that they were held outdoors in sequestered places, so as to evade the law forbidding Catholic education. Later the name was retained, though master and pupils worked in a barn, a cabin, or any building that could be given or lent for the purpose.

2. Or *shanachie*. A peasant story-teller versed in folklore. In ancient Gaelic society, a *seanchaidh* was a historian or genealogist attached to the household of a king or chief.

3. See his unfinished autobiography in D.J. O'Donoghue : *The Life of William Carleton*, London, Downey, 1896, or in *The Autobiography of William Carleton*, with a preface by Patrick Kavanagh, London, McGibbon and Kee, 1968.

4. *Traits and Stories of the Irish Peasantry*, first series, Dublin, Wm. Curry, Jun. and Co., 2 vols., 1830 ; second series, Dublin, W.F. Wakeman, 3 vols., 1833. Complete illustrated edition, Dublin, Wm. Curry, Jun. & Co ; London, W.S. Orr & Co., in monthly parts, 1842-43, in 2 vols., with an autobiographical introduction, 1843-44.

Included in *The Works of William Carleton*, New York, P.F. Collier, 2 vols., 1880 ; reissued, Books for Libraries Press, Freeport, New York, 1970.

A selection was published by the Mercier Press in 1974.

5. *Tales and Sketches Illustrating the Character, Usages, Traditions, Sports and Pastimes of the Irish Peasantry*, Dublin, James Duffy, 1845. Reprinted, Garland Publishing, Inc., New York, 1978.

Henry Lea,

6. « The Rival Kempers » opens with these words referring to « The Fate of Frank M'Kenna » : « In the preceding paper, we have given an authentic account of what the country folks... », *Tales and Sketches*, 70.

7. « Alley Sheridan, or the Runaway Marriage », *The National Magazine*, Dublin, 1830.

8. « The Fair of Emyvale », *The Illustrated London Magazine*, 1852.

9. For historical details, see Daniel J. Casey : « Carleton in Louth » in *County Louth Archaeological and Historical Journal*, XVII, 2, 1971.

10. D.J. O'Donoghue : *The Life of William Carleton*, II, 305.

11. See Vivian Mercier : *The Irish Comic Tradition*, Oxford, The Clarendon Press, 1962.

12. « Phil Purcel, the Pig-Driver » in *Traits and Stories*.

13. *John Bull's Other Island*, act I.

14. « Phelim O'Toole's Courtship » in *Works*, II, 1052.

15. « The Station » in *Works*, II, 746.

16. « The Geography of an Irish Oath » in *Works*, II, 953-4.

# JOSEPH SHERIDAN LE FANU.
# THE PRINCE OF THE INVISIBLE

**Jean LOZÈS**

At his death at fifty-nine years of age Joseph Sheridan Le Fanu had achieved a reputation as so dedicated a recluse that in Dublin he had been dubbed « The Invisible Prince ». Dubliners were perhaps responding to the element of mystery that seems to have surrounded Le Fanu in his life time. His writings have certainly created mysteries for those critics who have attempted to relate the works to the man. The author of fifteen novels, more than thirty short stories, some unsigned articles, verse and even drama, Le Fanu remains an enigma to all those who have attempted to penetrate his personality (1). And even the biographical sketches left by members of the author's family (2) are curiously unsatisfactory for they don't manage to convey a coherent sense of an individual.

Le Fanu was born in Dublin on August 28th, 1814, the second child and the first son of a cultivated ecclesiastical father and a sweet-tempered literary-minded mother. As a child Joseph was retiring and bookish (3) though not beyond enjoying practical jokes (4). His childhood was spent close to the Phoenix Park, the vast park situated near the heart of Dublin where the British military drilled and monuments of Vice-regal splendour could be glimpsed between the trees. Undoubtedly the young boy's imagination was stirred by his environment.

When in 1926 the family moved to Abington, Co. Limerick, a private tutor was engaged to care for the education of Joseph and his brother William. The tutor was keener on fishing than on instructing his charges in the mysteries of Latin verse, and the boys were left almost entirely to their own pursuits. Despite this Joseph managed to acquire a sufficiently sound education in his parents' cultivated, scholarly, literate home for him to enter Trinity College, Dublin.

At T.C.D. he studied law and was a fluent President of the College Historical Society (one of the college's undergraduate debating societies) where his gift for oratory suggested that he might eventually bring distinction on himself in a career at the Irish bar. But this was not to be, for, surprisingly, he abandoned the law for the practice of letters, becoming a short story writer, a novelist, editor of the *Dublin University Magazine* and a financially successful proprietor of several Dublin newspapers.

Perhaps heredity made it likely that Le Fanu should display an extremely versatile personality and an original talent. He came of a family of Huguenot descent which had included lawyers, churchmen and army officers. On his mother's side, he was the great grandnephew of Thomas Sheridan and the grandnephew of Richard Brinsley. Be that as it may, upon graduating Le Fanu threw himself into the life of letters and publishing.

There were two sides to his work as a man of letters. There was the brooding creator of his tales and novels of mystery (5) and there was the editor and newspaper proprietor who used his powers to influence the great public debates of his time on behalf of the class to which he gave his loyalty, the Irish Protestant Ascendancy. One imagines that the essential Le Fanu was the creative artist, who would have preferred the company of men like Paddy O'Neill, a fiddler and poet he encountered as a child in Co. Clare and who supplied Le Fanu with material for one of his most famous ballads, « Shamus O'Brien », to the company of politicians and journalists. But Le Fanu as well as being a writer was an Anglo-Irishman conscious of the anomalies and dangers inherent in that class's political stance in Ireland.

Much that may appear ambiguous, unlikely, in Le Fanu's behaviour may be explained in terms of his position as a sensitive self-aware Anglo-Irishman. As such he would have been conscious of the debt his own family owed to the Protestant Nation in Ireland which had allowed them, exiles from France, an honourable role in the country's life. On the other hand he would, despite his love of the Irish landscape and for the amiable inhabitants of the island, have been conscious of the dangers of a nascent Irish nationalism. Some of his writing indeed can be seen as an effort to trace the roots of Ireland's social, political and cultural dilemma. And his preference for literature over the law may have its sources in a desire to have a less conventional, less sterile, more open relationship with a country that he intuitively knew was undergoing great change, than that provided by a career at the Irish bar. His debts to England and the Ascendancy he paid in his strenuous advocacy in the *Dublin University Magazine* and through his various newspapers, urging a literary nationalism which would not shake the Union nor disturb what Le Fanu the business man believed were unbreakable economic ties between England and Ireland.

All this suggests a troubled, complicated case of divided loyalties, and the possibility of guilt, for it was impossible for Le Fanu to be true to all sympathies at once. Now seeking to be true to his awareness of the Irish possibilities that he seems to have sensed at an early age, now trying to engage English and Irish attention for the Irish world he knew, then defending the Ascendancy in the midst of political hubbub, it does not seem, after all, so very mysterious that his eerie tales should have guilt as one of their dominant motifs. Perhaps Le Fanu heard the creaking in the fine structure of Anglo-Ireland, feared that it could collapse and was not entirely sure that guilt was not one of the forces destroying it from within.

Le Fanu's short pieces fall into three main categories : humorous Irish stories, realistic stories and stories of the irrational, each of which offers a different view of mystery, depending on what effect that mystery produces and on whom.

If, for example, we read *Jim Sullivan's Adventures in the Great Snow* or *The Quare Gander* which Le Fanu wrote at the beginning of his literary career in the 1840s, we are simply confronted with what N. Browne calls « the obsolete tradition of the Stage Irishman (...) conceived originally for the entertainment of Anglo-Irish readers (...) » (6). All the characters are good-natured, gullible, loyal Irish peasants whose ancestral superstitions make them believe they are experiencing mysterious adventures. Their fears and terrors, however real they may be, are simply ludicrous bubbles that eventually burst in their own faces. The reader is offered entertainment at the expense of naive sympathetic beings whose sole merit is to have existed as such, to allow the story-teller to report their picturesque idiom and colourful behaviour. Here, dramatic irony is the keyword of the author's technique while his energetic imagination manifests itself in numerous excellent plots and subplots. The reader may enjoy the mysteries without any real disturbance of his comfort or convictions. These stories reveal Le Fanu the folklorist at his best as, without disparagement, he lovingly puts to use Irish cultural material and traditions. Characters like the « fairy doctor » or the Catholic priest who takes advantage of his parishioners' fears, although he is as ready as they are to believe in supernatural manifestations, or again superstitions like the idea of an animal being inhabited by the spirit of a dead man, could not have found a better literary conjurer than Le Fanu, who, as a young man, had spent hours listening to folktales from the lips of renowned story tellers.

If we now turn to *The Last Heir of Castle Connor*, which Le Fanu wrote in 1838 when he started contributing to the *Dublin University Magazine*, we find an entirely different vein of mystery. This grim, realistic narrative is supposed to be told by one Father Purcell — a mythical narrator, obviously Le Fanu's mouthpiece — who is preoccupied with the ancient glory of Ireland that strikingly contrasts with its present dismal condition. As his melancholy mood evokes the old families that once were the country's magnificence and splendour, Purcell is logically led to the matter of the story — how the last heir of one of these noble families met his death. What is unnatural, almost supernatural, here, is the dogged obstinacy with which a professional duelist, Fitzgerald, is set upon killing O'Connor. Fitzgerald is a rather mysterious character. He speaks little. He secludes himself from the world only welcoming social intercourse as an opportunity to precipitate an immediate duel. O'Connor, a frank, gay, generous, amiable aristocrat, loved by the peasants who recognize him as their lord because of his generosity and gallantry, is an ideal prey for Fitzgerald. As one for whom honour comes foremost, he too willingly responds to Fitzgerald's challenge, so much so in fact that the latter, as if to enjoy the sadistic pleasure of postponing the moment of a confrontation they both know is inevitable, sends him a note saying that the argument they had is no sufficient reason for a duel. This of course is only a further, more subtle provocation revealing that Fitzgerald is not simply a brute but a refined villain with

psychological insight. Here Le Fanu's strong sense of characterization as well as suspense appears at its best, together with
his sure gift for painfully photographic descriptions. Natural
description is also employed to stress the dreadfulness of the
whole affair. After many skilful delays — the comparing of the
pistols which Le Fanu terms « surgical instruments », O'Connor's
intentional miss of Fitzgerald, the spectators' indignantly crying
« Butcher, butcher », Fitzgerald's witness's stopping the action
to ask O'Connor if he is wearing two coats, which he says might
impede the progress of the bullet — after Le Fanu has thus built
the action up to a high shrill pitch of dramatic agony, the lethal
shot is eventually fired. When O'Connor dies a few days later,
absolutely terror-stricken, uttering a few words marked with « the
incoherence of distraction », his head sinks forward because, Le
Fanu concludes, « horror and despair had unstrung every nerve
and sinew ».

We must not forget that this story takes place in Ireland, that
an Irishman has dispatched another Irishman without cause.
That Le Fanu meant this to be an allegory of the fate of what
after all was his own country is quite probable considering Father
Purcell's prologue that we mentioned earlier. Should an Irishman
treat a fellow-countryman as Fitzgerald treated O'Connor ?
Should fellow-countrymen waste their sense of honour — and too
often lose their lives for such trifles ? Poor Ireland, Le Fanu
seems to say, if no nobler issues than this can offer a proper field
for the gallantry of its inhabitants and if blind savagery directs
the theatre of its history.

It is mostly as a writer of ghost stories and of tales of the
supernatural or the irrational that Joseph Sheridan Le Fanu is
now remembered. It would be hard to over-estimate the difficulty
of writing effective, successful stories of this kind. The risks are
considerable for as E.F. Benson has suggested : « The fearful lies
but a hair's breadth away from the grotesque and the ludicrous » (7).

But in view of our analysis of Le Fanu's achievement in the
writing of what was essentially a realistic story where we saw
how he could masterfully convey a sense of fear and dread
through the recounting of a purely « earthly » event like a duel,
we can be sure that he was equal to the task when it came to
ghosts. Of the thirty or so irrational stories he wrote, some like
« Dickon the Devil » or « The Child that Went with the Fairies »

were inspired by Irish folklore but not this time by its humorous vein. « Dickon the Devil » tells the story of a farm boy who is carried off by a spectre and whose wits are permanently unsettled as a result of the experience. « The Child that Went with the Fairies », a tale familiar in all Celtic lands, is treated by Le Fanu in a rather original way since, contrary to many other versions of the same theme, it does not tell us how the child is rescued or if he is ultimately rescued at all. Other stories such as « The Village Bully » or « The Sexton's Adventure » tell us about sombre destinies and supernatural or irrational revenges that come to redeem past injustices. « Sir Dominick's Bargain » and at least three other stories take up the well known Faustian legend of the pact with the devil.

Although they either retell common Irish tales or employ the ancient themes of a universal folk or literary legendry, all these stories bear the mark of originality. None of the ordinary Victorian practitioners of the ghost story — we think of authors as famous as Rhoda Broughton, Charlotte Riddell, Amelia Edwards or even Charles Dickens — whatever their excellence may have been, ever equalled Le Fanu in one particular point.

Le Fanu seems to have had the exclusive privilege of realizing that in a ghost story the individuality of the « hero » is much more worthy of notice than the supernatural or irrational phenomena proper. This is why his masterstroke in the handling of irrational mystery is to be found in some of the stories reprinted in 1872 with the title *In A Glass Darkly*. Indeed, tales like « Green Tea » or « The Familiar » deserve to be ranked among the highest pieces in the genre — we think of Walter Scott's « Wandering Willie's Tale » and Edgar Allen Poe's « The Fall of the House of Usher ».

Whereas the events of all Le Fanu's stories we have mentioned so far take place in a more or less remote past, « Green Tea » and « The Familiar » offer but the very vague background of a timeless present which the reader might well assume to be his own. Whereas most of the characters in the other tales belong to the portrait gallery of history, Reverend Jennings in « Green Tea » and Captain Barton in « The Familiar » are just ordinary people the reader might well meet any day.

Jennings and Barton both try hard to understand why they are pursued, and eventually cornered. They both vigorously attempt to discover who or what is « haunting » them and it is this question that creates the mystery of the tale, for it is never clearly answered. A total ambiguity therefore persists to the ends of the stories, to those conclusions that bring death to Jennings and Barton. Throughout Le Fanu attempts to rationalize the irrational and by so doing he subtly adds new mysteries to the main one. Jennings is « haunted » by a black hairy monkey. Barton is watched and followed by a little man. Both stories are presented by Le Fanu as being scientific cases studied by a mythical German physician — one Doctor Martin Hesselius who owes much to Swedenborg and who has himself written a book on Metaphysical Medicine.

Are the two characters the victims of those evil spirits that, according to Swedenborg, are lodged within every man ? Are they prey to hereditary tendencies, to self-destruction ? Are they guilty of some obscure crime, some transgression of a moral code ?

All these are the various explanations offered by Le Fanu for our speculative consideration. This method of suggesting parallel solutions completely puzzles the reader. Is the monkey a real one ? Is Doctor Jennings really talking with a beast ? Is the beast really talking to him or is he simply talking to himself and unable to recognize the voice or the eye of his own « interior vision » or « sense » as Swedenborg called it ? We are at a loss to answer these questions and so are the protagonists — all the more so in Barton's case where the little man who is chasing him and who, according to the laws of physical medicine, should have been dead for a long time, is actually seen and even brushed past by perfectly neutral witnesses ! Le Fanu's literary technique is very skilful. The persecution of Jennings and Barton is gradual, increasingly pervasive in direct proportion to their attempts to escape it. In the end they both retire fearfully to live in seclusion, trusting to sealed rooms where every precaution for their safety has been taken. In these apparently impregnable places they both experience the torture of a most horrible death.

Doctor Hesselius is definitely sure that he might have cured those he terms his « patients » had he been called earlier. Through him, Le Fanu offers a rational or seemingly rational scientific interpretation that enhances all the more the ambiguity of the whole and makes it look and sound all the more irrational. Both interpretations being equally unsatisfactory, we above all remain confronted with physical horror and mental terror that reach a degree of refinement which is not easily forgotten. Whatever the interpretation, we are faced with guilt on every page. Barton and Jennings seem guilty of something, of some abnormality, some mysterious crime. The mystery of the rational, or the irrational, is in fact the mystery of guilt.

The pangs that a guilty conscience has to endure, the various levels of consciousness of guilt that one may uncover if one has the will to do so, the inevitable retribution, the constant suggestion of the dual or even triple aspects in man's psyche — all these definitely suggest a new science, a new way of studying the human personality. Le Fanu undeniably sensed the birth of psychoanalysis.

Doctor Hesselius is neither a physician nor a metaphysician. His vocabulary is puzzling and his conception of medicine rather special. « I speak of medical science », he says, « as I hope some day to see it more generally understood, in a much more comprehensive sense than its generally material treatment would warrant » (8).

The study of Swedenborg had given Le Fanu a crucial insight. He had an intuition that Swedenborg's *Arcana Coelestia* (9), those « celestial » secrets, would one day appear as essentially human or terrestrial ones. However, evil spirits or subconscious layers of the human psyche, are not the only standards provided by Le Fanu for measuring the mystery of guilt.

« However the truth may be », he writes at the end of « The Familiar », « as to the origin and motives of these mysterious persecutions, there can be no doubt that, with respect to the agencies by which it was accomplished, absolute and impenetrable mystery is like to prevail until the day of doom » (10).

His *Personal Diary* (11) is there to prove that his faith was real and that his reference to God is neither a complacent literary allusion to conventional Victorian creeds nor an easy shelter against the unknown. God, and God only, has the masterkey to the sealed rooms of man's mind. It is useless for man to seek to hide from judgement ; evil will out.

Le Fanu's essential merit is to have probed so deep into man's psychology, to have provided a really clinical analysis of human behaviour, to have suggested in fact that the ghosts of our minds are those that we are to fear most and that man is to strive vigorously — not alone, but with the help of God — if he wishes to be saved.

In the Ireland of the nineteenth century, how many Anglo-Irish members of the Ascendancy were prepared to face the knowledge of guilt ? Why did the structures of this society start creaking, soon to collapse ? Because of the mark of guilt, a guilt as ancient as the history of the relationship between England and Ireland, a guilt perhaps as ancient as the history of man's relationship with man. Let us quickly evoke here the recurrent dream Le Fanu had of a house collapsing and the sad judgement of the doctor when the dreamer died : « I feared this — that house fell at last » (12).

Man's fall into the dark abysses of his own guilt is what Le Fanu pictured in most of his best short stories. Invisible but to himself, man's faults are projected on the blurred screen of his mind. Because he managed to shoot the film of these mysterious pictures, Le Fanu deserves to be called the Prince of the Invisible.

# NOTES

1. Critics who have been puzzled by Le Fanu include A.P. Graves, M.R. James, E. Kenton, E.F. Benson, M. Summers, S.M. Ellis, N. Browne, F.B. Shroyer, E.F. Bleiler and E. Bowen.

2. Thomas Phillip Le Fanu : *Memoir of the Le Fanu Family*, largely from materials collected by W.J.H. Le Fanu ; privately printed, 1924.

3. Thomas Phillip Le Fanu, cf. supra., p. 56 : « Joseph Le Fanu was a lonely boy devoted to his own thoughts and his father's books, climbing to the roof of the house and drawing his ladder after him on the approach of visitors, and though active and muscular taking no part in the field sports in which his brother excelled ».

4. S.M. Ellis : *Wilkie Collins, Le Fanu and Others*, London, Constable, 1931, p. 141 : « (Le Fanu's) high spirits and delight in practical jokes... ».

5. Thomas Flanagan : *The Irish Novelists, 1800-1850*, New York, Columbia University Press, 1959, p. 46 : « It is significant, perhaps, that both of these highly gifted members of the Ascendancy (Maturin and Le Fanu) should have turned to tales whose somber and uncanny atmosphere seeks to transcend the immediacies of social fact ».

6. Nelson Browne : *Sheridan Le Fanu*, London, Arthur Baker, 1951, p. 69.

7. E.F. Benson : « Sheridan Le Fanu » in *The Spectator*, Feb. 21, 1931, pp. 263-4.

8. Sheridan Le Fanu : *In A Glass Darkly*, with an introduction by V.S. Pritchett, London, John Lehmann, 1947, p. 18.

9. This book, originally written in Latin by Emmanuel Swedenborg, was published in London from 1749 to 1756. Here is the title of the complete edition in English : « *Arcana Coelestia : The Heavenly Arcana* contained in the Holy Scriptures, or Word of the Lord, unfolded in an Exposition of Genesis and Exodus : together with a Relation of Wonderful Things seen in the Worlds of spirits and in the Heaven of Angels ». Publications of the Swendenborg Society, 1 Bloomsbury St., London.

10. Sheridan Le Fanu : *In a Glass Darkly*, cf. supra., p. 82.

11. Jean Lozes : « Fragment d'un journal intime de Joseph Sheridan Le Fanu : document inédit en date du 18 mai 1858 » in *Caliban XI*, Annales de l'Univerité de Toulouse-Le Mirail, Tome X, Fascicule I, 1974, pp. 153-64.

12. Nelson Browne, cf. supra., p. 31.

# THE COMPOSITION OF SOMERVILLE
# AND ROSS'S «IRISH R.M.»

## Guy FEHLMANN

The *Irish R.M.* exhibits the two types of linkage described by Chklovski (1). It is clear that the essential structure of the collection is none other than Major Yeates and this is the clear suggestion of Somerville and Ross who have given their book the title *Some Experiences of an Irish R.M.*. At the same time the fact that Yeates' surname is not mentioned in the title shows that his person is not meant to influence the course of events. On top of that his anonymity is intended to suggest the total submission of Yeates to the unpredictable turns of the plot which is meant to develop freely without being shaped by the will of one of the protagonists. In this perspective Yeates is the anti-hero par excellence always present and never active. The following are the terms in which he presents himself in the first story of the *R.M.* :

A resident Magistracy in Ireland is not an easy thing to come by nowadays ; neither is it a very attractive job ; yet on the evening when I first propounded the idea to the young lady who had recently consented to become Mrs. Sinclair Yeates, it seemed glittering with possibilities. There was, on that occasion, a sunset and a string band playing « The Gondoliers », and there was also an ingenuous belief in the omnipotence of a godfather of Philippa's — (Philippa was the young lady) — who had once been a member of the Government.

I was then climbing the steep ascent of the Captains towards my Majority. I have no fault to find with Philippa's godfather ; he did all and more than even Philippa had expected ; nevertheless, I had attained to the dignity of mud major, and had spent a good deal on postage stamps, and on railway fares to interview people of influence, before I found myself in the hotel of Skebawn, opening long envelopes addressed to « Major Yeates, R.M. » (2).

For the agent, that is to say Yeates, to have a role in the action that would be as neutral as possible he must not be Irish and must know nothing of Irish life. These conditions of « nonexistence » were admirably fulfilled by the Major and for this A. Rivoallan judged him to be a foreign body in Irish society (3). This judgement need not be taken as a fault in Somerville and Ross but on the contrary as proof of their mastery of the device of composition by linkage. This is why they felt it necessary to let Yeates explain how after some petty intrigues encouraged by the unpredictable humours of the administration he found himself installed one fine day with the powers of an Irish R.M. Philippa his wife usefully completes his character like a variation created to enrich a melody. Deeply similar to Yeates she nevertheless acts or reacts in a contrary manner that reflects the moods of her feminine nature. Generally she is calm when he is irritated, optimistic when he is down-hearted, naive when he is distrustful etc. Other characters like Flurry Knox, his grandmother Mrs Knox, and Slipper also appear frequently but their role is less one of giving cohesion to the linkage than one of creating a high dramatic intensity in the story.

The composition of an *Irish R.M.* is thus solidly founded on two complementary systems remarkably harmonious with each other. This does not mean however that the composition of each story taken separately is itself of the same high quality. One can easily imagine an excellent collection of mediocre stories. Frank O'Connor defined this problem and suggested one possible solution for it. In his introduction to *The Lonely Voice* he analyses the creation and the particular qualities and shortcomings of the *Irish R.M.*

Kipling, a remarkable storyteller with some of Leskov's virtues, has had little influence outside the English-speaking countries, and even in them it would be hard to deduce from the work of any serious storyteller that such a writer as Kipling had ever existed. Even in his own country he has had no influence on Lawrence, Coppard, or Pritchett.

In Ireland, one could certainly deduce his influence on Edith Somerville and Martin Ross, the authors of *The Irish R.M.*, but the history of their work in their own country is almost an object lesson in the way storytelling develops.

*The Irish R.M.* — to adopt a general title for the books of stories that began with *Some Experiences of an Irish R.M.* — is one of the most lovable books I know. Edith Somerville was an art student in Paris and came under the influence of the French Naturalists, as we can see from a novel like *The Real Charlotte*. George Moore, another member of the Irish landowning class, was also an art student, and also came under the influence of Naturalism, and his novel *Muslin* stands comparison with *The Real Charlotte*. But there the similarity ends. When Somerville and Ross wrote stories, they forgot all they had ever learned from the French Naturalists and apparently wrote just to enjoy themselves. George Moore did not forget, and the influence of Flaubert, Zola, and the Goncourts — even of Turgenev — can be seen even in the slightest of the stories in *The Untilled Field*.

The contrast between these two books is extraordinary. I have reread *The Irish R.M.* off and on for forty years for the mere pleasure of it. The stories in it are yarns, pure and imple. They have a few of the virtues of Leskov's stories ; they are of the open air, of horses and animals, and people who have much in common with both. The humor is of the slapstick variety I remember from boys' books of my childhood (...) The number of mishaps that occur at the local agricultural show pass all reckoning (4).

Frank O'Connor then quotes a famous passage from « A Royal Command » in which the organizers of an obstacle race discover that the stream is dry and fill it with quicklime. Every one of the horses refuses the jump and amid the cheers of the public unseats its rider. These are the final sentences of O'Connor's commentary :

It is only when one asks oneself what the stories are about

that one begins to have doubts of one's own judgment. There, indeed, is a man's voice speaking — or a woman's — and it calls for an audience, but take the audience away and what are we left with ? Nothing, certainly, that responds to analysis (5).

What seems most to disconcert Frank O'Connor is an elusiveness that defies concrete approaches. As he sees it, it is impossible to dissect the stories critically before they melt away without leaving the slightest trace. It would appear that Frank O'Connor's intuition has been spoiled a little by his desire to make a detailed comparison between their work and that of George Moore. It is evident that a naturalist technique can be found in Moore's short stories as well as in his novels while only the novels of Somerville show this influence. Must one then conclude with O'Connor that Somerville and Ross are blind to the example of Flaubert, Zola and the Goncourt brothers ? This is an unlikely hypothesis as it would mean accepting that Somerville was highly conscious of naturalist models in *The Real Charlotte* published in 1894 and had completely forgotten them in an *Irish R.M.* published five years later in 1899. Surprisingly Frank O'Connor did not ask himself if in fact the forgetfulness is not deliberate. While his explanation of the circumstances of the writing of the *Irish R.M.* — « ...apparently... just to enjoy themselves » — is certainly not false, it may not be the whole truth. There is no doubt that the two authors enjoyed composing the *Irish R.M.* but this does not mean that the composition is due to chance or fantasy. The humour and the comic spirit of the *Irish R.M.* show an obvious perfection that can only be the fruit of a long preparation. The manuscripts contain precious revelations of the care with which Somerville and Ross worked out the form of their stories.

In 1945 and 1946 Professor Coghill closely studied the manuscripts and it is of interest to quote from his work. Somerville and Ross undertook detailed research during the preparation of the *Irish R.M.* Firstly they reviewed the motifs that might usefully support the plot and then they composed a brief outline of the action. After that the characters were drawn in ink by Edith Somerville as well as the animals, the houses and the furniture. This work was generally corrected by Martin Ross. The following are some details from the third folio of manuscripts.

*Preliminary Sketches for Plots of the Above R.M. Stories*
Page 1
a) some privates notes
b) « *Possible Motives — Bad. Mag. April 98*»
1 — Squatting, foxcatchers. 2 Bocok. 3 Underbred dog. 4 Longford Ghost. 5. Swimming Dog. 6. Private still. 7 Kennel horses, buried horses. 8. Landleague ? 9. Driving on Cab Dublin. 10. Hunting foxes by naked pursuers Tragumena Hatchetha Creature. Grand Jury Wake. Flurry's proposal for young lady — or two young ladies. His friend is Tomsy Flood. Doing up hair out hunting. Hounds in bed. I Rum. 2 Moonlighter's run away. Yachts with wreck and Dog killing. 5. Private still. 6 Flurry's elopements.

Page 2-5 : *Preliminary Abstracts of R.M. Stories*
| | | |
|---|---|---|
| *Great uncle McCarthy* . . . . . . . . . . . . | 25 lines (approx.) | |
| *Trinket's colt* . . . . . . . . . . . . . . . . . . | 26 » | » |
| *In the Curranhilty Country* . . . . . . . . | 22 » | » |
| *Lisheen races, Second-hand* . . . . . . . . | 18 » | » |
| *Philippa's foxhunt* . . . . . . . . . . . . . . . | 18 » | » |
| *The Waters of Strife* . . . . . . . . . . . . . | 50 » | » |
| *A Misdeal* . . . . . . . . . . . . . . . . . . . . . | 2 » | » |

*Sketches :*
About sixteen scribble-sketches scattered through the left and pages, e.g. Men's heads, crazy house, horse head, horse and cart, child by table, fox, dog, man on horseback, elephant, etc, but particularly facing page 45, which is numbered page 6, *Portrait of Martin Ross* under which is written (in the hand of E. OE. S.) « V.F.M. (libelled) », and facing page 75, which is the foxterriers of E. OE Somerville, of whom she has written in various books ; also another (recumbent) portrait of CANDY, facing page numbered 12, ten pages from the end. Another of MUSK, pregnant, three pages from end.

*Remarks :*
Some red-ink corrections *in the hand of Martin Ross*, facing page 88, numbered p. 2, and elsewhere. With regard to the list of *Possible Motives* given on this page, above, some of these « motives » are obviously the germs of the *R.M.* stories : e.g. *N° 2 Bocock* is clearly the germ of « Lisheen races, Second-

hand », etc. But E. OE. Somerville says she cannot now remember what most of them refer to. See also *Happy Days* by E. OE. S. and M.R. 1946, for chapter on the start of *R.M.* (6).

It is thus quite clear that the plot, the characters and the setting of the *Irish R.M.* were worked out, written down and discussed long before being integrated into a story. N. Coghill notes for instance the *Bocock* which is the starting point of the story « Lisheen Races Second-hand ». Most of the other motifs were also used, number 4 « Longford Ghost » can be found in « Harringtons », etc. The fact that in 1946 Edith Somerville could not clearly remember what inspired these motifs is not surprising when one takes into account that she was then ninety eight years of age. In the chapter of *Happy Days* to which Nevill Coghill alludes he stresses the deliberateness of the composition of the *Irish R.M.* and gives the example of the origins of *Trinket's Colt* :

I have had to grope in the dark corners of an indifferent memory in order to find some few facts about the infancy of our friend the *Irish R.M.*, and as a result of my gropings, I find myself marvelling at the patience and pertinacity of the Divinity that shaped his beginnings, even more than his ends. Both were undoubtedly rough-hewn. Polish had to come later, and I can truly say that none of Major Yeates' varied experiences received rougher or more « tavern-usage » than did the affair of « Trinket's Colt ». But the colt had his revenge. We couldn't escape from him (...) It has been said of Irish people that they do the right thing in the wrong place. Thus did Martin Ross and I employ any of the idle moments that happen in holiday times ; moments of waiting for Madame Lâ-Lâ's kettle to boil at the tea-party she was giving for our guests ; or of waiting while the Dean caught and harnessed the donkey which by sheer Irish instinct she had materialized in the marshes, and compelled to our uses. During any one of these chance intervals, one of us would scribble the haunting notion that had tormented us — a half-remembered saying of Slipper's, an elusive adjective that had evaded us. Somehow, scrap by scrap, the story unfolded itself for us, and I think we enjoyed its culminating instant as much as did old Mrs. Knox (7).

Thus Edith Somerville's humorous memories of the infancy of the *Irish R.M.* totally corroborate the observations of Professor Coghill.

Once the motifs have been found, the protagonists chosen, and their appearances and dress fixed in their details ; once the setting has been established and the local geography worked out, there still remains the problem of giving the story an interior rhythm which will efficiently bring it to its close. Sometimes the anecdote chosen is one similar to those discovered by Mark Twain. In such cases it has enough inherent force to enable it to dispense with supplementary procedures of composition. « A Royal Command » falls into this category of stories as its, anecdote is sufficiently dynamic to give it a rapid development in an alternation of comic moments that come ever closer to each other until the neutral dénouement is achieved. The first great moment of the story shows the visit of a Sultan to a jumping competition organized by an Agricultural Society in a small Irish town. After different incidents the competition turns into a farce to the great embarrassment of the organizers who are ashamed to have offered such a spectacle to the Sultan. During the next two days Major Yeates resumes his normal occupations which take him away from house. He then returns, convinced that life in his house has gone back to normal and that he will be able to relax after his day's work. It is at that point that the second great moment of the story begins when Yeates finds out that his servants are shifting furniture and in a bad humour about it. Before he can discover the reason for this upset his cook tells him that the local butcher is looking for a spear to kill the animal that is going to supply the main meat course at lunch. She adds that the butcher is indignant at being obliged to slaughter in such a barbaric way even if it is to satisfy the wishes of an oriental potentate. It is then that Yeates realises that his wife has invited the Sultan to lunch. The preparation continues feverishly. A piano tuner arrives whom no one dares send away. Excitement mounts until a turbaned individual presents himself. Yeates welcomes him with deference and then discovers that it is only Slipper. At this point of the story the neutral dénouement begins. Its function is to lower the dramatic tension replacing it with comic relief. Slipper has brought a telegram announcing that the Sultan's visit is cancelled. In the second part of the dénouement the piano tuner calmly states that he has had this information all the time but that he felt that no one would be interested in it. The two steps in the dénouement correspond to the two principal moments of the comic development of the plot thus giving a perfect symmetry to the overall economy of the story.

In other cases the anecdote in itself is not sufficient to give a story the necessary dynamic rhythm. For them Somerville and Ross adopt a form of composition that creates lack of balance that will bring the necessary dynamism to the development of the story. This procedure generally involves the notions of contrast or inequality. The unbalance of the combinations English/Irish English/Anglo-Irish, Anglo-Irish/Irish is capable of giving such a dynamism.

This procedure is used with effect in a good number of stories like « A Misdeal », « The Friend of her Youth », « The Comte de Pralines ». Besides inequalities and contrasts one can find the ordinary procedures of mystification, excess or absence of coincidences. The Comte de Pralines for instance is neither a count nor a Frenchman and the misfortunes of poor Chichester are made still more comic by an admirable series of unpleasant events which affect his person. The structure of the short stories of Somerville and Ross owes nothing to the principles of the French Naturalists. Notwithstanding Frank O'Connor's affirmations, it is the result of a deliberate organization, capable of being analysed, and not a mere wandering of the fancy among a few vague themes.

# NOTES

1. V. Chklovski : « La construction de la Nouvelle et du Roman » in T.Todorov, *Théorie de la Littérature*, Paris, Editions du Seuil, 1965, p. 194.

2. « Great Uncle McCarthy » : *The Irish R.M.*, London, Faber & Faber, 1962, p. 9.

3. *Littérature Irlandaise Contemporaine*, Paris, Hachette, 1939, p. 73.

4. Frank O'Connor : *The Lonely Voice*, London, Macmillan, 1963, Introduction, pp. 33-34.

5. *Id.*, p. 35.

6. Nevill Coghill : *Works of E. OE. Somerville and Martin Ross, Collection of Manuscripts*, 1946, p. 13.

7. *Happy Days*, London, Longmans, Green & Co, 1946, chap. VI, pp. 73-74.

# GEORGE MOORE : «THE UNTILLED FIELD»

## John CRONIN

The strange origins of George Moore's seminal collection of short stories, *The Untilled Field*, reflect the writer's idiosyncratic response to the Ireland of his time. They also throw a revealing light on the linguistic ferment of the age, a period during which many writers deliberately fed into their work the creative impulses of Ireland's two vigorous languages. All Moore's great contemporaries, from Yeats to Lady Gregory, from Douglas Hyde to J.M. Synge, were constantly involved with what Yeats himself had identified as the central preoccupation of the Anglo-Irish writer, the creation of an idiom. Lady Gregory's « Kiltartan » dialect, the vigorous speech of Synge's *Playboy*, the cogently dramatic idiom of Yeats's mature poems, all owe their peculiar vitality to various kinds of linguistic fusion. Moore had come to Ireland in May, 1899 for the performance of Yeats's play, *The Countess Cathleen*, in the Antient Concert Rooms. By 1902 he had established himself as an important figure among the writers of the Irish Literary Revival. Although he felt that he was himself too old to learn the Irish language he did not hesitate to try to impose it on his nephews, the sons of his brother, Colonel Maurice Moore, even going to the extraordinary lengths of threatening to disinherit them if their parents did not arrange for them to become fluent speakers of Irish. He now also set about making his own contribution to the efforts of the Gaelic League to revive the Irish language. To this end he undertook the composition of a book of stories for use in schools. The writing of a collection of stories had originally been suggested to him by John Eglinton (W.K. Magee) who had urged Moore to make his contribution to the Irish revival by writing stories of Irish life in the manner of Turgenev's *Tales of a Sportsman*. « As well ask me to paint like Corot » was Moore's reply but, in spite of this disclaimer, he began work on a set of stories.

He described *The Untilled Field* as « a book written in the beginning out of no desire of self-expression but in the hope of furnishing the young Irish of the future with models ». All experienced readers of Moore have to come to terms with the subtle hazards of his comments on himself and his work and learn to pick a wary way through the minefield of his personal ironies and shifts of tone. We may, however, permit ourselves the tiny luxury of taking this comment of his literally, only noting the importance of the qualifying phrase « in the beginning ». The work may well have begun with the simple didactic intention propounded by Moore. His biographer, Joseph Hone, commenting on Moore's response to the Ireland of the turn of the century, seems disposed to believe that Moore did indeed possess quite serious ambitions :

> It is more than hinted in *Ave* that he had already a lively sense of the comedy of his situation, but the evidence of his Irish associates and of his own correspondence between 1895 and 1900 reveals him as a man who was in deadly earnest, determined to interpret the facts of Irish life according to his desires, and fully persuaded that something was in the air which offered him a chance of influence if not of leadership (1).

Thus, *The Untilled Field* may well have been begun quite simply as Moore's offering to the language revival movement but it was soon to become much more than a mere text-book for the primary schools of the new Ireland. It was to grow into an elaborately conceived exploration of all that attracted and repelled Moore in the Ireland of his day and, in so doing, was to become eventually a profoundly important influence on many subsequent exponents of the form, from Joyce to Frank O'Connor.

It made its first appearance in 1902 as *An T-úr-Ghort*. Moore was very pleased at seeing his name in its Irish form of « Seórsa Ó Mórdha » on the title page on which also appeared the name of the translator, one Pádraig Ó Súilleabháin of Trinity College, Dublin. The little book, published by Sealy, Briars & Walker of Dublin contained six stories. One of these, « An Gúna-Phósta », was signed by « Tórna » (i.e. Tadhg O Donnchadha) as translator and it would seem reasonable to assume that the remaining five were translated by Ó Súilleabháin since « Tórna's » distinguished name is not attached to any of them. The work attracted very little notice, the Gaelic League even failing to display it in their window. Its English version, *The Untilled Field*, came out in April 1903. Moore got T.W. Rolleston to render some of the stories in *An T-úr-Ghort* back into English and worked from Rolleston's versions to produce his own renovated stories, declaring that they were « much improved after their bath in Irish ». Tracing the many variations of the stories from one language to another and back again, and following their progress from periodical to book publication would constitute a major piece of literary detection and tabulation which is hardly to our purpose at present. Nevertheless, a brief comparison of *An T-úr-Ghort* with the first edition of *The Untilled Field* is not without interest. Few of the stories in the Irish volume tally exactly with their versions in *The Untilled Field*. Indeed, the first story, « Tír-ghrádh », is missing altogether. It is a curious tale of an heroic figure who undergoes a mystical experience on a mountain-side, feels called upon to join the Boers in their fight against British imperialism and emigrates to South Africa to join in the battle there. This has, one presumes, some connection with Moore's avowed interest in the struggle of the Boers but he would seem to have decided to omit it from the English volume. A few of its details survived to appear in « The Wild Goose ». The second Irish story, « 'San n-Diothramh Dubh », becomes « A Playhouse in the Waste » and here also Moore departs in large measure from the Irish original. In the latter the playhouse planned by the priest is never built whereas, in the English version, it is built but falls in ruins. The amusing incident concerning the Catholic priest who lends his large congregation to his friend, the local Protestant clergyman, to enable the latter to impress his visiting bishop is dropped from the English version, whereas the conclusion of « A Playhouse in the Waste » is more extensively developed and includes the details of the girl « Good Deeds » and her illegitimate child whose dreadful death is held to be responsible for the fall of the playhouse.

The story translated by « Tórna » appears as « The Wedding Dress » in a version very close to the original Irish and « Home Sickness », one of the most acclaimed stories, also tallies very closely with the Irish « Galar Dúithche ». « The Exile » reproduces the detail of « An Deóraidhe » pretty faithfully though the treatment of Peter Phelan, the brother who wins the girl, is more effective in the Irish story where the mild satire of his general incompetence is more subtly presented than in the English version. The last story in the Irish volume becomes the fifth and final section of « Some Parishioners » but here again there are substantial variations. The Irish story of the woman who becomes obsessed with the notion of donating a stained-glass window to the local church is told in much greater detail which Moore reduced considerably in the later volume.

In general, when we compare the two works and note how they sometimes overlap and sometimes diverge from each other it is possible to suggest that the changes made by Moore throw some light on the writer's over-all design in *The Untilled Field*. The omission of the Boer War story, for example, would seem to imply that Moore found its romantic nationalism unsuitably idealistic for the English book. Perhaps we may also hazard a guess that the casual friendship between the Catholic priest and the Protestant minister in « 'San n-Diothramh Dubh » did not altogether accord with Moore's general satiric attitude to the Catholic clergy of the 1903 volume. Such alterations suggest that he excised all traces of sentimentality and idealism in his search for a more realistic and satirical tone. When he set about developing his Irish school primer into a full critical survey of Ireland's aesthetic and cultural deficiencies he deleted much that was unsuited to the new conception of the work.

The resulting book has often been linked with Joyce's *Dubliners* on which it may have exerted some influence (2). The two sets of stories are alike in a number of ways. They are both ambitiously conceived national panoramas devised by writers whose involvement with their chosen material was at once profound and richly ambivalent and whose creative confidence ensured distinctive tonal ironies. Moore's book, however, is more genial than *Dubliners* and much less tautly constructed. It does not, for example, confine itself rigidly to a single geographical location. The stories in *The Untilled Field* provide both urban and rural settings, being centred on North Mayo and the Dublin of the

1880's. They are given a loose framework in the persons of a sculptor named Rodney and his friends, Harding and Carmady. Rodney and Harding figure in the first story, « In the Clay », and also in the last one, « The Way Back ». Rodney voices in both stories Moore's most forthright condemnation of Irish philistinism in the arts and its origins in clerical domination. The specific occasion of the attack is contained in the opening story. Rodney has been sculpting a Virgin and Child, a commission from the local priest, Fr.McCabe. He has been employing as his nude model for the figure of the Virgin a local girl named Lucy Delaney. When Fr.McCabe discovers that Lucy has been modelling for Rodney, he informs her parents and on the very next day Rodney arrives at his studio to find his Virgin and Child in ruins and other recent works also destroyed. It eventually transpires that this vandalism has been perpetrated by Lucy's two young brothers who happen to overhear Fr.McCabe's revelations to their parents. The incident thus emerges as a consequence of misunderstood priestly prudery and we are clearly meant to interpret this as a representation of the damaging role played in Ireland by the Catholic clergy who are seen as pious bunglers exerting powerfully repressive influences on an uncomprehending and childish laity. The angry sculptor decides to abandon his « unwashed country » and betake himself to Paris or Rome where art and the artist are esteemed at their true worth. The closing story of the volume enunciates precisely the same condemnation of Irish philistinism. In « The Way Back » Rodney and his friend, Harding, meet in London. Harding, who is a painter, has encountered in London Rodney's former model, Lucy Delaney. The girl has fled from Ireland and, after a half-hearted attempt to seduce her, Harding genuinely befriends her and even visits her parents in Ireland on her behalf. Lucy eventually marries an American and is thereby safely stowed in Moore's other exilic refuge. The artist flees to Europe, the Irish peasant to America. In both the first and the last story we are offered a suitably simplified version of the history of art to buttress Rodney's assault on the artistic obscurantism of the Irish. The Gael is presented as a cultural yokel. « Since Cormac's chapel he has built nothing but mud cabins », Rodney informs us. Harding suggests the possibility of a Celtic renaissance linked with the revival of the Irish language (a side-glance this, perhaps, at Moore's own slightly absurd brush with the Irish language movement) but Rodney will have none of it :

> You know as well as I do, Harding, that the art and literature
> of the 15th and 16th centuries were due to a sudden dispersal,
> a sudden shedding of the prejudices and conventions of the
> middle ages ; the renaissance was a joyous returning to
> Hellenism, the source of all beauty. There is as little free love
> in Ireland as there is free thought ; men have ceased to care for
> women and women to care for men. Nothing thrives in Ireland,
> but the celibate, the priest, the nun and the ox. There is no
> unfaith and the violence of the priest is against any sensual
> transgression. A girl marries at once or becomes a nun — a
> free girl is a danger. There is no courtship, there is no walking
> out, and the passion which is the direct inspiration of all the
> world's music and art is reduced to the mere act of begetting
> children (3).

Ireland, then, is a cultural desert presided over by spiritual
dictators. The anti-clerical case could scarcely be more explicitly
enunciated and these two stories, discursive and didactic to a
tedious degree, would hardly engage our serious interest were it
not for the characteristically surprising twist which Moore
provides in the conclusion of the final story. This lies in
Harding's amazing decision to go against the artistic logic so
pungently propounded by Rodney, for Harding decides at the end
that he will return to live in his native Ireland. In its context the
effect is as striking as though Stephen Dedalus had concluded his
diary entries in the *Portrait* by announcing his firm intention of
taking a teaching post with the Christian Brothers. Harding
informs Rodney of his decision in the final paragraph of the
story :

> One day looking across a park with a view of the mountains
> in the distance, I perceived a pathetic beauty in the country
> itself that I had not perceived before ; and a year afterwards
> I was driving about the Dublin mountains, and met two
> women on the road ; there was something pathetic and wistful
> about them, something dear, something intimate, and I felt
> drawn towards them. I felt I should like to live among these
> people again. There is a proverb in Irish which says that no
> man ever wanders far from his grave sod. We are thrown out,

and we circle awhile in the air, and return to the feet of the thrower. But what astonished me is the interest that everybody takes in my departure. Everyone seems agreed that nothing could be more foolish, nothing more mad. But if I were to go to meet Asher at Marseilles, and cruise with him in the Greek Islands, and go on to Cairo, and spend the winter talking to wearisome society, everyone would consider my conduct most rational. You, my dear friend, Rodney, you tempt me with Italy and conversations about yellowing marbles ; and you won't be angry with me when I tell you that all your interesting utterances about the Italian renaissance would not interest me half so much as what Paddy Durkin and Father Pat will say to me on the roadside (4).

If the merging and conflicting themes of the first story and the last are properly grasped they will provide the best possible key to the rest of the book which is pervaded by the same oscillation from outright intellectual condemnation of Ireland's many cultural and spiritual deficiencies to a warmly emotional attachment to the Irish people and their lonely and beautiful land. The tone constantly shifts from the sardonic to the tender. There is no stylistic consistency such as we find in Joyce's meticulously integrated *Dubliners*. The characteristic flavour of *The Untilled Field* derives not from a single clearly articulated authorial viewpoint but rather from Moore's leisurely and contrived prose style with its deliberate Gaelic overtones.

Enclosed within the argumentative boundaries provided by « In the Clay » and « The Way Back » we have the untilled field itself, Moore's Irish « field full of folk ». The picture he paints of the place and its people, though often bleak, is never merely reductive. As is almost invariably the case with such collections, only a few of the stories achieve full independence of their setting in the volume while most of the others serve to fill out the general picture of characters and setting. This is the case also, for example, with the « R.M. » stories of Moore's celebrated contemporaries, Somerville and Ross. Some of their best stories anthologise well on their own (« Poisson d'Avril » and « Lisheen Races, Second-Hand » are cases in point) while many others serve merely to fill out the comic world the writers have set in motion and would not be fully viable if torn from their setting. Even in the case of Joyce's sedulously crafted *Dubliners*, it is arguable that one or two of the individual tales (« After the

Race » is one which springs to mind) might seem rather thin if separated from the parent book. In the case of Moore's collection a few of the stories stand out clearly enough. « Home Sickness », a story lavishly admired by Frank O'Connor, is perhaps the book's most successful item and « The Wedding Gown » and « The Clerk's Quest », though less substantial, can also stand being read in isolation.

Much of the rest of *The Untilled Field*, however, consists of the ruminative filling out of a landscape. « Some Parishioners » by its very title suggests the descriptive role it plays in the book's general fabric. It is a long, leisurely unfolding of rural incidents with pride of place in the controlling of the action inevitably assigned to one of Moore's domineering, thick-skinned priests, Fr.Maguire, who is depicted enacting the customary Moore-ish clerical practices, whipping lovers out of hedges, fulminating against village dances and drinking, making matches with scant regard to the wishes or inclinations of the men and women involved in the matter and collecting money for the building of his new church. In general, Fr.Maguire seems to rule the village unopposed but occasionally he runs full tilt into an insuperable obstinacy as in the case of Biddy McHale, a village woman who wants to pay for a stained-glass window in the new church but persistently refuses to part with her money until she can extract a full guarantee from Fr.Maguire about the positioning and the design of her window. Regularly also, Fr.Maguire has to depend on the greater wisdom and experience of his uncle, Fr.John Stafford, and here we encounter one of the saving graces of the book, Moore's determination to temper his anti-clerical asperities with fairly frequent depictions of gentle and reasonable priests. The outstanding example is the Fr.Mac Turnan of « A Letter to Rome ». Borrowing his central idea, perhaps, from Brian Merriman's celebrated satirical poem, *The Midnight Court*, Moore has Fr.MacTurnan come up with the entertaining notion that the only way to save Ireland from Protestantism is for the Catholic clergy to abandon their vows of celibacy, marry and beget large families. In Ireland, he decides, priests are the best housed, the best fed and the best educated of all Catholics and would clearly make the best possible parents who would beget strong children, rear them well and bring them up as faithful followers of the Church. Once in the snare of this new idea, poor little Fr.MacTurnan must carry it through by writing a letter about it to Rome. The gentle comedy of his attempts to translate his letter into good Latin for the Pope's secretary « who was doubtless a great Latin scholar », leads to a vastly entertaining interview between Fr.MacTurnan and his bishop who, to begin with, embarrasses his visitor horribly by hinting that his plans for Ireland may emanate from some lustful inclinations of his own. Fr.MacTurnan hastily disclaims any such desires on his own part and begs to be excused from marrying even if his proposed reforms are accepted. The bishop finally concludes the matter diplomatically by giving the priest the five pounds which will enable two of his parishioners to marry. So Fr.MacTurnan abandons his grand matrimonial plans for the clergy in favour of arranging the humble nuptials of two of his penurious parishioners.

Sometimes, of course, village humours of this kind give way to darker matters. A number of stories have as narrator an agent for the Irish Industrial Society who travels through Ireland in the last decades of the nineteenth century and visits the bleakest areas of a land denuded by famine and depopulated by emigration. The lonely landscape is seen as having bred the peasants in its own image :

They were scanty fields, drifting from thin grass into bog, and from bog into thin grass again, and in the distance there was a rim of melancholy mountains, and the peasants I saw along the road seemed a counterpart of the landscape. « The land has made them, » I said, « according to its own image and likeness, » and I tried to find words to define the yearning that I read in their eyes as we drove past. But I could find no words that satisfied me (5).

This is the land cursed by Julia Cahill, one of several independently minded young women who figure in Moore's stories and defy the authority of the priest. Julia, in some sense a forerunner of the heroine in *The Lake*, refuses to accept the match made for her by the priest, is condemned from the altar and shunned by her fellow villagers. Before departing for America she curses the village and from that time on « every year a roof has fallen in » and the place is emptied of its people. In a story which links with « A Letter to Rome » through the figure of the mild and selfless Fr.MacTurnan, the narrator encounters this priest characteristically engaged on yet another of his improbable schemes. This time, he has planned to build a playhouse in the wilderness to attract people from Dublin to come and see plays there. The project is inevitably a failure and its failure is linked to the starkly horrible story of the girl who was to have played Good Deeds in the miracle play but succumbed to temptation, bore an illegitimate child and was dreadfully punished for her sin by her implacable mother. At this point Moore's prose attains great heights of realistic horror coupled with grim fantasy :

> The girl had been led astray one evening returning from rehearsal — in the words of my car-driver, « She had been 'wake 'going home one evening, and when the signs of her 'wakeness 'began to show upon her, her mother took the halter off the cow and tied the girl to the wall and kept her there until the child was born. And Mrs. Sheridan put a bit of string round its throat and buried it one night near the playhouse. And it was three nights after that the storm rose and the child was seen pulling the thatch out of the roof (6).

Moore's urban stories resemble the rural ones in that they usually have a strong central preoccupation with loneliness and poverty and various kinds of despair. Edward Dempsey, central figure of « The Clerk's Quest », is strongly reminiscent of some of the pathetic clerks of Joyce's stories. He recalls both the Ignatius Gallagher of « A Little Cloud » and Mr.Duffy in « A Painful Case ». Joyce would not have permitted himself the rather sentimental ending which Moore employs in « The Clerk's Quest » nor, one imagines, would he have approved of the rather contrived happy ending which Moore fastens on the very short story, « Alms-Giving ». While one is entitled to link the characters and the settings of these stories with Joyce, the narrative manner employed in them recalls rather the Stephens of *The Charwoman's Daughter*. Moore never attains the disciplined detachment, the authorial objectivity which is Joyce's great strength in *Dubliners* and, as a result, the figures in *The Untilled Field* never achieve the sharply etched independence of Joyce's most memorable creations. Very few of Moore's characters linger in the memory like Gabriel Conroy or Michael Furey. *The Untilled Field* is overpopulated by intrusive narrators who intervene between us and the characters of the various tales. Rodney, Harding, the agent of the Irish Industrial Society, all surrogates of the incessantly intrusive Moore himself, come before us to direct our thoughts and feelings about the material and as these authorial personae occupy the front of the stage the people in the stories get pushed into the background, distanced from us by the general slackness and indecisiveness of the form. An exception might be made in the case of « Home Sickness », perhaps the most anthologised of all the stories in the book. In this one story Moore memorably encapsulates most of his major themes, the loneliness of the individual soul, the pain of exile, the power of the Catholic clergy, the sad beauty of the land itself. In Irish literature generally the agony of the departing exile is equalled only by the painful disillusionment experienced by those foolhardy enough to return. Joyce's Richard Rowan of *Exiles* and, more recently, Brian Friel's Cass Maguire come quickly to mind. Moore's returned exile in « Home Sickness » (a brilliantly meaningful title this) is James Bryden who makes his way back to his native place after long absence, in search of health. Physical health he manages to find but the whole drift of the story suggests a ruinous spiritual malaise as the pervasive condition of Ireland. Bryden has had thirteen years in America and is no longer able to tolerate the magisterial authority of the local priest, with his puritanical disapproval of drinking and dancing and merry-making. His heart warms to the remembered peace and beauty of his little native place but his sturdy independence will not brook the priestly control of his love-making and his future marriage to Margaret Dirken. In this story, Moore handles his touchy themes with great sensitivity and tact and manages to elevate the whole fictional structure into a moving commentary on the heartbreakingly unsatisfactory business of human choice itself. Bryden hates the grossness of his American existence, he knows it has cost him his health and longs to remain in his beloved birthplace where he can regain his strength, marry and settle down to a peaceful existence with a loving woman. Yet, in the end, he deliberately puts it all behind him and flees to the violent freedom of his Bowery slum. Moore imparts a Hardy-like tension to Bryden's difficult parting with Margaret Dirken. The stresses of this story are held in the sort of tremulous balance accessible only to a great stylist engaging with congenial themes which are of vital importance to him.

In pursuance of his favourite artistic credo that « art is correction » Moore tinkered with the contents of the book at intervals over the next thirty years. Colin Smythe's recent edition provides a useful compendium of the changes which the work underwent during that time (7). An edition of 1914 excluded both « In the Clay » and « The Way Back ». The edition of 1926 contained a revised version of the long story, « The Wild Goose » and the edition which appeared in 1931, the year before the author's death, included a new story entitled « Fugitives » which was based on the two stories omitted from the edition of 1914. Moore's own judgements on his book were characteristically volatile. On its completion he wrote wearily to Dujardin that « fourteen priests in ten months are too much ». Later, in a letter to a friend, he commented « It is a dry book and does not claim the affections at once. » Yet Joseph Hone records that, at the very end of his life, Moore voiced the opinion that *The Untilled Field* contained his best work. Like his own character, Harding, he would seem to have left an important part of his heart and his affections in the « unwashed country » which had irritated, tantalised, delighted and saddened him in turn. One of Moore's most perceptive and sympathetic commentators, Helmut Gerber, has remarked the vital change which Moore made from a didactic to a truly artistic purpose :

He may have regarded his invasion of Ireland as a missionary opportunity. He may have begun by having some Messianic notions of himself, but he ended by being an artist first and foremost... In *The Field*, like his sculptor Rodney, George Moore discovered that the model is not his vocation, art is (8).

# NOTES

1. Joseph Hone : *The Life of George Moore*, London, 1936, p. 218.

2. See, for example : Philip L. Marcus : « George Moore's Dublin 'Epiphanies' and Joyce » in *James Joyce Quarterly*, V, 1967-68, pp. 157-61. Sister Eileen Kennedy : « Moore's *Untilled Field* and Joyce's *Dubliners* » in *Eire-Ireland*, V, 3, 1970, pp. 81-9. John Raymond Hart : « Moore on Joyce : The Influence of *The Untilled Field* on *Dubliners* » in *The Dublin Magazine*, 10, 2, 1973, pp. 61-76. D.K. Scott : « Joyce's Schooling in the Field of George Moore » in *Eire-Ireland*, IX, 4, 1974, pp. 117-41.

3. George Moore : *The Untilled Field*, London, 1903, pp. 416-7.

4. *Ibid.*, pp. 419-20.

5. *Ibid.*, p. 202.

6. *Ibid.*, p. 237.

7. George Moore : *The Untilled Field*, Gerrards Cross, Colin Smythe Ltd., 1976.

8. Helmut E. Gerber, ed. : *George Moore in Transition*, Detroit, 1968, p. 279.

# JAMES JOYCE'S METHOD IN «DUBLINERS»

## Donald T. TORCHIANA

Most critics remind us that Joyce held up a mirror to the
average Irishman in *Dubliners*, his first major publication. The
ending of the famous letter to Grant Richards is usually cited to
good advantage : « I seriously believe that you will retard the
course of civilization in Ireland by preventing the Irish people
from having one good look at themselves in my nicely polished
looking-glass ». Aside from this mirror image of paralysis,
commentators also point to Joyce's frequent use of the epiphany,
especially at the end of his stories, to cast sudden illumination, a
kind of radiance, that distinguishes the whatness of the story.
Other critics insist on autobiographical interpretations. These
stories, so the account goes, follow Joyce's four divisions of
childhood, adolescence, maturity, and public life. Recent critics
increasingly stress the psychosexual slant of these pieces. Joyce
himself in his letters frequently reveals an almost obsessive
demand for accuracy in the details of these works, as though only
the accurate fact insured the meaning. Even when on the
Continent, he seems to have had access to Irish newspapers,
maps, and even John T. Gilbert's three-volume history of Dublin.
His final effort, « The Dead », may well partly attempt to sum up
and conclude the entire volume, for it has, simply put, the most
facts and details. Now all these hints, speculations, and approaches go a long way to help a general reading of *Dubliners*.
Yet they don't go very far in clarifying Joyce's method, one that

is oddly enough neither the method of literary naturalism, a term early settled on him, nor that of the mere symbolist, the identity that graces him in so much American criticism.

Instead *Dubliners* strikes me as a series of representative pictures. That is, they catch a permanence in Irish life that has a timeless quality as though each detail in any story had about it a built-in significance that no educated native Irishman could really miss and no outsider, armed with a guide to Ireland and a bit of imagination, could fail to detect. Yet these stories are also startlingly new, for all their occasional resemblance to Turgenev's *Sketches*, a scene from an Ibsen play, or the forceful truth of Tolstoi's short novels. This newness, as I take it, comes largely from Joyce's writing of Dublin as she had never been viewed before and, at the same time, writing against the mode of the Irish Literary Revival. Before, then, turning to the many-sided permanence that *Dubliners* registers in such telling detail, let me first pursue this matter of literary strategy.

## I

As I have argued elsewhere, the opening story, « The Sisters », pictures a boy's fate, his likely future defeat as a priest of the imagination, something like the fate of Father Flynn, a genuine and no less scrupulous priest. Misunderstood by his sisters and the boy's aunt, condemned by the uncle and Mr. Cotter, the priest in his relationship to the boy serves as an ironic parallel to the figure of Father Christian Rosencrux, Yeats's symbol for the imagination dormant for some two hundred years in both his essay « The Body of the Father Christian Rosencrux » and the later poem, « The Mountain Tomb ». Yeats frequently went on to speculate that his imaginative rekindling in literature would soon break out in Ireland, the hoped-for effulgence of the Irish Literary Revival. I hold Joyce's first story to be a strong demurrer against such a possibility in the Dublin of 1895 and after. Part of Joyce's method would then seem to be his setting his face against such extravagant hopes. For example, his derision at the publication of AE's *New Songs* in 1904 figures powerfully in his letters and in his probing the character of Little Chandler in a story like « A Little Cloud ». We recall that he contemplated signing his name T. Malone Chandler in hopes of recognition as a poet of the Celtic Twilight, much like the writers in AE's gathering. It is just possible that one of the more egregious among the mediocrities that contributed to *New Songs*, George Roberts, a man who was to give Joyce trials enough in the publication of *Dubliners*, is openly glanced at in the character of Little Chandler. For, while he recognizes himself as « a prisoner for life », he does not recognize that he is also enacting the role of the famous Prisoner of Chillon, in Chandler's case a mean love marriage, perhaps made doubly ridiculous by the inclusion of Robert's poem « The Prisoner of Love » in *New Songs*.

Nor have critics been slow to recognize the spoof of the Revival in the story « A Mother ». The Kathleen of the story is partly betrayed by Holohan, and partly by her own mother's outraged propriety and legality. Yeats's play may certainly be mocked, no less his poem, « Red Hanrahan's Song About Ireland », Kathleen is not the daughter of Holohan. One might even go on to say that by the time we reach « The Dead », the boy of the first story has dutifully grown into the nervous yet complacent Gabriel — reviewer, teacher of languages, Continental traveler, critic, but not imaginative poet. His speech at table is clearly derived from the last of Browning's poetic volumes, *Asolando*, which Gabriel probably reviewed earlier in 1903. Gabriel's speech, very close to the easy sentiments of the « Epilogue » to that volume, also serves as something of a dramatic monologue to expose him at his most fatuous. The method, then, so far has been to mock the literary ideals of the Revival and to show instead the paralysis of the imagination in Ireland.

## II

But Joyce's larger method — a laying on of national, mythic, religious and legendary details, often ironically, as we shall also see — may discover itself in the simplest of references and place names. For instance, early in the pages of « Two Gallants » we behold a mournful harpist playing « Silent, O Moyle » not far, we are informed, « from the porch of the club ». Unobtrusively Joyce has placed the key to the interlocking scenes of the story into our hands. For, instead of aimless wanderings through Dublin that the story seems at the best to afford, we recognize a landscape some two hundred years old. The club is the Kildare Street Club, bastion of a declining Ascendancy, and an off-shoot from the older Daly's Club, where half the land of Ireland was said to pass through the gambling hands of a sporting nobility and gentry. In Corley (Lord Corley in *Ulysses*) and Lenehan we get the Garrison remnant of those former Ascendancy Bucks, still doing in Ireland and getting paid for it to boot. As Joyce once said of British rule, and its instrument the Ascendancy in Ireland, « She enkindled its factions and took over its treasury ». Consequently, every place name in the story speaks of that Williamite and Georgian period and its profitable betrayal of Ireland's interest. From Rutland Square to the Shelbourne Hotel to Hume Street, the half-sovereignty, exposed in the small gold coin at the end, merely attests to that formula.

In the same mode, more briefly but no less powerfully, I would call attention to Farrington's final steps home upon alighting from the Sandymount tram in « Counterparts », and then to the furniture in Mr. Duffy's room in « A Painful Case », and last to the dead priest's books in « Araby » and no less to the death notice in « The Sisters ». All these objects seem to me charged with a significance that goes to the heart of the stories.

If indeed a counterpart can be a legal document, a duplicate, or like person, it can also be for Farrington himself another whose complement makes for a completeness. From first to last we see Farrington — whether at work, at play, or at home — in hell. Most readers recognize that he in fact commits all seven of the deadly sins. Tom his son pleads vainly that he'll say a Hail Mary for his father — of no avail for a man in hell. Yet we sympathize with Farrington, and Joyce in a letter has expressed the same sympathy — he may be more sinned against than sinning. Hence, as we watch Farrington enter Mr. Alleyne's office at the onset, a place centered by « the polished skull which directed the affairs of Crosbie and Alleyne », we are literally in the place of a skull, Golgotha. At the end of the story, when Farrington steps from the tram at Shelbourne Road, we hear of him propelling « his great body along in the shadow of the wall of the barracks ». This is the famous Beggars Bush Barracks, still standing today but no longer used by the military. A famous 18th-century engraving by Giles King shows the real meaning of the area before the barracks was built : a haunt of beggars, thieves, footpads, and rapparees. In his way, Farrington is one of them, yet he too has suffered crucifixion that day and may, like the fortunate thief in Luke, his counterpart, receive some release from his hell.

Mr Duffy has another counterpart. Perhaps enough has been said about his library in « A Painful Case », but no one has looked at the fact that « he himself had bought every article of furniture in the room ». That furniture includes « a black iron bedstead, an iron washstand,... a coal scuttle, a fender and irons... a black and scarlet rug... A little hand-mirror... a white-shaded lamp ». All these may seem of a piece when we realize that Mr. Duffy's counterparts are the two slow trains, one from Kingstown that knocked Mrs. Sinico down, the other from Kingsbridge moving laboriously towards Cork, parallel on its track to the Liffey but puffing in the opposite direction. Yes, Mrs. Sinico had tried to « cross the lines », had died of « shock and sudden failure of the heart's action », and « had gone out at night to buy spirits ». So she had also sought him out after their first meeting, so she had crossed the lines when pressing his hand to her cheek, and so he had rebuffed her and broken her heart. Chapelizod, South George's Street, and the Magazine Hill, identified with the beginning, middle, and end of the story, are also Dublin's three associations with Isolde, her chapel, her tower, and her fount, all adding the ironic application of the Tristan and Isolde story to Mr. Duffy's mistake. Just as quietly, the dead priest's books perused by the boy in « Araby » are all about or by double agents. Vidocq is perhaps the most celebrated, yet he must also vie with Pacificus Baker, compiler of the *Devout Communicant*, who brought the young Edward Gibbon into the Catholic Church, Gibbon who was to become one of her greatest enemies. *The Abbot*, despite its title, settles on a supposed waif taken up by Protestant nobility who later, in disguise, spies upon Mary Queen of Scots, but not without sympathy, and only at the end returns to find himself indeed the scion of that Protestant nobility. Only at the end of « Araby » does the boy, earlier aware of his « confused adoration », learn the futility of transferring his love of the Virgin to Mangan's sister, who so much resembles the girl in the charity bazaar on the Saturday after Whit Monday. He is in a world of double agents that include himself, his father surrogate, the uncle, Mrs. Mercer, « a pawnbroker's widow who collected used stamps for some pious purpose », and the Irish girl making up to bank holiday visitors from England. Perhaps the same boy, the boy in « The Sisters », will also reflect, after his telling silence at the end of the story, on the implications of a death notice that makes Father Flynn's life virtually correspond with the Church in Ireland since Catholic Emancipation in 1829, attaches his death to the defeat of another James at the Boyne on the same day, holds up the Feast of the Precious Blood for a man who fancied himself responsible for a broken chalice, and may point to another St. Catherine's Church where Emmet was executed. To these enemies of promise, one is bound to add that the good father had also retired to a shop in Great Britain Street where articles were sold to keep water from infants. Even an unscrupulous man might have found himself disappointed and crossed before his death in such an ethos. The opposite irony springs from Mrs. Mooney's decision in « The Boarding House » to « catch short twelve at Marlborough Street ». For she will be going to the Pro-Cathedral, the Church of the Immaculate Conception, only after insuring that Polly her daughter, a pregnant and « perverse madonna », will be married.

How much and how deep the pedestrian and ordinary flashed out meanings to Joyce is a subject usually reserved for discussion of *Ulysses*. Yet even the titles alone of the above stories suggest that meanings may be more than one, as we shall see in titles like « Clay », « Grace », « A Mother », and « The Dead ». Yet I would continue here to show how Joyce's method also makes for an expansion of his effects by linking the paralysis of Dubliners to all Ireland and insisting that its impress is something more than a contemporary malaise. Joyce's frequent appeals to a historical memory strike an almost timeless note for the bane that afflicts all Ireland.

### III

For instance, during the boys' wanderings in « An Encounter », time and again we happen on places of historical encounters where the Irish always ultimately lost, however apparent the victory might have seemed. Following the North Strand Road and then the Wharf Road, the boys also trace the line of the Battle of Clontarf, a famous Irish victory over the Norsemen, yet also a Pyrrhic one in the loss of Brian Boru. Their final encounter with the pervert is in part a meeting head on with a cruel twisted Puritanism going back to Cromwell's time and not unknown to the Catholic Church in Ireland. Cromwell also landed at the Pigeon House, the boy's failed destination. Yet they are also encountering a perpetual figure in Irish life, the combination of priestly and political repression that stretches back further than Cromwell. Moreover, the field where the boys come to rest, within sight of the River Dodder, is very close to the confluence of that river and the River Liffey, site, given its shallow beach, of the original Scandinavian landings in Dublin. In just such a field, the Norsemen would often construct a Thingmote where trials were held before a combined priest and magistrate, a *godi* as described in Haliday's *Scandinavian Kingdom of Dublin.* A convicted malefactor's only chance to escape execution was to run the gauntlet of surrounding warriors and escape the ring of by-standers. So the boy in the story goes over the wall, escaping his goggle-eyed pious sadist with silence, cunning, and something like exile. An encounter on ancient grounds turns out to be an encounter with a possible version of himself, given religious and political forces, did he stay. Stephen Dedalus' weapons will be his.

No less drastic historically appears the likely necessity of defeat when, as in « After the Race », an Irishman gains the allegiance of the French in any contest with the English. The sense of triumph that flushes the face of James Doyle while riding in a winning French car after the 1903 Gordon-Bennett Cup Race sharply recalls Irish enthusiasm after another such famous race won by the French. I speak of course of the famous Races of Castlebar, the jibing appellation affixed to the British rout by a small French and Irish force under General Humbert in 1798 after the landing at Killala. But it's the aftermath, as Joyce's title suggests, that must preoccupy us. In the story, aboard the yacht in Kingstown harbour, the Englishman Routh wins the final game of cards over the Frenchman Ségouin. But the heaviest losers are the Irish-American Farley and the Irishman Jimmy Doyle. Just so after the Races of Castlebar. A second engagement lasted but a half hour when the French surrendered. Their officers and men were well treated, even feted in Dublin. The Irish were massacred on the spot and their officers summarily executed. « Our friends the French », the traditional slogan said to link patriotically Catholic France to Catholic Ireland in their joint enmity for England, turns out to be inevitably disappointing, perhaps even collusive in Ireland's usual defeat.

But defeat at home or exile abroad may be much the same ; surely neither is much different historically, or so a story like

« Clay » might insist. While Maria is clearly a symbol of Ireland, the Little Old Woman who appears to be ugly and has for her reward a remembrance of her mortality in the neighbor girls' trick, still I would point to a further emphasis in the story. For a neighbor girl wins the ring in the games while, of the four Donnelly children, one receives a prayer book and the others get the water. In other words, the predominant likelihood of children in such a family is either the Church or emigration. Might it be too much then to think of those mischievous girls next-door as somehow resembling Caledonia and Britannia ? The evening is not just Halloween or All Hallow's Eve. It is also the beginning of Samhain, the Irish winter when the druidical god of death sets evil spirits abroad in the darkness without disguise — such a history and such a time of year play nicely into Joyce's hands.

### IV

The timelessness of Irish paralysis reinforces what I might call mythic, religious, and legendary patterns that Joyce seems to place so frequently at the very center of a story. The method is openly visible in books like *The Portrait* and *Ulysses*, but I strongly believe that Joyce has invested very similar paradigms in most if not in all these *Dubliners* tales. John Kelleher's justly famous essay, « Irish History and Mythology in James Joyce's 'The Dead' », cleverly establishes the mythic center of the final story as the fate of King Conaire in the saga « The Destruction of Da Derga's Hostel ». But more on the ramifications of this piece must wait on my concluding discussion of The Dead ». For the moment let me show Joyce's method as equally prone to employing religious and legendary imprimaturs.

In « Eveline », for instance, if we can accept the title as directing us to a little Aoife as well as a little Eve, we may strongly question Eveline's rejection of Frank. To be a little Aoife is to emulate a number of legendary and mythic women, none a very great friend of the Irish family. To be a little Aoife may mean to be like the mother of Conla, or to be like the wicked stepmother of the Children of Lir, or even to follow Dermot MacMurrough's daughter and marry Strongbow in the smoking ruins of Waterford. In the same story, « Eveline », the religious pattern is taken ironically from the life of the Blessed Margaret Mary Alacoque, whose colored print is on the wall. Her sufferings led to her meeting with Christ at the grille, the merging of his burning heart with hers, and the eventual founding of the Order of the Sacred Heart so dear to family life in Ireland. Yet in the name of that Order and the promises made to the Blessed Margaret Mary, Eveline dumbly refuses to accompany « openhearted » Frank to Buenos Aires. In short, she who left a home consecrated to the Sacred Heart for that very cause refuses a similar call to her own heart and soul. A heritage of Christ's blazing love for man, caught in the visions of a provincial French girl of the 17th century, now denies the heart and renders chastity trivial in a later provincial and Catholic Dublin.

Sometimes Joyce's audacity in pursuing the ironies of religious assumptions in Dublin almost surpasses belief. If we count the money-lenders, questionable political figures, and ordinary run of failed businessmen and castle officials attendant upon the red-faced Father Purdon in « Grace », they add up to a round number twelve. We might well call the group apostles enough, if not children of light, as they ingest the Word, the sanctifying grace from a businessman's Christ. One critic, Joseph Blotner, has detailed the many parallels with the crucifixion to be found in « The Boarding House ». But he has neglected Joyce's clear-cut division of the story, the second part assuming less than a page of text yet seemingly equivalent in weight to the first. For here Joyce appends his sequel to the crucifixion that is any Irish forced marriage, that is, he gives us the likely drama of the Annunciation. In *Ulysses* we learn that Bob Doran on his yearly bender had identified himself to prostitutes as Joseph. Here at the end of « The Boarding House », Polly suddenly drifts into a dream full of « hopes and visions » until her surroundings fade from her mind before being recalled by her mother's voice. If her role has been that of a Magdalen in most of the story, now — pregnant, dreaming, and hopeful — she may be no more than « a little perverse madonna » yet she is in the same human predicament as her saintly sister of old, the Mother of Christ. To observe further the threats of Mrs. Mooney, a butcher's daughter, and the implacable attitude of Doran's employer, a great Catholic wine merchant, should Doran be exposed and refuse the sacrament of marriage, in no way lessens the ironic pertinence of the birth and crucifixion of Christ for another loveless Irish marriage sanctified by a mass.

Just as pertinent, though more muted as befits legend, is

Joyce's use of Dun Laoghaire in « After the Race », at the time
called Kingstown. To contemplate Doyle senior, the former
butcher and merchant prince, and his son Jimmy is also to glance
at the continuing fates of Niall of the Nine Hostages and his son
Laoghaire. Niall had embraced the hag Royal Rule to get the
kingship at Tara ; he had sought to advance himself on the
Continent ; one story has it that he was slain by a British arrow
shot by a rival backed by the Franks. Laoghaire was known for
his attention to Irish law, his formulating the Senchus Mor, and
then for resisting the Boromean Tribute — cattle, sheep, and
swine — due King Tuathal of Leinster. Captured during that
resistance, he swore by the four elements never to repeat his
refusal. However, he broke his oath and was immediately struck
down by them. In the face of this legendary account, the
flickering ironies in the fortunes of the Doyles, whose money and
position are dependent upon meat, need not be drawn out. Yet
the father is a kind of prince collaborating with royal rule ;
despite his patriotism, police contracts had allowed him to
expand his business. He is also a parent who has sent his son to
college and then to Cambridge in England. The son in turn has
lost him a good deal of money to a Briton while in the company
of Frenchmen in whose enterprise the father had encouraged the
son to invest, thus hoping to extend both their social lives into
Continental circles. Jimmy had dabbled in law at Trinity and now
has returned to the family stronghold, formerly Dun Laoghaire,
after a foray near Naas, once King Tuathal's base in exacting the
Tribute. Breathless and excited, Jimmy is struck by the dawn's
light on a body of water, Dun Laoghaire/Kingstown Harbor,
where, disarmed, relieved of his money, slumped toward earth, his
head in his hands, he must nevertheless face his friends, the
French.

Perhaps the expanding shadow of Old Jack on the wall as his
fire momentarily flickers may also set us thinking as we begin
« Ivy Day in the Committee Room ». For in fanning the flame he
unwittingly stirs memories of the Phoenix Flame associated with
Parnell, and before him with the Fenian efforts to rid Ireland of
England. Interpretations of the story that identify Parnell with
Moses and the martyred Christ are well enough known. Yet the
enlarged shadow of a decayed old man may also be juxtaposed
not only with Parnell and the Fenian tradition but also with the
original Finn and his Fianna. Finn and his warriors also cruelly

contrast with the mayor-maker Fanning, his tool Dicky Tierney, and their seedy vote-canvassing underlings in the Committee Room. The popping of corks from Guinness bottles may also contrast with the real meaning of the Irish words behind the misnamed Phoenix, pure water.

## V

Let me conclude then with a look at « The Dead ». I have already hinted that it not only brings together most of the themes of the previous stories but that it also shows off Joyce's method in *Dubliners* most conclusively. John Kelleher's essay offers grand support for some of my claims for this method. For instance, Lily the servant girl pronounces almost unnoticed Gabriel's surname in three syllables, and in that stroke, Kelleher demonstrates, aligns him with that King Conaire who broke the nine tabus that stood between him and death in « The Destruction of Da Derga's Hostel ». One by one Kelleher ingeniously ticks off those same tabus now broken by Gabriel. Part of his fate Kelleher sees as also deriving from his heedless levity at the expense of his grandfather Morkan, associated with the unofficial Back Lane parliament, and no less from his flippant salute to the O'Connell statue, the memorial to the Liberator of his grandfather's generation. Thus a word, a historical memory, and the mythic story of a destruction all bear on Gabriel's diminution and bitter self-knowledge come at the end.

Yet there is more. For at least three other omens point to the grimmer view of the evening that will prevail when Gabriel reassesses it in his room at the Gresham. In his repeated mention of the song « The Lass of Aughrim », his depicting Mr. Browne as a figure of death, and his saddling Gabriel with a review of Browning's poems, Joyce underlines the realities of the death-in-life that lurk beneath the party's noisy surface.

« The Lass of Aughrim » pretty clearly defines Gabriel's role as Lord Gregory, as a number of critics have seen, both to Lily at the beginning and then to Gretta, at least for a stubborn moment, at the end. This unconscious role was probably abetted by his mother's ambitious nature, yet it sets Gabriel apart from a family gathering, much like the cold father or villain in every opera mentioned at the table, long before he discovers his distance from Gretta's true heart. To punctuate almost every scene at the party with something like a full stop, Joyce also uses Mr. Browne as might Holbein in his series of woodcuts, *The Dance of Death*. He smiles, he grins, waxes ironic with Gabriel's speech, claims Julia as his discovery, and « laughs as if his heart would break » before gathering Freddy and his mother, certainly two more of Death's likely victims, into something like the Irish death coach which he directs to the gates of Trinity College. No less foreboding must be Gabriel's bumptious remarks at the banquet. Since the story takes place on Wednesday, January 6th, 1904 — *Mignon* started the next day, the conference on the University Question had met that day in Galway, and the Negro chieftain had just been introduced to Dublin — Gabriel had probably reviewed the last and 17th volume of the Macmillan Browning. Its principal content was *Asolando*, the collection of poems that had appeared at the time of Browning's death, dedicated to the American hostess Mrs. Arthur Bronson and celebrating her hospitality. The lines Gabriel probably had in mind might well have come from the « Epilogue », the last poem of *Asolando*. The final stanza is symptomatic and all too reminiscent of the Browning of those years and the Gabriel who urges his audience to leave off memories of dead and absent faces and turn instead to the strenuous claims of the living :

No, at noonday in the bustle of man's work-time
   Greet the unseen with a cheer !
Bid him forward, breast and back as either should be,
« Strive and thrive » cry « Speed, — fight on, fare ever
     There as here ! »

Fatuous enough, as he later admits, in orating to vulgarians, Gabriel will finally distinguish another kind of hospitality.

This I identify with that of the Reformed Cistercians of the Strict Observance, the monks at Mount Melleray. Mr. Browne cannot understand their hospitality ; Freddy Malins, who is going there to dry out, can. In any case, the hospitality Melleray signals is a charity that cares for the sick and needy, the charity synonymous with the Knights Hospitaler of St. John of Jerusalem. However warm and nourishing the Morkan evening, the human atmosphere seems only occasionally charitable. The counter to the Dance of Death — cavorting, singing, laughing, and applauding amid a superabundance of food and drink — lives,

I take it, in the charitable spirit that finally overwhelms Gabriel with « generous tears » at the end. Their force lies in the quiet and hardly ironic insistence of place names linked to this bracing charity. Although Gabriel lives in Monkstown, he may not know that the name comes from the castle there that had once been affiliated with Cistercian monks from the 12th century on. Indeed Usher's Island and the near-by Phoenix Park were once the possessions of the Knights Templar and the Knights of St. John. Moira House since 1826 had been the Mendicity Institution serving paupers over 100,000 meals a year right into Gabriel's century. Likewise the later mention of Nuns' Island admits to the story another haven of charity, the convent of the Poor Clares in Galway City whose austerities and prayers for the sinners of the world approximate those of the monks at Melleray. This counter hospitality of charity becomes then Joyce's religionless yet Catholic companion to the human grace of the falling snow.

His method, I think, finally proves itself in Gabriel's transfiguration. He has a night vision. His attitude toward his wife and Michael Furey changes. Gabriel may be said to be converted to another understanding. Like the legendary St. Patrick, he decides that the time has come to make his journey westward and he makes it by following the falling snow west to a grave in Oughterard. As Joyce once said of St. Patrick, he did not convert the Irish, the Irish converted him. Something of the same legendary change overtakes Gabriel.

The parallels that bind the two men are striking. Miss Ivors brands Gabriel a West Briton ; Patrick came from the western sector of Roman Britain. Patrick was enslaved by Irish sea pirates at sixteen and brought to Ireland to herd swine. The name Morkan derives from a Gaelic term meaning sea warrior or pirate. Every year Gabriel has been captured and enslaved by his aunts Morkan, and this year he must shepherd the gross-appearing Freddy. Later Gabriel recognizes himself as the pennyboy or slavey for his aunts. The name Malins was long associated with the traditional keepers of St. Patrick's bell in the North. Rightly, and now only Freddy understands Mount Melleray — at the table he beats time with his pudding fork ! Patrick also contended with the druids at Tara. Gabriel contends no less with a modern druidess wearing a Tara brooch who is also a Gaelic enthusiast. Gabriel's night vision is of Michael Furey, « the form of a young man standing under a dripping tree », in the west of Ireland. Patrick tells us in his *Confessions* that the voice that called him back to Ireland after his escape as a slave came from the man or angel Victor in the forest of Fochlut by the western sea. Previously, Patrick had traveled and gained his learning in Germany, France, and Italy, the places where Gabriel takes his cycling holidays to keep up his languages. Patrick's final route on his penitential journey westward follows Gabriel's naming the locales where the snow touches down all over Ireland : « the dark central plain », « the treeless hills », « the Bog of Allen », « the mutinous Shannon waves », and « the lonely churchyard on the hill where Michael Furey lay buried ». All are sacred to the memory of St. Patrick : Westmeath and its Hill of Croghan ; the treeless hills of Tara where Patrick encountered King Laoghaire and his druids ; the Bog of Allen associated with Patrick's colloquy with Finn's son ; the Shannon estuary and Knockpatrick ; and the Lugnaeden Stone at Oughterard on Lough Corrib.

According to Yeats's description of the literature of the past two hundred years, Gabriel, the boy from « The Sisters » grown up, seems to have been fated to represent it as mere reviewer, teacher, speaker, and commentator given to summing up. Yet at the end of « The Dead » he contemplates fondly a dead singer or poet. The parallel, however faint, could well be that of St. Patrick — teacher orator, West Briton — contemplating Oisin lured to his death by a vision of beauty, Niamh, and his own charity in leaning from his saddle to help a burdened man. Gabriel's accommodation with such a modern Oisin — self-sacrificing lover and poet — is a glimpse of the *Colloquy* at its most hopeful. Joyce's method tends to the hard and accurate facts of Dublin obviously enough. But it also appeals to the farthest reach of the Irish imagination, especially when excited by the illustrious dead in religion, legend, myth, history, place-name and literature.

# SEAMUS O'KELLY

## Anne CLUNE

When Seumas O'Kelly was buried on 17 November 1918, the torrential rain which drenched the city did not deter the many thousands of admirers who lined the route from Clarendon Street to Glasnevin for the two hours it took the funeral procession to pass. The coffin was draped with the Irish Republican colours and escorted by an honour guard of the Irish Volunteers. Sinn Féin, Conradh na Gaeilge, Cumann ba mBan and the Corporation of Dublin were represented. It was, as has often been remarked, a funeral more suited to a national hero than to a journalist and writer. Yet, in the circumstances, it was felt that O'Kelly had, in P.S. O'Hegarty's words, « died for Ireland as surely, and as finely, as if he had been shot by a Black-and-Tan » (1). Still, what amounted to a state funeral was a strange end for a man who was affectionately regarded by his friends as a most gentle, peaceable person. Seumas O'Sullivan, a close friend with whom O'Kelly was staying at the time of his death, recalls that friendship.

We met on a Saturday at Webb's bookshop on Crampton Quay. I had gone there to keep an appointment with Arthur Griffith and when Griffith came along he had with him a stoutly-built little man — he was of about the same height as Griffith — who seemed to me, at first sight, to be the most good-natured-looking person I had ever seen (and I may add that on this occasion my first impression was correct). For sixteen years following that introduction I had the great joy and privilege of enjoying his friendship — a friendship which only ceased when he died in 1918. And never throughout those years did I hear a harsh word spoken by him, or of him — a record which must have been well nigh unique in those years of storm and stress through which the country was passing. His was, indeed, one of those very rare natures which have the faculty of spreading a sense of well-being, of security, good-fellowship, healing, by their very presence. Bitterness seemed to fade out in the presence of Seumas O'Kelly, and quarrelling was impossible when he was in the company. I can still hear that pleasant voice, see the almost priestly gesture of his hand as he said « That will be all right »…. Yet beneath that gentleness lay hidden a very real strength which could evince itself splendidly when occasion demanded (2).

Similar tributes came from Arthur Griffith, from Maire nic Shiubhlaigh and even from Joseph Holloway who walked in O'Kelly's funeral procession and noted in his diary of 19th November, « One of our most brilliant young writers and dramatists, Seumas O'Kelly, died suddenly of heart failure last week and was given a public funeral on Sunday last — a most solemn, impressive affair... We all dearly loved the poor fellow for his gentle ways and kindly manner » (3).

It is surprisingly difficult to ascertain the actual details of O'Kelly's life. We know that he was born in Loughrea, Co. Galway but the date is uncertain. Consequently there is dispute about his age at the time of his death as well as about the causes and circumstances of that death (4). It seems most likely that he was born in 1878 and was only 40 when he died. He was the youngest of six or seven children. His mother, Catherine, was renowned for her piety. His father, Michael Kelly, though said to be « one of the sufferers amongst the evicted tenants of the Clanrickarde estate », was a successful businessman running the family's old-established corn-carrying business. Seumas himself does not seem to have received much formal education. There are references to him attending the local « hedge-school » of John Furey and St. Brendan's College, Loughrea, but no records survive. The earliest positive information we have, is of his becoming editor of *The Southern Star*, the local newspaper in Skibbereen, Co. Cork. He was said to be the youngest editor in

Ireland. If he was born in 1878, he would have been only 25 in 1903. For the rest of his life he was to be associated with the provincial press. During a life characterised by hard work and self-sacrifice, he dedicated himself to improving the quality of provincial journalism in Ireland. He wished to interest his readers in both local and national events. He had been an early recruit to the Sinn Féin movement and its aims were to be united with his own insights in forming his editorial policies. In 1906 he became editor of *The Leinster Leader* and moved to live in Naas, Co. Kildare. It seems likely that it was while living in Naas, possibly in 1911, that he contracted the rheumatic fever which was to weaken his heart. From 1912-1915 he edited the *Dublin Saturday Post* until ill-health forced an early retirement. He returned to Naas to live with his brother Michael who had succeeded him as editor of the *Leinster Leader*. When Michael was arrested and imprisoned as a member of the Irish Volunteers, Seumas, though he had been warned of the dangers of exertion, resumed his old editorial post. After Michael's release, Seumas returned to live in Dublin and, while sharing a house with Seumas O'Sullivan, undertook the task of replacing Arthur Griffith as editor of the Sinn Féin paper *Nationality* during Griffith's imprisonment. Three days after the armistice, soldiers and their wives, incensed by Sinn Féin policies on the war, invaded and wrecked the offices of *Nationality*. After they had left, O'Kelly was found unconscious, (some accounts say he tried to defend himself and the printing presses with his walking stick), and did not recover consciousness. The official certificate records « cerebral haemorrhage/coma » as the cause of death. Sinn Féin, in recognition of O'Kelly's complete lack of self interest in carrying on Griffith's work, and in view of the events preceding his collapse gave him a hero's funeral.

In retrospect his death now appears as a much greater loss to the world of letters than to the world of journalism and politics. It is as a dramatist, novelist and short story writer that O'Kelly is now remembered. Most commentators have, in fact, regretted his obsession with politics and have felt that the intrusion of political concerns adversely affected the quality of his work. It is certainly true that in plays like *The Homecoming* and *The Parnellite*, in the somewhat melodramatic ending of the novel *Wet Clay* and in some of the short stories, the political message is so direct, so crude as to resemble propaganda more than art. The ending of « A Wayside Burial » provides a good example of the lack of artistic distancing which was to mar some of O'Kelly's work.

> The priest stood for a moment.
> « You see the great mounds at the end ? » he asked. « They are the famine pits ».
> « The famine pits ? »
> « Yes ; the place where the people were buried in heaps and hundreds, in thousands, during the famine of '46 and '47. They died like flies by the roadside. You see such places in almost every part of Ireland. I hope the people will never again die like that — die gnawing the gravel on the roadside ».
> The rusty iron gate in the demesne wall swung open and we passed out (5).

O'Kelly's youth, spent in the vicinity of the Clanrickarde estate and the poor lands of East Galway had given him an intense awareness of poverty, deprivation, and the evils of emigration and depopulation. His involvement with Sinn Féin had added another, historical and theoretical, dimension to that essentially emotional reaction and was to colour everything he wrote in the future. It is easy to see why critics should have been impatient or embarrassed with some of his writing. Nevertheless, it is difficult to agree with Eamonn Grennan when he argues that O'Kelly, aware of the conflict between art and politics, had « to retreat into a world of total privacy and to concentrate upon single human lives occupied with the simplest and so the most profound business of living in a landscape that is not cluttered with political abstractions » (6). O'Kelly's best stories are intensely political. In his finest work he found a means of integrating the major concerns of his life. « The Weaver's Grave », a story of old men, is also a story of the desolation of the land, the destruction of an old and integrated way of life, the loneliness and despair of a people without identity. The tone of O'Kelly's last story is a refinement of the mood of one of his earliest tales.
The style of « A Land of Loneliness » may seem unduly ponderous but its concerns underlie the vision of many of the best stories which are, mercifully, free of its excessive didacticism :

It was all a level country as far as the eye could reach — a grey, cold, cheerless country, and the only thing that relieved the monotony of the landscape — that broke the spell of flatness — were the faint blue outlines of the Clare mountains to the West which bounded the South of Galway Bay, and the range of dark hills to the south-east, which made a zig-zag outline from distant Mount Shannon and looped themselves on to take a peep at their heath-clad brows in the mirror of the clear waters of the Grey Lake, and then stretched themselves on to Gort and finally bowed their rough heads in mute homage before the crumbling fane of Kilmacduagh of the Saints. It was indeed a barren land, this part of the territory of Hi Many. And yet, as I looked to the north, to the south, to the east, and to the west, I reflected that once a vigorous, prolific race, industrious, intelligent, large of heart and pure of soul, made the territory ring with the mirth of their laughter and the joy of their lives. They were scattered like the leaves from the sickly poplar trees that are wasted mourning over their fallen homes ; melted like the snow which mantled the mountains belting the Western bay — denied the patches of ground between the prolific rocks ! The only vestige of the race I had seen was a bare-legged urchin scurrying into a windowless cabin with a sagging thatched roof and the thick streaks of sodden rain down-striping its uneven mud walls (7).

Yet, if O'Kelly was occasionally to succumb to this kind of writing, he was also capable of the humorous detachment of the story of Gobstown, (« The Shoemaker ») (8) a town which suffers the awful fate of having a good landlord, where guns can be used only to stir the tea, where everyone is content and so talent stifles for want of grievances to set it aflame. Humour is, indeed, one of O'Kelly's greatest qualities — a gentle humour quite unmarked by satire. He seems to have had a genuine regard for the people who populate his world and wrote about them with warmth and affection, an attitude he articulates in one of the stories of *Hillsiders* ; « Blame not the shanachie, for the shanachie took the people of Kilbeg as he found them, the good and the bad, and sometimes he liked the bad better than the good » (9). It is, of course, easy for that kind of warmth to become mere sentimentality and O'Kelly could degenerate into the cloying sweetness of for example, always referring to Fardy Lalor's mother as « the little mother ». « But one night the little mother quietly slipped the moorings of her earthly barque, moved out calmly from the harbour of life, and set sail for a far sea where a lost voice was calling » (10).

Other major characteristics of O'Kelly's work are his realism and the sense of tragedy which pervades his writing. Yet tragedy can become melodrama and does in the dreadful second section of « Both Sides of the Pond » which pictures the almost infernal horrors suffered by a young countryman forced to emigrate to the Bowery. Melodrama and sentimentality were certainly faults but are more than compensated for by the intensity of O'Kelly's imagination, the accuracy and lyricism of his evocation of the natural world and the importance of his position as the chronicler of a dying culture.

O'Kelly published six volumes of short stories. He wrote two novels, *Wet Clay* and *The Lady of Deerpark,* some poems collected as *Ranns and Ballads* and a number of plays. He was associated with the Theatre of Ireland from its earliest days. His first play *The Matchmakers* was produced in 1907 by the Theatre of Ireland which was to have one of its greatest successes with another O'Kelly play, *The Shuiler's Child,* in 1909. Most of the plays deal with the same matter as do the short stories. O'Kelly had a tendency to try to turn his stories into plays and indeed many of the stories are inherently dramatic. « The Weaver's Grave », dramatised for radio by Micheál O hAodha was awarded the Prix d'Italia. Most of the stories were first published in the numerous newspapers to which O'Kelly contributed, among them *The United Irishman, The Irish Weekly Independent* and *The Manchester Guardian.* The dates of publication do not always co-incide with the dates of composition. It is, therefore, more helpful to discuss the stories in order of composition (12). *By the Stream of Kilmeen* (1904-1906), *The Leprechaun of Kilmeen* (1908-9) and *Hillsiders* (1909) to some extent form a composite group unified by certain attitudes and concerns. « The Golden Barque » (1912) is somewhat of an oddity in the O'Kelly canon for, with *Waysiders* (1910-17) and « The Weaver's Grave » (1918) he continues earlier themes but with more sophisticated stylistic modes. There are two, as yet, uncollected groups of stories, some more leprechaun stories which appeared in *The Irish Weekly Independent* in 1910, and some 'Padna' tales which were published first in the *Manchester Guardian* in 1916 and 1917 and the *Sunday Independent* in 1919 and 1920.

The greatest influence on O'Kelly was the environment of Loughrea. The Grey Lake itself, (from which the town takes its name), the small townlands with their « characters », the burial field, the local traditions and legends and the characteristic hiberno-english dialect of the people only a short way removed from their original Irish speech, are evoked in story after story. Only in « The Golden Barque » does O'Kelly deal with another landscape.

It is a country in which the story-telling tradition was very strong (elements survive even to-day). The stories told by the seanchai, on whom O'Kelly was to consciously model himself, were of traditional things and of the daily incursion of the marvellous. The stories were all known, what was appreciated was the skill of the story-teller in finding new turns of phrase, original forms of description. Although O'Kelly was to learn the use of symbolism, and was to write at least one story that seems classical in its perfection, he was also to incorporate into that story the habits of the seanchai, the direct address as if to a listening audience, the ritualistic repetitions and formalised addresses.

> Mortimer Hehir, the weaver, had died and they had come in search of his grave to Cloon na Morav, the Meadow of the Dead. Meehaul Lynskey, the nail-maker, was first across the stile... Following him came Cahir Bowes, the stone-breaker... Hot on their heels came two dark, handsome, stoutly-built men, alike even to the cord that tied their corduroy trousers under their knees, and, being grave-diggers, they carried flashing spades. Last of all... the widow of Mortimer Hehir, the weaver and she followed the others into Cloon na Morav, the Meadow of the Dead (13).

This is a refinement of the style of the earliest stories, those of the cunning leprechaun which bests the people of Kilmeen and whose doings are chronicled by Tom Kelleher in the genuine storyteller tradition.

> Oul' Tom was sitting with his back up against one of the hay cocks, and when Padraic asked him if he'd tell them a story, he looked hard at him for a good bit, for it wasn't everyone Tom would give out a story to. So when he said he'd try, Padraic felt that proud that he could leap a five foot bar

gate. Little delay any of us made until we were settled around about Tom Kelleher in the meadow, as quiet as mice, to hear the story.

Oul' Tom Kelleher looked over the field, and the eyes of him rested on a fairy fort that you could see near the hedge... « 'Tisn't for me or for you to be puttin' the evil word on them that has the fort beyond, but if there is a man from here to Hong Kong and back that has cause to say the bad word of them, I'm that same man. And I'll tell you how that is » (14).

All these stories rely for their effect on the vivacity of the telling. O'Kelly's attempt to render the dialect, whilst sometimes accurate and colourful — « I'm sorry I can't strengthen your knowledge » ; « For that's always in the four bones of me » — is often overdone, and particularly so in the earliest stories. By the time O'Kelly came to write *Hillsiders*, his style was becoming more « literary ». There seems to be a clear influence from Synge and from Lady Gregory. There is less of the directness of the oral tradition. The storm scene in *The Elks* seems almost like a set piece. There is some fine writing in it but it had, even by then, become a literary cliché.

It was just as well for Fardy that he could not witness the scene on the headland. His little mother had her eyes fixed on the figure that clung to the broken mast on the wreck upon the Elk. She would throw an odd quick glance to *The Bean Sidhe* as if measuring the distance that separated it from the wreck, an excited, feverish look in her eyes. When the figure on the wreck had lurched a little, lost its grip, made an apparently feeble effort to regain its hold, and in doing so was caught in a wash of the leaping water — water which sprang like a panther for its prey — and the figure went down to its doom right between the Elks the little mother threw up her arms with a gesture of despair.

« Stephen ! Stephen ! » she cried, for she knew it was her man who had gone to his death before her eyes (15).

In the best stories of *Waysiders*, « The Can With the Diamond Notch », and « The Grey Lake » and in « The Weaver's Grave » O'Kelly integrated the style of the seanchai with the more literary ' high ' style he was to learn from his contemporaries.

O'Kelly wrote stories about a community disrupted by the activities of a leprechaun ; of the drowning of a town because the seven springs imprisoned there wished to leap out of their bounds to embrace their lover, the moon ; of a man who, clinging to life by means of a rope attached to the end of his bed, still asserts that the world is all a dream ; of a woman lying ill in the workhouse who describes her little house as if it were a palace ; and of a golden barque sailing through a magic landscape. His storytellers and their audiences are people who believe in miracles and in magic, who accept unquestioningly that the world is suffused with wonder. O'Kelly does not himself question these beliefs. Indeed his writing is at its best when he is dealing with the borderlands of fantasy, when his poetic imagination expresses itself primarily through an evocation of the beauties of the natural world, as in Mary's vision of the golden barque, or the legend of the grey lake.

He could hear a great cry of joy down in the well. He put the key in the lock, turned it, and immediately there was the gliding and slipping of one steel bar after another into an oil bath. The great lid slowly revolved, moving away from over the well. The Seven Sisters did the rest. They sprang with a peal of the most delirious laughter — laughter that was of the underground, the cavern, the deep secret places of the earth, laughter of elfs and hidden rivers — to the light of the moon. The shepherd boy could see seven distinct spiral issues of sparkling water and they took the shape of nymphs, more exquisite than anything he had ever seen even in his dreams. Something seemed to happen in the very heavens above ; the moon reached down from the sky, swiftly and tenderly, and was so dazzling that the shepherd boy had to turn his face away. He knew that in the blue spaces of the firmament overhead the moon was embracing the Seven Sisters (16).

Yet in spite of this poetic intensity, O'Kelly never loses sight of reality. Even the six stories of *The Leprechaun of Kilmeen*, (which Vivian Mercier called « the most satisfying re-working of latter-day traditions about these little people ») (17) are set within a recognisable rural community. The leprechaun will be found sitting on the demesne wall, he will want a cup of tea and he will ultimately be triumphant as much because of the failings of the people of Kilmeen as because of his own cunning. In an important sense the real focus of interest in the three early collections is the community itself. O'Kelly was intensely aware of the subtle undercurrents, bonds and enmities of Kilmeen and Kilbeg. He shows his people busy with the job of survival but even more concerned with feuds, gossip, greed and jealousy, and local standing. The ties of community are strong and so Tom Kelleher has to cease his pursuit of the leprechaun to follow the funeral of his old enemy Martin Moran for « if it was the blackest stranger that was in it instead of poor Martin I couldn't let the funeral pass me by without joining it, and I wasn't going to bring disgrace on all that ever belonged to me by letting the corpse of a neighbour pass me by on the road » (18). At the end of *Hillsiders*, the reader knows as much about the eccentricities of its inhabitants as the audience of Lady Gregory's comedies knew about the inhabitants of Cloon. The stories are concerned with traditional crafts, and pastimes. Matchmaking, funerals, annual visits space out years so devoid of great events that any small happenings assume epic proportions. People who are cha-racterised by their trades, weaver, cooper, nailer, stone-mason, grave-digger, or by their position in a closely knit and conser-vative society, « the wife of the bed-ridden man », the widow Lowry, the fourth wife of the weaver, have to face the problem of attaining individuality. Where uniqueness is difficult to achieve and names and family associations are of long-standing, where the very faces and bearing of the people are conditioned directly by the landscape in which they exist, it is enough to be a scold, or a little stand-offish to gain a place in society. Miss Mary Hickey learns the misery of separation from her community but is received back into it with joy for

If Miss Mary Hickey had only known it, Kilbeg wanted a social centre, a person of high breeding and great gentility, as ardently as she was eager to supply it. By her return she would restore the social ballast of Kilbeg and give its feminine craving a lost outlet. She was as necessary to Kilbeg as is a queen to a kingdom or an empress to an empire, and they would make the same use and abuse of her. Also she was no more make-believe than the best or the worst of queens (19).

The reality is often painful. Emigration and death are constant factors. Nan Hogan, left behind in Kilbeg and lying sick in the Union, has only two comforts for her loneliness, to scold and to invent great stories about her house. In a vein similar to that struck by Lady Gregory with her two old paupers in *The Workhouse Ward* O'Kelly realises that it is better to be quarrelling than to be lonesome. Loneliness is an ever present condition only staved off by talk, society or, perhaps, a protective circle of hills. After the lyricism of « Michael and Mary » in *The Golden Barque*, the ending with Mary's abandonment to a life of loneliness is tragic.

The landscape adds to the sense of loneliness, overpowering the people with its vast spaces, separating lovers and forcing a grinding poverty on those in thrall to it. Yet O'Kelly's vision is so essentially benign that it is rare for this tone of melancholy and loneliness to remain dominant. While there is always the underlying awareness of the possibility of grief the resolution of most of the stories is hopeful. Nan Hogan finds company, Miss Mary Hickey resumes her place in society, Fardy Lalor marries Meg Sullivan, Hannah is not evicted from her role in the church, even Pa Cloon's lies pay off. In *Waysiders* whilst the tone is more sombre the major stress is still on vitality, on the fierce cunning of the tinkers and their great line of talk in « The Can with the Diamond Notch », in the humour of « The Shoemaker », the lyricism of « The Grey Lake », the sense of a natural balance restored in « The Building » and the promise of recovery for the young man in « The Sick Call ». The mood of the stories of *The Golden Barque* is lightened by the loving descriptions of the wild life of the canal, the antics of Billy the Clown and the gentle humour of « The Man with the Gift ». These elements help to balance the somewhat uncharacteristic evocation of hatred and unrelenting passions in the stories « Hike and Calcutta » and « The Haven ».

O'Kelly's masterpiece is, undoubtedly, his story « The Weaver's Grave ». Sub-titled « A Story of Old Men » it is also a story of the attainment of individuality in the young. The story is dominated by four old men — the dead weaver, the stone-breaker, the nailer and the cooper. All these men are highly individualised within the terms of their traditional crafts but most dominant is the cooper, Malachi Roohan, who has

a weird face, not in the least pale or lined, but ruddy, with a mahogany bald head, a head upon which the leathery skin — for there did not seem any flesh — hardly concealed the stark outlines of the skull. From the chin there strayed a grey beard, the most shaken and whipped-looking beard the widow had ever seen... (20).

Malachi Roohan, so aged that he is almost mummified but possessed of a fierce independence and a totally dominant personality, has the kind of memory shared by Cahir Bowes and Meehaul Lynskey ; the kind of memory which can trace the epic history of all their contemporaries.

« So you're Sally MacCabe, from Looscaun, the one Mortimer took off the blacksmith ? Well, well, that was a great business surely, the pair of them hot-tempered men, and your own beauty going to their heads like strong drink ».
He looked at the widow, a half-sceptical, half-admiring expression flickering across the leathery face. It was such a look as he might have given to Dervorgilla of Leinster, Deirdre of Uladh, or Helen of Troy (21).

The widow is not Sally MacCabe, nor Delia Morrissey, she is only the fourth wife of the weaver and does not have a name, nor a place of her own. Neither do the two grave-diggers. Only the old and the dead are individualised. The widow, significantly enough, hates genealogy. Genealogy is however, the greatest joy of the old men, « passionate, cantankerous, egoistic old men » (22), old men who are as distinct as trees, a distinction which the widow does not like.

She could understand calling fruit trees fruit trees and all other kinds simply trees. But that one should be an elm and another an ash, that there should be name after name, species after species, giving them peculiarities and personalities, was one of the things that the widow did not like. And at this moment, when the elm tree of Malachi Roohan had raised a fresh problem in Cloon na Morav, the likeness of old men to old trees — their crankiness, their complexity, their angles, their very barks, bulges, gnarled twistiness, and kinks — was very close, and brought a sense of oppression to the sorely tried brain of the widow (23).

Yet the widow has to learn to accept the importance of this distinctiveness. As she becomes more and more aware of the presence of one of the twin grave-diggers the importance of that essential individuality is revealed to her.

> That most subtle and powerful of all things, personality, sprang silently from the twins and made them, to the mind of the widow, things as far apart as the pole (24).

From the moment that one of the twins springs across the grave to embrace the widow, they have personality. They will no longer be merely a grave-digger and the nameless fourth wife of the weaver, but the man who claimed his wife at the mouth of her husbands grave and the woman who accepted that this be so. They will be, in Yeats' phrase, Olympians, unlike their colourless modern counterparts.

> The overflow from Cloon na Morav had already set a new cemetery on its legs a mile away, a cemetery in which limestone headstones and Celtic crosses were springing up like mushrooms, advertising the triviality of a civilization of men and women, who, according to their own epitaphs, had done exactly the two things they could not very well avoid doing : they had all, their obituary notices said, been born and they had all died   (25).

The truth is that the traditional, close society which nurtured the passions and eccentricities of Malachi Roohan and Mortimer Hehir is dying, its only remnants being the two old men who cannot remember where the grave is. The old-established patterns of memory, folk memory are breaking down, to be replaced by the written word which destroys the need for a community memory. Cloon na Morav though it is the field of the dead, houses a community which is still integrated into the living community.

> The ground was billowy, grotesque. Several partially suppressed insurrections — a great thirsting, worming, pushing and shouldering under the sod — had given it character. A long tough growth of grass wired it from end to end. Nature, by this effort, endeavouring to control the strivings of the more daring of the insurgents of Cloon na Morav (26).

The wishes of the dead must still be respected, their traditional rights and privileges observed. It is for this last task Cahir Bowes and Meehaul Lynskey are called from their useless retirement.

> Both old men had the air of those who had been unexpectedly let loose. For a long time they had lurked somewhere in the shadows of life, the world having no business for them, and, now, suddenly, they had been remembered and called forth to perform an office which nobody else on earth could perform (27).

With this profound sense of an integrated, if dying, community goes O'Kelly's sense of the importance of particular places, a sense he shared with many other writers in the Anglo-Irish and Irish traditions. All the people who are named are given their place of origin. The graveyard itself, their final place, influences and is in turn influenced by the community, of which it is a symbol.

The sense of traditional values, influenced by a particular landscape had been a constant element in O'Kelly's work. To it is added, in « The Weaver's Grave », a deeper, more reflective level. Malachi Roohan hanging on to life, « hoisting himself up from the dead on a length of rope reversing the usual procedure » (28) is a strange symbol of life in death. In a story dominated by death, his rope is an umbilical cord attaching him to life. In the resolution of the story, the great young star which shines above the head of the grave-digger before he embraces the widow, is a similar symbol of life.

> The widow could see the dark green wall, above it the band of still deepening red, above that the still more pallid grey sky, and directly over the man's head the gay frolicking of the fresh star in the sky. Cloon na Morav was flooded with a deep, vague light. The widow scented the fresh wind about her, the cool fragrance of the earth, and yet a warmth that was strangely beautiful... The widow thought that the word was strange, the sky extraordinary, the man's head against the red sky a wonder, a poem, above it the sparkle of the great young star (29).

In making a story about death into a promise of life, O'Kelly is uniting the diverse traditions of the wake and a motif common to most cultures and so raises the story of Cloon na Morav to an almost universal significance. In the process an elegy becomes a poem about youth and continuance. It is this vein, the vein of comedy (and there are many forms of rich humour in the story), which is, ultimately, most characteristic of O'Kelly dominating the moods of melancholy or tragedy which are also to be found. The note of warmth, of vitality, of love for scratchy eccentricities, allied with descriptive intensity and above all with that precise evocation of the difficulties and triumphs of traditional communities represents O'Kelly's unique contribution to the tradition of storytelling in Ireland.

# NOTES

1. Quoted by Seumas O'Sullivan in *Seumas O'Kelly : Essays and Recollections*, Dublin, Talbot Press, 1944, p. 122.

2. O'Sullivan : *op. cit.*, pp. 118-9.

3. *Joseph Holloway's Abbey Theatre*, ed. R. Hogan and M.J. O'Neill, Southern Illinois University Press, 1967, p. 199.

4. Joseph Holloway says that O'Kelly was 36 when he died. This conflicts with the discussion in George Brandon Saul : *Seumas O'Kelly*, Lewisburg, Bucknell University Press — Irish Writers Series, 1971 which I have followed for the biographical details given here. It also contains an excellent bibliography.

5. « A Wayside Burial » in *Waysiders*, Talbot Press, n.d., p. 139.

6. Eamon Grennan : Introduction to *A Land of Loneliness and Other Stories by Seumas O'Kelly*, Dublin, Gill and Macmillan, 1969, p. 6.

7. « A Land of Loneliness » in *A Land of Loneliness, op. cit.*, p. 21.

8. « The Shoemaker » in *Waysiders*, pp. 92-103.

9. «The Apparitions of Oul'Darmody » in *Hillsiders*, Talbot Press, n.d., p. 179.

10. « The Elks » in *Hillsiders*, p. 173.

11. « Both Sides of the Pond » in *Waysiders*, pp. 50-3.

12. George Brandon Saul argues for a later date of composition for *The Leprechaun of Kilmeen*, see *op. cit.*, Dublin, p. 34 and bibliography.

13. *The Weaver's Grave*, Dublin, A. Figgis, 1965, p. 5.

14. « The Big Man of the Fairies » in *The Leprechaun of Kilmeen*, The Leprechaun Press, 1964, p. 8.

15. « The Elks » in *Hillsiders*, p. 165.

16. « The Grey Lake » in *Waysiders*, pp. 165-6.

17. V. Mercier : *The Irish Comic Tradition*, London, Oxford University Press, 1962, p. 38.

18. « The Last of Martin Moran » in *The Leprechaun of Kilmeen*, p. 52.

19. « The Prodigal Daughter » in *Hillsiders*, p. 55-6.

20. *The Weaver's Grave*, p. 39.

21. *The Weaver's Grave*, p. 44.

22. *Op. cit.*, p. 38.

23. *Op. cit.*, p. 64.

24. *Op. cit.*, p. 62.

25. *Op. cit.*, p. 7.

26. *Op. cit.*, p. 7.

27. *Op. cit.*, p. 5.

28. *Op. cit.*, p. 41.

29. *Op. cit.*, p. 79.

# PLACE AND PEOPLE IN THE SHORT-STORIES OF DANIEL CORKERY

## Sean LUCY

All writers are more or less rooted in place and time, and Irish writers sometimes seem to be particularly so : the process of their history is an obsessive theme with them, and the place itself, Ireland, is so powerful a presence, in all its moods and demands, as to be one of the dominant *dramatis personae* of their story-telling.

Daniel Corkery was a man who believed passionately in Ireland as a culture, a people, and a nation. He represents a particular kind of cultural nationalism which was the response of many of the Irish to the challenge of identity under the increasing pressure of the English language and English attitudes. His was the nationalism of the Gaelic League, of Sinn Féin, and of the 1916 Rising and the War of Independence. It is an exclusive nationalism : Gaelic is Irish, English is not ; Catholic is Irish, Protestant is not ; countryman is Irish in ways that town or city man is not ; Republican is Irish, Loyalist is not.

In Irish studies in both languages Corkery stands for certain critical and historical attitudes which are closely connected to this nationalism, are in fact part of it. He is a point of nationalist reference, and the more extreme passages of cultural generalisation from *Synge and Anglo-Irish Literature* and from *The Hidden Ireland* are far more generally known and discussed than is his creative work. He is a useful stalking-horse ; or, to change the metaphor slightly, an attractive weapon or target — depending on the reader's own views of Irishness and of Irish language and culture.

He himself would probably have been pleased to be associated with the more extreme, exclusive, « pure », anti-English cultural positions which he expressed with such force and conviction, but, in so far as these distract us from, or even prejudice us against his prose fiction and his more detailed criticism, they are a nuisance.

At his best, rooted in the same obsessions that nourished his prejudices, there was in him a knowledge and love of his own place and people which made him a powerful writer, and a critic in whom intuition and intelligence held a fine and exciting balance.

This short study is an attempt to tease out some of the strands that are woven into many of his best and most characteristic short stories.

It seems that it is fashionable to think that, as a short story writer, Corkery was left far behind by his sometime disciples, Seán O'Faoláin and Frank O'Connor. To anyone who has really read Corkery this must seem muddle-headed. The first real observation is that Corkery is very different to either of the younger men ; the second is that he is more *uneven* and that his worst stories like some of those in *The Hounds of Banba* (propagandist parables rather than stories) are far worse than the worst work of the other two ; the third is, that, at his best, his stories, like his novel *The Threshold of Quiet,* have a deeper tone, a more impressive *gravitas* than we almost ever find in the work of the younger men. Interestingly enough, on the rare occasions when O'Connor and O'Faoláin achieve tragic or epic tone they sound most like their old mentor : when the calm irony of O'Faoláin deepens into sorrow or compassion, as at the end of *The Great O'Neill,* or when O'Connor's ready tenderness and humour are shadowed by a real sense of mortality, as in such stories as « The Weeping Children », or « Expectation of Life », or « The Long Road to Ummera ».

We might express the difference between Corkery and the younger men simply by saying that he was a countryman, or that he understood the country while they were essentially « townies ». This statement must be carefully qualified, for O'Faoláin has a rich gift for describing landscape and weather, and O'Connor has some brilliant stories of country life and attitudes. Yet they are always, to some extent, strangers in the countryside, always, somehow, outside observers, and often patronising or ill-at-ease.

Corkery on the other hand shows that identification, that sense of belonging which, in all its moods from desolation to a sense of glory, marks him truly as *in* and *of* the landscape. He is like Father Reen in his story « The Priest » :

> Whenever in his pacing he faced the west his eye traversed not only the river but the village beyond it. He saw the evening smoke of its homely fires ascending, each spire of it alive with the sunshine streaming through it. He had been so long in the place, first as curate and then as parish priest, that he had got into the way of whispering to himself such pet phrases as : My valley, my river, my river, my hills. This afternoon, the ascending smoke spires taking his eye. My people ! was the phrase that possessed his lips (1).

To expand a little : for our three writers the town, the city, is almost always Cork, folded into and climbing up out of its snug river valley ; Cork, so well evoked time and again by all three, and not least memorably by Corkery himself in his novel *The Threshold of Quiet*. The river Lee, which embraces « the flat of the city » and then spreads into a series of fine tidal lakes linking it to the sea, has come down from the West between the Red Sandstone ridges of those East-West Armorican foldings which determine so much of the whole varied feature and character of County Cork. In the Eastern and North-Eastern County and in the central area round the city these ridges seldom rise to mountain but are green to their crests with fields and woods — rich lands of fat farms and big estates ; but to the south they are steeper and closer with poorer land and smaller farms, until they meet the sea in a complication of bays and cliffs and inlets ; while to the North and North-West they rise and rise and break out into the stony mountain landscape of West Cork and Kerry, where farm and lake are folded close between the wild uplands until at last the major ridges move out their long mountain ranges into the Atlantic and hold between them the great bays of South-West Munster.

It is West Cork with its mountains that forms the sharpest arena of imaginative challenge — beloved landscape or howling wilderness — where a man alone in the open air can really test whether he is free in nature or whether he is incurably urbanised.

In this landscape and also on the Atlantic coasts, Corkery set many of his finest stories.

O'Faoláin and O'Connor both came to know West Cork very well during the War of Independence and the Civil War and each reacted ambiguously. The challenge of the mountains was increased by the fact that it was here as in other wild places that some of the last of Gaelic Ireland had survived, clinging to the small fields of high remote valleys. The Irish language, symbol of renascent nationalism, was still the speech of the place. Thousands of years of the same language in the same place — an idea, like the size of a mountain, to inspire or to terrify.

O'Faoláin's story « Fugue » from *Midsummer Night Madness* follows young rebels on the run through these mountains and ends with the hero alone in the vast, wet, strange landscape :

At last I came upon a lonely ruin upon the mountain, three walls, and I lay on the lee side of it while the rain dripped on me from the remnants of its eaves. When I awoke a dim radiance lit the falling haze, but whether it was the dawn or the sinking moon or any hour past three or before three I could not say. No sound was to be heard : no living thing moved ; no bird stirred the wet air : the falling haze made no sound. I rose chattering and trembling, and my feet plashed through the wet earth and the drowned grass, and when I halted there was quiet. I crossed a little stone wall and one of the stones fell with a mighty sound. I might have been the last human creature to crawl to the last summit of the world waiting until the deluge and the fortieth night of rain would strain him upwards on his toes while the water licked his stretched neck. Yet everywhere they slept sound abed, my dark woman curling her warm body beneath the bedclothes, the warmer for the wet fall without, thinking if she turned and heard the dripping eaves — that the winter was at last come

> Cold till doom !
> The storm has spread.
> A river is each furrow on the slope,
> Each ford is a full pool (2).

The verse, to fit the landscape, is from the old Irish.

In « The Long Road to Ummera », one of his finest and most

moving stories, O'Connor pays tribute to an old countrywoman living in the city, whose final obsessive wish is to be buried in her own mountain place among her own people. The old lady is based on O'Connor's paternal grandmother, who appears in so many of his writings, and who terribly embarrassed and annoyed him as a boy by her country manners, going barefoot in the house, eating potatoes with her hands from the table, drinking porter, muttering in Irish — the old hag herself, you might say. « The Long Road to Ummera » may be seen as a sort of peace-offering to his country ancestors, and it is full of affection and understanding ; but, in the end, O'Connor is closer to the son in the story who cannot for the life of him understand the old woman's rooted longing to go back in death to such a place :

All West Cork was in it : the bleak road over the moors to Ummera, the smooth grey pelts of the hills with the long spider's-web of the fences ridging them, drawing the scarecrow fields awry, and the whitewashed cottages, poker-faced between their little scraps of holly bushes looking this way and that out of the wind (3).

The essential difference, then, between the attitudes of the two younger writers and that of Corkery is that, whatever the rich range of emotions they may feel about the country, and particularly the wild country of West Cork, it remains for them, as it always is for the true townsman, somewhere « out there », almost as though the only real, human, dry land was the town and all the rest was an uncharted and shifting ocean.

Corkery, it is true, was a country boy by adoption rather than by origin, for he too was born and bred in the city of Cork, and indeed only came to the Irish language and to Irish Nationalism as an adult. Yet he knows and thinks about the countryside as one who belongs there. And he brings the artist's eye, for he was also a painter, to the places he visits in his words. Landscape for him is a matter, not just of physical feature, but always of light and weather ; and this must be so for an Irish writer or painter because there is probably no other country on earth that changes mood and character so often and so strangely as Ireland under the shifting skies of the Atlantic. There is hardly a story by Corkery for which one could not write a fairly detailed weather report ; and this weather moves over specific, vividly conjured-up landscapes which have a real geography, and have names which, even when invented, are based on the names of a thousand places like them. Here are the cliff fields by the sea on an October night :

> The sun had gone down that October evening sullenly in dusky crimson and flaming gold ; afterwards the clouds cleared and a frost had fallen. The wide stretches on the cliff tops were white with it, the silent sheep were white with it ; but wherever a streak of shadow was laid at all it was as black as ink, and sharp and strong. The moon was behind us, however, and only little jabs of shadow were visible : we were looking at a sharp-edged slope of white ; beyond it was a grey mass, whether sea or sky one could not say except when out on the reef a run of foam would catch the moon's rays for a moment, wriggle silver bright, like an eel caught in the hand, and then go out, leaving the darkness vast and vacant.
> We made upwards across that white slope to the *lios* ; and as we swept through the newly-frozen grass and heather we left dark wet-looking tracks behind us (4).

And here are a group of men climbing a stony mountainside called Knockanuller on a moonlit night in late November :

> As he spoke he raised his stick towards the brow of the hill, which was gapped and rugged with boulders and rocks. There the sky was becoming more and more luminous and the stars were gone. The moon they understood to be away towards the right. When they pierced through among the boulders they saw it suddenly, rising in splendour. Slabs of blanched stone, pillar stones of shadow, gaps of darkness — sharp-edged, were all about them in confusion. They felt astray (5).

Here, in contrast, is a warm evening on a rich farm of land called Dunerling East which has been bought and fiercely cared for by a farmer from the stony hills :

> ...The ground fell away downwards to a bracken-covered stream. Beyond the bracken it rose again ; much more suddenly however, so suddenly indeed that the red earth showed in patches through the tangled greenery. Those reddish

patches looked like corbels supporting the cornice-like ledge of the upward-sloping grazing grounds above. Just now, along that sun-drenched ledge, a procession of shapely deep-uddered cattle was moving from left to right, the beasts in single file or in pairs or groups, deliberately pacing. Thirty-one milkers were to pass like that, making for the unseen bridgeway across the stream in the hollow. Presently they would dip from sight and again be discovered in the tree-covered passage trailing up towards the milking sheds, the rich sunshine catching their deep-coloured flanks and slipping swiftly and suddenly from their horns and moving limbs (6).

For Corkery the people and the land are inseparable, different dimensions of the same reality. His eye is exact and fierce, but never patronising. His style matches it : being at its best, spare, vivid and energetic. He is a master of the physical detail that will give you both the person and the situation ; and, particularly in gesture, he shows a precise eye for the mannerisms of the particular area in which his people live. They are both individuals and also representative of types and attitudes which are accurate local examples of universal country types :

He was big, bony high-coloured, with large flashing eyes, like an excited horse's, and a drooping moustache of strong hairs with dew drops pendulous at the tips of them ; when speaking he threw up his head as if to give the voice free passage from the strong gristly throat. In gurgles and splashes it gushed from him ; and the moods of his impetuous heart were felt in the uneven flow of it. « The awkward squad that can't learn nothing », and he threw his hand carelessly in the air as if there never could be question of amendment (7).

Or again :

They were an ill-matched pair ; Lambert, the ex-soldier, brazen-eyed, straight-lipped, withered-skinned, impudent, and with a reckless way of striding along : old Redney, shy and tongue-tied, looking out from under his shaggy brows, his head down, his left hand clenched across the small of his back, his right hand tight and heavy upon the knob of his stick. With quick, uncertain steps, he made forwards as if his secret knowledge was no happy cargo. The neighbours would see him hobbling along with Lambert, always a little in the rear (8).

And here is a wordless exchange about a sick man :

> He shook a silent head in the direction of the listener's room, a look of inquiry in his eyes, and this look Mary answered with a sort of hopeless upswing of her face. Things had not improved in the lower room (9).

And a stupid passionate man going to pieces :

> ...In such a state that you wouldn't like to be looking at him — the big purple face of him so blue and shivery (10).

Corkery's accuracy is based on a deep understanding of place and people. In *Synge and Anglo-Irish Literature* he said that the three great forces which have formed the Irish consciousness and which he thinks should be the themes of any really Irish literature are :

1 — The Religious Consciousness of the people ;
2 — Irish Nationalism ;
3 — The Land (11).

He finds all of these forces most vividly in focus in the country-side, where, in fact, the last great force, the concern with the ownership of the land itself is the very condition of everyday life. For the farmer the ownership of land is identity itself, an absolutely personal, sometimes even a mystical, relationship.

One of Corkery's finest stories is « Carrig-an-Afrinn » which is the story of one farmer and two farms. The first farm is Carrig-an-Afrinn itself, the rocky West Cork farm from which he, and his people the Hodnetts have come. He is old when the story begins and it is long years since he sold the old farm and moved to Dunerling East, a far richer holding :

> ...ten miles farther from the hardness of the mountains, the cold rains, the winds, the mists. In those ten miles the barren hills that separate Cork from Kerry had space to stretch themselves out, to die away into gentle curves, to become soft and kind (12).

The story is about what the two farms have meant in the life of Hodnett. Carrig-an-Afrinn means « the Mass Rock », and was named for the pile of stone that stood in one of its fields where the Mass had been said many times in the old days when the law forbade it. Poor though the land is, it is a holy place where the angels stand guard forever over the consecrated ground. In selling it, in leaving, Hodnett suffers a sense of loss from which he never recovers, though he grapples fiercely with life and makes his new farm a showplace of order and prosperity. As an old man he is telling the tale of his last night in the mountains and of how he faced the challenge of the new life ; to get the feel of it we must quote at some length :

So I said to myself, and I listening to the clock ticking at the foot of the bed, I'm undertaking that big place, and maybe 'twon't thrive with me. And if it fails me, where am I ? That's what I said. It it fails me, where am I ? I tell ye, I was broken with thinking on it. And all the time, and this is the queerest thing of all, I heard someone saying, « Carrig-an-afrinn, Carrig-an-afrinn. Carrig-an-afrinn, Carrig-an-afrinn ». And not once nor twice nor three times, but all the night long, and I thinking and thinking. Of course, there was no one saying it at all, only maybe the beating of my own heart to be like a tune. But I was afraid. I thought maybe music might come rising up to me out of the *cummer*, and it thronged with angels, or a great light come striking in at the window. And sure enough at last I starded up and I cried out, « There it is ! There it is ! » But 'twas no unnatural light at all, only the dawn of day breaking in on top of me. 'Tis how I was after dozing off for a little while unknown to myself, and I woke up suddenly in confusion and dread.

That morning and I rising up my limbs were like wisps of straw. I was terrified of the long day before me, and that's the worse way a man can be. But when I came out and stood in the broad sun, and 'twas a morning of white frost, I drew in the air to myself, and I took courage to see my poor animals grazing so peacefully on the hill, just like what you see in a picture. If the big farms broke the men that were born to softness and luxury, Dunerling East wouldn't break me, and I reared hard and tough ! That's what I said, with great daring in my breast.

Not long after that we moved our handful of stock east to this place. I laughed to picture the two scraggy beasts, and all the deep feeding of Dunerling East to themselves. And that same evening myself and Michael, Michael that's dead, God rest him, went over and hither and in and out through the length and breath of this estate and round by the boundary ditch ; and 'tis a thing I will not forget till my dying day what he said to me, my son Michael, that same evening, and we killed from the exertion. He stopped and looked up at me before he spoke :

« Look », he said, « why have you your hands like that ? »

My two hands, clenched and stiff, *stiff*, like you'd have them in a fight, watching your opponent, watching to catch him off his guard, or for fear he'd spring on you. That's how I had my hands. And 'twas natural for me to have my hands like that, for what I was saying to myself was : I'll break it ! I'll break it ! And I was saying that because if I didn't break it I was sport for the world. Like a bully at a fair I was, going about my own land the first day I walked it ! (13).

Corkery manages to focus into Hodnett not only a vivid portrait of a certain sort of man but also the whole struggle in a proud person between success and peace, almost between Mammon and God — a point sharpened by the fact that, unknown to the old man, the beloved Mass rock, whose memory he still reveres, has been blasted away to widen the road.

In « Carrig-an-Afrinn » and other stories Corkery weaves together the forces of religion and land as neither O'Connor nor O'Faoláin did or tried to do. These stories are passionate, but seldom sentimental : there is a hardness of detail and an almost pitiless realism of psychological insight that saves them from that. It is only in his nationalistic stories like many of those in *The Hounds of Banba* that Corkery's own passions cloud perception and lead him into that emotional rhetoric which is often the plague of Munster writers.

It is when Corkery gives us figures not just *in* but *of* a landscape that he is at his best. Those who studied English literature at University College Cork, when he was Professor there, often speak of his lectures on Wordsworth, particularly on the poem *Michael*. He believed, like Wordsworth, that the struggle with natural forces and the presence of natural process and form can develop and change a man, as they did Michael :

And, truly, at all times, the storm, that drives
The traveller to a shelter, summoned him
Up to the mountains : he had been alone
Amid  the heart of many thousand mists,
That came to him, and left him, on the heights.
So lived he till his eightieth year was past.
And grossly that man errs, who should suppose
That the green valleys, and the streams and rocks,
Were things indifferent to the Shepherd's thoughts.
Fields, where with cheerful spirits he had breathed
The common air ; hills, which with vigorous step
He had so often climbed ; which had impressed
So many incidents upon his mind
Of hardship, skill or courage, joy or fear ;
Which, like a book, preserved the memory
Of the dumb animals, whom he had saved,
Had fed or sheltered, linking to such acts
The certainty of honourable gain ;
Those fields, those hills — what could they less ? had laid
Strong hold on his affections, were to him
A pleasurable feeling of blind love,
The pleasure which there is in life itself (14).

In the countrymen Corkery found an independence and a
strength which attracted him, but also in the Irish country people
he found another quality, some sort of wildness, of recklessness,
that fascinated him — some sort of restless dissatisfaction with
the common round, a dissatisfaction which can turn a man into a
hero or a saint or a madman.

For Corkery was attracted to imagination and to will, and
fascinated when these came together in obsession. The focus of
story after story is on a man gripped by a vision, more or less
real, and led beyond the ordinary everyday boundaries of his life.
In a natural setting, particularly a wilder more challenging
setting, the individual human being shines out more strongly and
more strangely than in the city, and Corkery has given us that
strength,without denying the narrowness that often goes with it,
and has given us the strangeness, without flinching from some of
its more gross and grotesque manifestations.

« The Priest » is a simple story of a priest in some West Cork mountain district, who is called out towards nightfall to minister to a dying farmer in a remote rough corner of his parish. The journey and the task bring out Father Reen's concern for the community under his care. He cares for their souls, but should he not do something to alleviate and to enrich the hard, bare struggle of their lives in that harsh landscape ? He comes to the little mountain farm crowded with relations greedy to inherit the few rocky fields and the scrap of money, and goes in to find the dying man still clinging to the thought of his land and of the eighty hard-earned pounds marked in his dirty bank book.

No sooner was Father Reen aware of this than he knew that it would be easier almost to wrench one of the rocks in the fields abroad from its bed than to wrench that long-accustomed support from the old man's little world of consciousness without shattering it to insanity. Yet this at last Father Reen felt he had succeeded in doing ; he thought he found a new look coming into the old man's eyes, overspreading his brow, some expression of hard-won relief, some return of openness, of simplicity, that may not have been there since early manhood ; in the voice he thought he found some new timbre, some sudden access of tenderness, of sweetness ; and, more surely telling of the new scale of values suddenly come upon by that old battler in a rough world, a flood of aspirations broke impetuously from the trembling lips : « Jesus Christ, O welcome, O welcome ; keep near me, I'm not worthy, I'm not worthy, but welcome. O Blessed Mother, pray for me, now now » — a flood onward and never-ending once it had started at all ; and Father Reen noticed how the two fists, twin knobs, equally hard and small, were pressed fiercely down upon the brows, side by side, covering the eye sockets, hiding almost the whole of the rapt countenance, except the moving chin. Limbs and all, the old peasant had become one knot of concentration, and the thought of what he was leaving behind him was not any longer its secret (15).

Leaving the house the priest gallops his horse home through the rocky landscape under the stars, trying to forget in his fierce ride the questions about life which have been resurrected in him by the old man's death.

It has been the intention of this study to bring out what is strongest and most original in Corkery's stories. His limitations are equally clear. He has almost nothing to say about women, or about the love between men and women which is, of course, the other great theme of Irish life and literature, and which he forgets in his famous list. His pupils, O'Faoláin and O'Connor, make him appear almost childish here, when we compare his stories to their rich fund of love chronicles, to their various and often brilliant explorations of the minds and hearts of girls and women as well as boys and men. Then again, there are times when Corkery's tragic vision and tragic style lapse towards cliché and melodrama, though this is because he runs the sort of risk which the younger men almost never take, the risk of taking people completely seriously.

This last risk finds its justification in stories like « The Priest » and in passages like the one quoted above from that story. At such times Corkery achieves something not often found in contemporary literature because his vision is based both in a rooted realism and also in the belief that, for all his limitations, man is capable of nobility.

# NOTES

I find I have taken all my examples of Corkery's craft from his book of stories *The Stormy Hills*. I suppose that this is because twenty years ago, in exile in England, I found that book in the library of a school where I was teaching, and was deeply impressed and moved, not only by its inherent qualities but by the way it brought me home in imagination. It is probably his best collection. For the convenience of the reader, my page references are to the Mercier Press paperback reprint which is still available (Cork, undated). These references are noted *S.H.*

1. *S.H.*, p. 117.
2. *Midsummer Night Madness*, London, 1932, pp. 112-3.
3. Originally published in *Crab Apple Jelly*, London, 1944 ; reprinted in the paperback *Day Dreams*, London, 1973, p. 75.
4. *S.H.*, pp. 58-9.
5. *S.H.*, pp. 87-8.
6. *S.H.*, pp. 31-2.
7. *S.H.*, p. 10.
8. *S.H.*, p. 83.
9. *S.H.*, p. 108.
10. *S.H.*, p. 95.
11. *Synge and Anglo-Irish Literature*, Mercier Paperback reprint, Cork, 1966, p. 19.
12. *S.H.*, p. 37.
13. *S.H.*, pp. 41-2.
14. *Michael*, pp. 56-77.
15. *S.H.*, pp. 124-5.

# LIAM O'FLAHERTY : THE UNCHAINED STORM.
## A VIEW OF HIS SHORT STORIES

### Brendan KENNELLY

It would be a mistake, I think, to lump Liam O'Flaherty with those other distinguished writers such as Frank O'Connor, Seán O'Faoláin, Mary Lavin and others, and say, with convenient finality, that O'Flaherty, like these, makes his own special contribution to the Irish short story tradition. He does, of course. And yet I must admit, at the outset, that it seems to me to be inaccurate to limit the scope and depth of O'Flaherty's art by pinning on him the label « short story writer ». It seems more precise to me to say that he is a poet in prose, who chose the short story as a medium. It follows that while his stories may be considered purely as stories, it is also helpful to look on many of them as poems in prose, poems of a peculiarly explosive, energetic and echoing nature.

I choose the word « energetic » deliberately. His stories are, for the most part, energetic responses to infinitely varied spectacles of energy. It is energy that obsesses him, that most draws his astonishing capacity for wonder and admiration into full play. There are times when O'Flaherty writes as though he were Adam opening his eyes on creation for the first time. Forms of boringness and dulling familiarity seem not to exist for him ; when they do, he attacks them savagely. He seems attuned to the astounding energies of life itself ; and this is why his prose frequently has the intensity and strong momentum of a poetry whose primary impulse is wonder, admiration and praise. It follows that what most repels O'Flaherty is death, all forms of death — inertia, boredom, emotional pettiness and fatigue. And it must be admitted that he is not at his best when dealing with what are for him forms of emotional death ; some of his worst writing, « The Wedding » for example, shows him floundering, bewildered and jabbering, among various forms of human ugliness and distortion. In stories like « The Wedding » O'Flaherty tries to compensate for a fatal uncertainty of perception with fake lyricism and strident melodrama. The reason is, I think, that there is singularly little energy in the story ; and where there is no form of energy to wonder at, O'Flaherty's prose relies on a kind of blind, simplistic swiping that might be insulting if it weren't so ridiculous. Saddest of all, in such stories, O'Flaherty seems to have no critical awareness of his flaws. Indeed, it seems that for O'Flaherty, the critic has little or no existence. It is well to remember, though, that while this lack of critical awareness can lead to writing of not easily equalled atrocity, it is also connected with O'Flaherty's highest and most uninhibitedly ecstatic flights, the splendid ferocity of his lyricism. All in all, therefore, one is glad to accept him as he is.

Not many of O'Flaherty's stories are as bad as « The Wedding ». For the most part, he writes with a vehemently sustained skill. Even when he is well below his best, he still writes grippingly. Because he writes out of excitement and wonder, he usually stirs excitement and wonder in his readers. It is precisely this capacity for primal excitement that helps us to understand the poetic qualities of O'Flaherty's prose.

In an issue of *The Irish Statesman* dated October 18th, 1924, there was a letter from O'Flaherty, headed « National Energy ». The letter was in reply to an essay entitled « Leaders of Indian Nationalism » which had appeared in the issue of October 4th. O'Flaherty was intensely moved by what he called the « vitality and force and passion and stinging truth of that essay, the surging rhythm of the prose, the ferocity of expression ». The essay had been in praise of peace, of « quiet culture ». To O'Flaherty, this didn't really matter, because « in literature it is the method and the manner that counts, the manner of expressing the passion that is within the heart ».

There follows a passage in the letter which I would like to quote in full because it is an eloquent statement of O'Flaherty's great love and great theme — energy. It is equally eloquent about his loathing for fraud, corruption, usury and sluggishness. In fact, this passage may be used as a condensed statement of O'Flaherty's aesthetics.

> But the human race has not advanced from savagery to culture on the feeble crutches of philosophy. What epics have there been written about the disputations of scholars ? Did Homer write of philosophy or of the hunting of wild boars and the savage wars waged around stone-walled cities ? Did Shakespeare live in the days of twenty per cent. interest on oil stocks and the loathsome mouthings of Ramsay MacDonalds at Geneva about Leagues of Nations that are based on fraud, corruption, and the usury of slim-fingered, cultured bankers ? Did he not live in the days when piratical adventurers carried the standards of Britain across the oceans and the continents ? Did he not live in the days when his race was emerging, with bloodshot eyes, lean, hungry, virile, savage, from the savagery of feudalism into the struggle for Empire ?
> In Ireland, to my mind, we have reached that point in the progress of our race, the point which marked the appearance of Shakespeare in English literature. Let us not be ashamed that gunshots are heard in our streets. Let us rather be glad. For force is, after all, the opposite of sluggishness. It is an intensity of movement, of motion. And motion is the opposite of death.

O'Flaherty concludes his letter by contrasting Irish culture with Indian culture which he sees as « a culture of sweet, beautiful words and of slim fingers, slim, long, aristocratic fingers that are effete and on their death-bed ». Irish culture, on the other hand, « is the wild tumult of the unchained storm, the tumult of the army on the march, clashing its cymbals, rioting with excess of energy ». I do not think that I would accept this as an accurate description of Irish culture as a whole or even at that point in time. As a way of appreciating O'Flaherty's own work, however, it seems to me to be helpful. I would like, therefore, to consider some of the stories under the following headings : Nature ; Wild Creatures ; Humans. In many stories these themes fuse with each other. I shall try to do justice to this fusion while pointing out the poetic qualities of the writing.

More than any other natural image, the image of the

sea pounds and roars through O'Flaherty's work. « In literature, it is the method and the manner that counts ». O'Flaherty's « manner » of presenting the sea in a story like « The Landing », for example, is both distinctive and effective. He creates a cosmic drama around the efforts of fishermen in a curragh to land safely during a storm, watched by their relatives and friends on the shore. O'Flaherty convincingly connects the tumult of the natural world with the confusion and terror of minds forced to witness such a spectacle. As O'Flaherty presents it, it is a massive, terrifying music filling sea, sky and every witnessing mind. He deftly gives us the « horrid distinctness » of sounds becoming mental visions on the threshold of madness. The effectiveness of this passage, as of so many other similar passages, is that the storm is no mere hullaballoo of nature ; it is inseparable from a tortured human drama, a wild music of minds on the brink of disintegration. Rhythm and images combine perfectly to dramatize the sense of being simultaneously together and isolated. Prose is heightened to the point of poetry.

The crashing of the waves against the cliffs to the east was drowning the wind. The wind came steadily, like the rushing of a great cataract heard at a great distance, but the noises of the sea were continually changing, rising and falling, with the stupendous modulations of an orchestra played by giants. Each sound boomed or hissed or crashed with a horrid distinctness. It stood apart from the other sounds that followed and preceded it as menacing and overwhelming as the visions that crowd on a disordered mind, each standing apart from the others in crazy independence.

Of O'Flaherty's sea-stories, it is those in which the sea is inseparable from the drama, human and inhuman, that best succeed. « The Rockfish » and « The Oar » are good examples. Less successful are the stories in which the sea is not convincingly evoked, or seems incidental to the drama. In « The Struggle », for example, two drunken men have a fight in a boat ; in the end they drown. The violence is strongly presented, but O'Flaherty fails to dramatize it convincingly ; after the initial shock, the violence is tedious. The fact that it takes place in a boat on the sea makes little difference to the story which in the end strikes one as having a sordid and mechanical character. At such moments, one regrets the absence in O'Flaherty of an intellectual questioning of his own themes ; instead of this questioning, one gets the sense of a deadpan satisfaction with the *fact* that he is actually treating violence in a way that is complacent, unmoved. Stories like « The Struggle » have the subtlety of a hammer-blow.

It is worth noting at this stage that the deadpan presentation of violence is often the mask for melodrama and sentimentality. Any critical appraisal of O'Flaherty's stories must acknowledge these faults before his merits can be properly appreciated. There are many examples in his stories of melodrama and sentimentality. Here, however, I am merely making the point that under the obsession with violence and bravado, in which self-congratulation masquerades as detachment, one can hear, if one listens carefully, the hearbeat of the softie, the romantic slob. This soft writing happens more when O'Flaherty is dealing with human beings than wild animals or birds. An excellent example of this is his treatment of motherhood in « The Outcast », which deals with the death of a girl and her child after an encouter with a brutal priest, and « The Cow's Death » which tells how a cow leaps to her death into the sea when she sees the body of her calf on the rocks below. In « The Outcast », almost nothing is credible. From the grotesquely exaggerated picture of the priest at the beginning to the girl's final leap into the lake (laughing « madly, wildly, loudly », mind you, as she does so) with the child in her arms, we are in a world of vivid incredibility. In « The Cow's Death », however, which presents a situation that would appear to pose a far greater problem of stylistic treatment, O'Flaherty is infinitely more convincing. Although at the beginning of the story he hovers on the edge of sentimentality, his narrative proceeds at a swift, relentless pace, matching the cow's increasingly frantic, self-wounding, and finally self-destroying quest for her calf. A primal impulse is captured in a primal style. From a comparison of these two stories, it would seem that there are times when O'Flaherty's imagination is more at home among the beasts in their fertile and dangerous world than among humans in their world of confused and tangled emotions.

And yet, even poor stories like « The Struggle » indicate one of O'Flaherty's major concerns — the struggle of men and women with the natural world of sea and land. When he avoids exaggeration and distortion, his treatment of this fundamental and

eternal struggle can be intensely moving. « Spring Sowing »,
which deals with the first day of the first spring sowing of a
young peasant and his wife, must surely be one of O'Flaherty's
finest creations. The young couple, still in the first joy of
marriage, face their struggle with the land. As the story unfolds,
so do the characters of the couple, and so do not only their lives
on this particular spring day but also their lives in future years.
In this struggle with the land, the young woman becomes afraid
of the « pitiless, cruel earth, the peasant's slave master, that
would keep her chained to hard work and poverty all her life until
she would sink again into its bosom. Her short-lived love was
gone ». But she also discovers « a strange joy » which over-
powers « that other feeling of dread ». The young man discovers
that he is capable of struggling successfully with the earth. The
final sentences of the story beautifully portray a picture of that
struggle — its hardship, its rewards, its devouring endlessness.

They stood for a few moments in silence, looking at the work
they had done. All her dissatisfaction and weariness vanished
from Mary's mind with the delicious feeling of comfort that
overcame her at having done this work with her husband. They
had done it together. They had planted seeds in the earth.
The next day and the next and all their lives, when spring
came they would have to bend their backs and do it until their
hands and bones got twisted with rheumatism. But night
would always bring sleep and forgetfulness.

My main effort in this article is to try to define or describe
what constitutes the poetry of O'Flaherty's prose. It is, as I have
said, connected with his response to energy, and to a lesser
extent with the workings of his imagination when it is freed from
the need to disentangle the emotional complexities of people.
That is why, I believe, his best stories are about wild creatures,
and why the distinctive O'Flaherty poetry occurs most of all in
those stories. This poetry has in it a genuine epic throb, an
unpolluted primitive wonder, a strong purity of narrative line
which, by reason of its very strength, is more like verse than
prose. I am convinced in fact that « Wild Stallions » falls
naturally into verse. If we listen to its rhythms, the varying cool
impassioned flow of its sympathies, its unfolding of anticipation,
conflict and resolution, we find ourselves in the company not of a

modern writer of short stories but of a bardic teller of tales, a narrator for whom the disclosure of marvels is as natural and inevitable as the ear for the rhythms of city-talk is natural to James Joyce. Here is the opening of « Wild Stallions ».

As he stood over his grazing herd,
on a hillock near the northern wall
of his lofty mountain glen,
the golden stallion's mane and tail
looked almost white in the radiant light of dawn.
At the centre of his forehead,
a small star shone like a jewel.

This beautiful rhythm is maintained right through the story which has a fierce sexual pulse. The final clash of the two wild stallions, which will decide the sexual supremacy for which they struggle to the death, shows O'Flaherty's poetry in full epic flight.

Neighing hoarsely in his throat,
the invader cantered forward slowly
with his head bowed. The golden stallion
stood his ground on widespread legs,
mustering the last remnants of his strength,
until the enemy swerved at close quarters
to deliver a broadside.
Then he rose and brought his forelegs down
with great force.
Struck above the kidneys,
the grey uttered a shrill cry and fell.
While rolling away, a second blow on the spine
made him groan and shudder from head to tail.
With his glazed eyes wide open,
he turned over on his back,
swung his neck from side to side
and snapped his jaws without known purpose
in the urgent agony of death.

It is worth noting here that « Wild Stallions » is an excellent example of the crisp, definite way in which O'Flaherty often manages to finish his stories. He rarely lingers indulgently in the drama he has created, or dallies complacently in lyrical climax.

The ending of « Wild Stallions » is as clean as the cut of the sharpest axe. The golden stallion, a maimed victor pursued by wild predators, is briefly defended by his mares but

Then two of the mountain lions
broke through the circle
and brought him down.

In « Wild Stallions » both stallions die. The wild swan, in the story of that name, loses his mate and, after a struggle, finds a new one, and brings her back to his nest. This particular ending pulses with the promise of new life, but two sentences are enough to express the full glory of that promise.

The two great white birds walked round the nest, flapping their wings and uttering harsh cries of joy. Then they began to prepare the place for their brood.

Contemplating his wild creatures, O'Flaherty's language is precise, confident, unstrained. These stories are visions of energies at work. Human eyes, conditioned by the civilized strictures of necessary moralities, may see such energies as cruel or barbaric. To O'Flaherty, however, these energies are the truest and deepest manifestations of reality. Of the hawk, in the story of that name, and of the wild swan, he uses the phrase « brute soul » to express his concept of that energy. This belief in a kind of brute spirituality or spiritual brutishness is a primary reason why these stories are immediately and permanently compelling. If it is possible to speak of a soul in action (and I believe it is), then O'Flaherty must be commended for his vision of the « brute soul » of the hawk in action as natural as it is superb.

The hawk waited until the songbird had almost reached the limit of his climb. Then he took aim and stooped. With his wings half-closed, he raked like a meteor from the clouds. The lark's warbling changed to a shriek of terror as he heard the fierce rush of the charging hawk. Then he swerved aside, just in time to avoid the full force of the blow. Half-stunned, he folded his wings and plunged headlong towards the earth, leaving behind a flutter of feathers that had been torn from his tail by the claws of his enemy.

When he missed his mark, the hawk at once opened wide his wings and canted them to stay his rush. He circled once more above his falling prey, took aim, and stooped again. This time the lark did nothing to avoid the kill. He died the instant he was struck ; his inert wings unfolded. With his head dangling from his limp throat, through which his lovely song had just been pouring, he came tumbling down, convoyed by the closely circling hawk. He struck earth on a patch of soft brown sand, beside a shining stream.

The hawk stood for a few moments over his kill, with his lewd purple tongue lolling from his open beak and his black-barred breast heaving from the effort of pursuit. Then he secured the carcase in his claws, took wing, and flew off to the cliff where his mate was hatching on a broad ledge, beneath a massive tawny-gold rock that rose, over-arching, to the summit.

It is very important to remember that O'Flaherty sees himself as presenting the workings of a « brute soul ». This is one reason why these stories are totally devoid of sentimentality. They are packed with the pressure of the author's love and admiration for his creatures or, as I prefer to call them, his visions of living energy. Not all these visions concern struggle and conflict, maiming and killing. One of the purest moments of tenderness I know occurs in « The Wild Goat's Kid » in which a wild goat encourages her new-born kid to stand, to face the world, to live.

How she manoeuvred to make him stand ! She breathed on him to warm him. She raised him gently with her forehead, uttering strange, soft sounds to encourage him. Then he stood up, trembling, staggering, swaying on his curiously long legs. She became very excited, rushing around him, bleating nervously, afraid that he should fall again. He fell. She was in agony. Bitter wails came from her distended jaws and she crunched her teeth. But she renewed her efforts, urging the kid to rise, to rise and live... to live, live, live.

I believe that this impulse « to live, live, live » is what O'Flaherty most admires in his wild creatures and what he would most like human beings to do. It is his deepest passion. As such, it helps to explain the intensely simplistic quality of most of his

stories dealing with people and their relationships with each
other. It is not enough to say that O'Flaherty deals mainly with
peasants and peasants are rather simple-minded and simple-
hearted folk. Nor is it enough to say that O'Flaherty is a sort of
emotional fundamentalist, one who is, quite simply, not interested
in the more elusive shades of emotional subtlety but is content to
prowl among the apparently sharply-defined blacks and whites of
the heart. No, I think it is fair to say that the main fault of most
of his stories about human relationships — their simplistic
intensities, their hammering unawareness of the heart's subtler
uncertainties — is due, paradoxically, to what is most admirable
in this writer, his almost messianic wish that his human characters embody and manifest the magnificent energy of his wild
creatures. Therefore, when he describes a beautiful woman, he
sees her in terms of a snake and a young tree. Red Barbara is
splendid but she is more of a wild, idealized creation than a
credible human being.

> She had a small head, like a snake, but with no malice or
> subtlety in her large, sleepy, blue eyes. She had long, golden
> eyelashes and pretty little teeth like a young girl. Her hair
> was red-gold. Her limbs were long and supple. She walked with
> a long raking stride, almost sideways, for her slim body
> swayed voluptuously, like a young tree swaying in the wind.
> And when she rested she appeared half asleep, without
> thought ; as if she knew she was only made for love and must
> always wait for and suffer admiration or caresses. Her lips
> were always half open, her lashes drooped and her little ears,
> peeping from beneath her red-gold hair, seemed to be perpe-
> tually listening for words of admiration.

The problem is this. O'Flaherty loves the free, the flawless, the
ecstatically abandoned, the amoral exultant spirit, but, confronted with human beings in all their weaknesses and failings, he
drives himself into a necessarily simplistic position by his
compulsion, understandable as a result of his love for perfect
embodiments of energy, to create characters who tend to be either
too flawless or too flawed. Either way, a certain distortion takes
place. In spite of this, I would like to say that O'Flaherty's heart,
if not his head, is nearly always in the right place. After all, he
*does* love freedom, and he would like his people to be free. In his

ironic, and often bitterly comic *Tourist's Guide To Ireland*, he attacks many of the enemies of Irish freedom, which, in his eyes, is freedom from « priests, politicians, ignorance and various other diseases ». In the following passage, he paints for the tourist a picture of pious scavengers.

He'll see other orders of religious clergy who make it their business to go around the country on missions terrorising the unfortunate lower classes with threats of fire and brimstone in the hereafter, while in their train march countless vendors of statues, medals, scapulars and *agnus deis*, which are used by the ignorant in the place of medicine. He'll find other orders that live simply by begging. And on every side, among all orders, he'll find a rapid accumulation of property, which threatens to turn the whole country into a clerical kingdom. He'll meet nuns, also accumulating property. He'll meet Christian Brothers, who are in the teaching business, midway between the secular clergy and the religious orders. And he'll finish up, if he is any way sensitive, by getting an impression of Ireland, as a beautiful sad-faced country that is being rapidly covered by a black rash.

The same clergy are portrayed as the enemies of freedom in several O'Flaherty stories. In « The Child of God », a priest banishes the young artist, Peter, from the community. In « The Fairy Goose », the priest is a black harbinger of fear. In « The Outcast », the priest is largely responsible for the deaths of the girl and her child. In all three cases, O'Flaherty is making a strong, humane point ; but it must be admitted that in no case is he fully successful in creating a totally credible priest figure.

O'Flaherty's love of freedom finds its most convincing artistic expression in those stories dealing with tramps and tinkers. « The Tramp », for-example, works as a story because the central figure's love of freedom gives him a Synge-like volubility in his talk, makes him a patient, discriminating listener, and above all, perhaps, endows him with a capacity for swift, decisive action which is firmly and acceptably contrasted with the slavish indecisiveness of Deignan to whom the tramp has been kind and generous and whom he has tried to persuade to set out on the exciting road to freedom. At the end, the tramp moves forward into freedom but Deignan remains behind, petrified by indecision.

Among the other enemies of freedom whom O'Flaherty loathes
are the single-minded money-makers, the usurers, the gombeen
men, the unscrupulous dealers, the mercenary opportunists,
callous and tireless. In *A Tourist's Guide To Ireland*, he savages
the greedy publican and his mean, sordid house.

> Here one must eat like a hermit in the desert, in order that
> the parish priest may have abundance for his table. Here one
> must drink, standing up like a cab-horse at a drinking trough,
> black beverages that remind us of the death that is the
> common destiny of us all. And one must drink quickly, on an
> empty stomach, drink after drink, diluted and weakened, so
> that the publican may rake in quickly, with little labour,
> enough money to make his sons priests, doctors, lawyers and
> politicians, and then to build a new church or repair an old
> one, as a duty to God and to save his immortal soul in
> payment for all the robbery he has committed.

Throughout the stories, O'Flaherty is bitterly critical of the
effects of greed and ruthless ambition on people. What he
deplores most of all are the dehumanizing effects on people of the
slavish dedication to the making of money. One of the most
powerful examples of this is « Two Lovely Beasts » in which
Colm Derrane determines to rise in the world by purchasing two
promising calves. Very soon, he becomes « as ruthless towards
his family as he is tender towards the calves ». At the end of the
story, he is « cold and resolute and ruthless ». The pursuit of
money has robbed him of his warm humanity. A new, implacable
ugliness has taken hold of him.

Conversely, the man who lives free from the tyrannies of
money-making is for O'Flaherty a natural aristocrat, a sort of
male version of Red Barbara. The tinker in « The Tent » is a
good example. He is a « slim, tall, graceful man, with a beautiful
head poised gracefully on a brown neck, and great black lashes
falling down over his half-closed eyes, just like a woman ». He is
one of those who are « cut off from the mass of society yet living at
their expense ». Clearly, he has O'Flaherty's unqualified admiration and approval. The tinker is as near as one gets to a human
version of one of O'Flaherty's wild creatures.

This is at once his appeal and his limitation. Once we accept
the limitation, the appeal becomes more convincing. This remark,

in fact, applies to most of O'Flaherty's stories about people.

One final point. It seems to me a pity that O'Flaherty did not attempt more stories in the comic vein of « The Post Office ». It is funny because it is, for the most part, understated. The creation of comedy shows O'Flaherty capable of an effective reticence in his writing.

O'Flaherty probably has more faults than any of the other outstanding Irish writers of short stories. But, with the exception of Joyce, he also rises to greater heights. His failures as a writer are directly connected with his ecstatic successes. He is a poet who has chosen to tell stories. He is capable of the most sustained imaginative intensity ; and he can sink into the most deplorable depths of melodrama. At times, his writing seems to have the pure energy of a natural force. « Ours » he claimed in that letter to *The Irish Statesman* in 1924, « Ours is the wild tumult of the unchained storm ». O'Flaherty's imaginative energy reminds one at times of « the unchained storm ». It can be rough and wild and whirling but it can also be profoundly exhilarating.

# FRANK O'CONNOR AND THE DESOLATION
# OF REALITY

## Roger CHATALIC

« *The country ! Oh, God, the bloody country* » (1)

Owing to a Yeatsean pronouncement on his early work, now
dutifully turned into a slogan by his publishers (2), Frank
O'Connor (1903-1966) has come to be known as the Irish
Chekhov. This title, which is also claimed for O'Faolain, high-
lights his standing as one of Ireland's foremost mid-twentieth-
century writers, but it obscures his originality. Whatever
O'Connor has in common with Chekhov, his genius is very much
his own, with its virtues and its faults. It is less reserved,
heartier, more emotional than the Russian master's. It reflects
the shifting moods of a personality at once diffident and
flamboyant, as quick to anger as to joy or despair, opinionated,
irreverent, rebellious, full of violent likes and dislikes. O'Connor
himself felt it dangerous to try to follow Chekhov : « He is
inimitable », he observed, « a person to read and admire and
worship — but never, never, never to imitate » (3).

And yet, judging by his criticism, he may well have drawn
from the latter something of what seems to form the mainspring
of his creativity : his haunting sense of man's isolation. Such a
sense, he contended, lies at the root of the short story — a form
best approached, to his mind, in a mood akin to that of Pascal's
saying : *Le silence éternel de ces espaces infinis m'effraie* (4). His
conception of it as « a lonely, personal art » (5) is unsatisfactory

as a theory, but it is not unfair to take it as a clue to his own vision and achievement. His was a very subjective mind, whose general views were coloured by his personal problems (6).

One of the « strayed revellers of the Irish literary revival » (7), he found himself out of place in the pious parochialism of post-revolutionary Ireland. But there was in him a deeper sense of alienation, traceable to his earliest life, and which shaped his vision of man and the world. A professed agnostic till his last years, he keenly felt the collapse of traditional beliefs and values, hence his reference to Pascal. This reference is paradoxical, for the main feel of his work is of warm humorous humanity rather than tragic metaphysical anxiety ; but even in his lighter fiction, one may discern the dread, manifest in his more sombre stories, of a world in which « there is no longer a society to absorb (the individual), and... he is compelled to exist as it were by his own inner light » (8). The warmth of O'Connor's fiction may be understood as a counter to this dread. Bracing his imagination against despair, he clung to faith in the individual, however insignificant the latter appeared in the alien vastness of the modern world. His art sprang from a need to overcome his sense of what he referred to as « the desolation of reality » (9).

His life was a long struggle to realize his own individuality within, and against the fierce pressures of, the world where he felt he belonged. Born and bred in Cork's slums, the only child of a common labourer and an orphan maid-servant, he was exposed from the first to a chaotic, dispiriting reality, and led to seek in his inner self the strength to endure it. His drunken father sometimes threatened his wife and son with his razor, and once threw them both out in their nightclothes. Such incidents inspired the writer with a distrust of authority, a deep feeling of in-security, and a craving for intimate warmth. « For me », he writes, « there has always been in imagination a stage beyond death — a stage where one says ' I have no home now'» (10).

He became intensely attached to his mother and in her care acquired ideals and a yearning for education that preserved him from the coarseness of his milieu, but also cut him off from his fellows. Overimpulsive, he failed to satisfy his teachers, and dropped out of school before he was thirteen, to educate himself on his own while working as a messenger boy. His lonely efforts earned him more gibes than sympathy until they were rewarded by the friendship and guidance of the writer Daniel Corkery, who introduced him to other young intellectuals like Sean 0'Faolain.

His commitment to the Irish cause further shaped his personality. He joined the Gaelic League at thirteen, the Volunteers at fifteen, fought with the Republicans in the Civil War, was arrested and imprisoned in 1923. Yet, put off by the abstract inhumanity of the fighting, he rebelled against his side, refusing to shoot unarmed soldiers out with their girls, or, in jail, to join in a mass hunger-strike.

After his release, he became a librarian, and, sponsored by A.E. and Yeats, established himself as a writer — poet, novelist, playwright, but chiefly as a master of the short story. As a new member of the Dublin intelligentsia, he displayed some arrogant individualism and, by his own confession, acquired the reputation of a firebrand (11). This became the basis of his public image in the forties, when having married and resigned his librarianship to live by his pen, he asserted himself as an outspoken opponent of Irish orthodoxy. Hostile to his country's neutrality in the war, he chose to work for the British government, and at home, with O'Faolain and others, set about denouncing the new Ireland's sectarian provincialism. As a result, he was treated as a political suspect, an impious sex-obsessed free-thinker, his books were banned, and he came to be shunned by almost everyone. The breakdown of his home-life in the late forties made his isolation worse, and determined as he was to live in Ireland, he had to go and stay in England to obtain a divorce.

In 1952, harrowed by difficulties of all kinds, he left for the United States, where he mostly remained for the next ten years, to regain his health and balance, renew his creative powers, and, marrying an American wife, rebuild his personal life. He could not, however, refrain from returning to his homeland for annual visits (12), and in 1962, secure in his international reputation, his books no longer banned by the Irish censor, he returned to Ireland, where Trinity College, Dublin, awarded him a D. Litt., and provided the opportunity for some lecturing and teaching. He was to spend the remaining few years of his life in Ireland, in comparative reconciliation (though still prompt to castigate) with his community, from which he had felt so bitterly excluded.

Between 1926 and 1966, O'Connor had over 150 stories published, all but a few of which have now appeared in book form. Most were collected by himself, under titles that form the landmarks of his career : *Guests of the Nation* (1931), *Bones of*

*Contention* (1935), *Crab Apple Jelly* (1944), *The Common Chord* (1947), *Traveller's Samples* (1951), *Domestic Relations* (1957). In *The Stories of Frank O'Connor* (1952) and *More Stories by Frank O'Connor* (1954), he tried to gather the best of his output from his beginnings. But as these collections (especially the second) include several largely rewritten stories and many yet uncollected ones, they also mark a specific stage in his evolution. O'Connor remained dissatisfied with *More Stories,* which he eventually recast as *Collection Two* (1964). The latter offers a more balanced sampling of his whole production, and may be taken to form with *The Stories* a final personal selection of his best short fiction. *Collection Three* (1969), a posthumous volume compiled by his widow, includes a few strong stories written in his last years, but consists chiefly of items he himself had abstained from gathering in book form, or left unpublished altogether. It falls short of the standard of the two volumes it purports to complement, and adds little to the essential Frank O'Connor. As far as possible, we shall in this paper take our examples from *The Stories* and *Collection Two.*

O'Connor's storywriting probably took its direction from his association with Corkery. He read the latter's *A Munster Twilight* as early as 1916 (13). Corkery later introduced him to the tradition in which he was writing, viz. that established in Ireland, under the influence of nineteenth-century Russian fiction, by Moore's *The Untilled Field* and Joyce's *Dubliners.* In this same tradition O'Connor in turn took his place, claiming Turgenev as his « hero among writers » (14). He did for the Irish provincial town what Moore had done for the Irish countryside and Joyce for the Irish capital. Corkery also introduced him to Browning, whose verse he admired all his life, and whose dramatic monologues helped him to shape his conception of his art (15). He has pointed out that he wrote the war stories in *Guests of the Nation* under the influence of the Soviet Jewish writer Isaac Babel, whose *Red Cavalry* came out in English in 1929 (16), but apart from some technical devices like the use of the narrative present, the resemblance is not striking. As Thomas Flanagan remarks, O'Connor chiefly responded to a similarity in his situation and Babel's — « young slum intellectuals swept into revolutions which overturned their societies and their inner world » (17). His mature work, at any rate, moved away from the « romanticism of violence » and the over-poetic style he later criticized in Babel (18).

It also departed from the cold naturalism and self-conscious formal elaboration of Joyce, whose influence may be discerned in stories like « In the Train ». It found its keynote in a realism that tried to « unite the idealism of Yeats with the naturalism, the truthfulness of Joyce » (19) : a gently satiric, humorous realism, which may owe something to the writer's familiarity with Gaelic literature — his translation of Merriman's *The Midnight Court* (20) obviously falls in with his fiction of the same period —, and yet fraught with emotion, never far removed from pathos ; a realism less candid than O'Flaherty's, and less intellectually sophisticated than O'Faolain's.

O'Connor's themes stem from his vision of modern man as the individual reduced to his private lights in a dark universe which is apt to make him feel, like the protagonist of « Guests of the Nation », « somehow very small and very lost and lonely like a child astray in the snow » (21). His sense of « the terror of the human soul alone with nature and the night » (22), of « the mystery of human existence, of humanity faced with the spectacle of infinity » (23), made him imagine life as « a warm vivacious lighted house in the midst of night and snow » (24). In his stories he celebrates the virtues of the familiar, of warm intimacy, companionship and love (25). At the same time he shows himself aware that it behoves man to hold his own against the external chaos, and keep his house « warm », « vivacious » and « lighted ». Reacting against the modern dissolution of humanism (26), he celebrates the individual's capacity to overcome his limitations by his subjective energy. This means that, to quote his own judgment of Chekhov, he writes « as a moralist, but his morality is no longer the morality of a group ; it is the short-story writer's morality of the lonely individual soul » (27).

His most conspicuous theme is Ireland. He tried to minimize its significance for him :

> I prefer to write about Ireland and Irish people merely because I know to a syllable how everything in Ireland can be said ; but... only language and circumstance are local and national ; all the rest is, or should be, part of the human condition, and as true for America and England as it is for Ireland (28).

Yet this (disingenuous ?) claim to universality amounts really to an admission that his imagination was tied to his homeland. As one of his friends remarks : « It is hard to imagine him writing about something else » (29). He wrote about the Irish in war and in love, about Irish life in the country, in cities and small towns, about Irish clerics, Irish children, and Irishmen abroad, etc... Above all, as he himself emphasized, he wrote about « the Irish middle class Catholic way of life, with its virtues and its faults... » (30). His work offers a wide-ranging, if sometimes partial, picture of post-revolutionary Ireland.

He claimed to have written about his country « without any of the picturesqueness of early Irish writing which concentrated on colour and extravagance », and « out of a nationalism that had achieved its results and was ready to look at everyday things with a new respect » (31) : he saw himself « turning away from the public to the private thing » (32). Such statements throw light on his deeper imaginative interests, but hardly allow for several aspects of his picture, especially the caustic, satirical bias he gave it in reaction to his country's socio-political drift. He was not above delighting in « colour and extravagance », as one may see, for instance, in « The Long Road to Ummera » or « The Miracle », which are reminiscent of his admiration for Synge, and Somerville and Ross (33). And even his early work is not free of concern for the « public thing ». His war stories often read like indictments of the inhumanity to which Irish nationalists were led by romanticizing abstractions and violence (34). His stories of rural Ireland (35) raise the question of the nation's identity, centered as they are on the opposition between traditional peasant mores and the law, police and judiciary, of the new bourgeois order. His fiction of the forties and the fifties is highly concerned with exposing what he called « the death-in-life of the Nationalist Catholic establishment » (36) : it pictures a choking, provincial Ireland of small towns and sleepy cities, debilitated by ignorance and prejudice, dominated by a vulgar, sectarian middle class, and ridden by an intolerant, obscurantist priesthood. He was led to focus his anger more particularly on his mother-country's fiercely puritanical attitude to love and sex, and her invidious treatment of unmarried mothers and illegitimate children (37). Even his stories of childhood often expose failings of Irish life (38). On the whole, O'Connor's vision of Ireland can hardly be said to spring from a readiness to look at everyday things with respect, or from « a nationalism that had achieved its results » ; but rather from one that felt itself betrayed. As several commentators have suggested, it is charged with the feelings of a « disappointed lover » (39).

If O'Connor's vision of Ireland turns « away from the public to the private thing », it is by avoiding the communal and deliberately seeking the personal — « romantic, individualistic, intransigent » (40). For that reason, O'Connor's Ireland, at once home and earthly hell, also stands, as he claims, for his vision of the world at large. He inclined to view short-story protagonists as « outlawed figures wandering about the fringes of society », or submerged in « a society that has no sign-posts, a society that offers no goals and no answers » (41), thus revealing a yearning for one that would. It is significant that he warmly admired Trollope. While it cannot be said that all his characters clearly answer such descriptions, it is true that many appear alienated from their group by their failure or refusal to conform to its norms and conventions. Several, like Stevie in « My Da », have to become exiles to realize themselves. Others, like Evelyn in « The Masculine Principle », find that, no more than Helena in « In the Train », or indeed O'Connor himself in real life, could they fulfil themselves away from home. This points to a major conflict in the writer. He celebrates the moral and spiritual independence of figures like Anna in « The Custom of the Country », who rebels against her society's mores ; like the boy in « Old Fellows », who finds in his imagination the strength to conquer his terror of the dark and reach his home by himself ; or like the old woman in « The Long Road to Ummera », who, by the sheer force of her personal vision, overcomes all obstacles to have herself buried in her faraway mountain village. But he also shows himself aware that such courses lead away from the security of the familiar, that the quest for personal integrity is apt to contradict the need for social integration, and — whatever his delight in reckless individuality (42) or quixotic triumph — that self-realization also demands a lucid recognition of life's harder realities. Many of his stories are stories of disillusionment (43), which show their heroes frustrated, if not always shattered, by forces that violate their personality or nature : they often present experience as a painful thing that fosters nostalgia for childhood innocence and, ultimately, the bliss of the maternal womb (44).

O'Connor's fiction expresses a search for inner balance. He conceived of psychic life as the opposition of two principles : the masculine (judgment, conscience) and the feminine (instinct, emotion, fantasy), and felt that, like dreams, works of art answered their creator's need to reconcile these two principles in himself (45). This opposition clearly underlies the central conflict of many of his stories, for instance that of the priest and his parishioners in « Peasants », of Rita and Ned in « The Mad Losmaneys », or, as emphasized by the title, of Jim and Evelyn in « The Masculine Principle ». O'Connor tentatively acknowledged a preference for « the instinctual as against the intellectual » (46), which can be recognized in his treatment of romantic characters like Charlie Cashman (47), and his interest in youthful heroes whose spontaneity is yet unspoiled, or in priests like Devine or Fogarty (as opposed to Jackson) whose emotional, imaginative nature frets under the discipline of their calling (48). But in other stories — « The Mad Losmaneys », « The Cheapjack » —, he shows the necessity of a balance between the two. Ironically, in « The Wreath », it is the judicious Jackson who has to extricate the imprudent Devine from his predicament.

O'Connor seldom touches overtly in his stories upon the metaphysical bearing of his vision. He does so, however, in « Guests of the Nation », « This Mortal Coil » and « Don Juan's Temptation ». He writes about the protagonist of the latter :

He had woken up from a nice, well-ordered, intelligible world to find eternity stretching all round him and no one, priest or scientist, who could explain it to him. And with that awakening had gone the longing for companionship and love which he had not known how to satisfy, and often he had walked for hours, looking up at the stars and thinking that if only he could meet an understanding girl it would all explain itself naturally (49).

Characteristically, Gussie's temptation takes the form of a yearning for some ideal or faith, « something bigger than life that would last beyond death » (50). This suggests that, symmetrically, his girl's « conversion » is an attempt, after the collapse of her simple « optimism » (51), to stand up to the mystery of experience by forging her own values and trusting to her own judgment. The individual's need to assert his freedom, however rashly, to live out his imagination of himself, and triumph by his inner light over the limiting pressures of his circumstances, remains, for all O'Connor's claim to being a « realist » (52), his most characteristic and essentially romantic theme.

His narrative technique and style can also be related to his central concern with human desolation. He felt that « literature is communication », that « it lifts the burden of solitude and puts us in contact with other minds » (53). And although he once declared himself « cursed at birth with a passion for techniques » (54), and has recently been praised by O'Faolain as « the finest craftsman in the art of the short story that Ireland has produced » (55), he objected to the cult of form for its own sake, because to him it meant turning one's back on the reader. Deliberately eschewing detachment, symbolism, and modernistic devices, he sought « the conversational movement of prose, the casual, sinuous, evocative quality that distinguishes it from poetry and is intended to link author and reader in a common perception of the object » (56).

His search for contact with the reader expresses itself first of all through his genial humour. As O'Faolain stresses (57), his gift for laughter could lead him to escapism (« The Drunkard », « Vanity »). Yet it is one of the mainstays of his art, most effective when used as a defense against excesses of fantasy or sentiment (« Uprooted », « The Pretender »), or to purify the emotion. O'Connor writes about Gogol's « The Cloak » :

> It uses the old rhetorical device of the mock heroic, but uses it to create a new form, that is neither satiric nor heroic, but something in between, — something that finally, perhaps, transcends them both.

He goes on to point out that short story protagonists are superimposed sometimes on symbolic figures whom they caricature and echo — Christ, Socrates, Moses » (58). This technique is also his, as suggested by titles like « Darcy in the Land of Youth », or compositions like the moving « The Long Road to Ummera », which reads like a mock saga. In the latter, the partly comic treatment of the old woman brings out her essential dignity.

O'Connor's greatest technical originality was his attempt to recover in his fiction what he called the « narrative impulse », i.e. the spontaneous vigour of oral storytelling. It has been suggested that he thus tried, like Moore before him, to relate himself to the Irish oral tradition (59). He himself reveals that his endeavour was motivated by his dissatisfaction with broadcast readings of his early stories :

> Those carefully arranged scenes and balanced sentences failed to get me beyond the microphone to listeners at the other side. Generations of skilful stylists from Chekhov to Katherine Mansfield had so fashioned the short story that it no longer rang the tone of a man's voice, speaking (60).

He had not done so badly with the written word in stories like « In the Train » or « Uprooted », and did not thoroughly avoid the danger of sinking into a mere raconteur when bending his art to the requirements of broadcasting. Yet he remained conscious of the difference between storytelling and storywriting (61). Besides, his fondness for the speaking voice can be traced to certain of his early stories, like « Guests of the Nation ». This shows that it was inherent in his attitude to men and the world.

His concern with the narrative impulse bore on his techniques of composition. Reacting against the modern short story's addiction to poetry and atmosphere on the one hand, to scenic over-concentration on the other, he insisted that a story should have a dramatic subject, statable in four lines, and comparable in its movement to the bending of an iron bar (62). Except for a few early sketches, his own fictions deal, if not always with such violent action as « Guests of the Nation », at least with striking incidents, like Fogarty's tacit recognition of his love for Una in « The Frying Pan ». He knew that a good story, having its principle in some « glowing centre of action » (63), often had to be handled, for the sake of intensity, in « one quick scene, combining exposition and development » (64) — as « The Majesty of the Law » or « News for the Church ». Yet he was also aware of the danger, that by sacrificing exposition and narrative to drama, he might deprive the reader of the information necessary for his imagination to work (65). His rewriting of « First Confession » shows that he preferred to « isolate the exposition in the first four paragraphs and allow the development to take place in three scenes or five » (66), which implied a re-evaluation of narrative and chronology (cf. the final versions of « The Mad Losmaneys » and « The Luceys »). While Chekhov

held that « it is better to say not enough than to say too much »
(67), O'Connor wrote : « If I have to choose between too much
and too little, I prefer too much » (68). His insistence on clarity and
logic, which sometimes led him to over-explicitness (69), reveals
his need to put down his awe of life's mystery.

The store he set on the tone of the speaking voice depended on
the strong aural quality of his imagination. He observed that his
impressions of people mainly came from their wording of things
— « the cadence of their voices, the sort of phrases they'll use »,
and he felt that « everybody speaks an entirely different
language » (70). This made him a master of natural, colloquial
dialogue. He makes his characters speak an easy vernacular,
sometimes dialectal, sometimes slangy, which he deftly modulates
according to their social conditions. He also shows himself very
alert to the emotional rhetorics of individual voices, giving
liveliness to his pages by having them converse more or less
tangentially, by questions and exclamations, as in the opening
scene of « The Long Road to Ummera ». In his best stories he
defines the conflicts of the characters in terms of their linguistic
idiosyncrasies :

> I cannot pass a story as finished... unless I know how every-
> body in it spoke... If I use the right phrase and the reader
> hears the phrase in his mind, he sees the individual. It's like
> writing for the theatre... It's transferring to the reader the
> responsibility for acting those scenes (71).

Thus, in « The Mad Losmaneys », there is a significant contrast
between Rita's rather vulgar, half slangy, half dialectal, exuberant speech, and Ned's, which is careful and formal. The thematic
relevance of this contrast is underscored by their final exchange :

> « Go on ! » she taunted him. « Say it, blast you ! »
> « I couldn't », he said bitterly (72).

But of course, O'Connor's cultivation of the speaking voice lies
chiefly in his treatment of his narrators. In his stories of
childhood, the point of view is that of an adult reporting what, as
a rule, was originally for him an excruciating experience. He now
presents it humorously, from a comfortable distance, but yet in
close, warm sympathy with his remembered young self. He

achieves this double focus by speaking as much as he can the language that was his at the time of the action (cf. « The Pretender »). Several of O'Connor's early stories are told by well defined narrators, often shown addressing a listener who stands for the author (« The Bridal Night ») in a colloquial dialectal idiom. In later stories like « The Holy Door », the teller becomes hard to identify, at once dramatically present and elusive. He speaks in a familiar, animated, sometimes testy, sometimes jocular tone ; implying that he is a neighbour of the protagonists, with remarks such as : « That was no joke in *our* church » (73) ; and yet enjoying an omniscient narrator's privilege to enter the characters' private minds — for instance, in « The Holy Door », mostly Charlie's, but also others', like Polly's during her wedding night (74). This inconsistency seems to reflect the writer's conflicting attitudes to his world : his anxiety to be integrated in it, and yet to escape its limitations. It shows him, as in his stories of childhood, trying to draw on the resources of both « instinct » and « judgment » to overcome his dread of alien realities.

As Vivian Mercier has remarked (75), O'Connor is a writer who would have to be included in a representative anthology of the world's short stories. If he has been comparatively ignored by academic critics, it is probably because his work can be readily enjoyed without the help of commentators. He shared in the reaction against modernistic experiment in fiction, against those whom he called « university » writers, and tried to remain a popular « natural » one (76).

This, of course, does not mean that he is without depth. Like many other contemporaries, he sought in his creation a remedy against existential anxiety — a sort of substitute for religion. By exalting individualistic self-realization in warm human intimacy, and seeking it for himself in his art, he tried to overcome his terror of the eternal silence of infinite spaces. In this light, his highly unorthodox *credo* at the end of *An Only Child* takes on its full significance :

From the time I was a boy and could think at all, I was certain that for my own soul there was only nothingness. I knew it too well in all its commonness and weakness. But I knew that there were souls that were immortal, that even God, if He wished to, could not diminish or destroy, and perhaps it was the thought of these that turned me finally from poetry to storytelling, to the celebration of those who for me represent all I should ever know of God (77).

These lines reveal what finally separates O'Connor from Chekhov. The former was not sufficiently sceptical, or emotionally disciplined, to stand up the bleakness of the modern welt-anschaung. He could not refrain from idealizing, or sometimes even sentimentalizing, whatever in his eyes could belie the ultimate possible emptiness of the world. Is this to say that his fictions are no more than « coloured balloons » (78) ? Someone has testified somewhere that « The Long Road to Ummera » had helped an old woman to die. O'Connor's enduring popularity suggests that he also helps people to live. For a writer, it is no mean achievement.

# NOTES

1. *An Only Child*, London, 1961, p. 271.
2. « O'Connor is doing for Ireland what Chekhov did for Russia ». Quoted on the dust-jacket of *The Stories of Frank O'Connor*, London, 1953.
3. Malcolm Cowley, ed. : *Writers at Work*, New York, 1958, p. 166.
4. *The Lonely Voice*, London 1963, the epigraph and p. 19.
5. « And It's a Lonely, Personal Art » in *The New York Times Book Review*, April 12, 1953, p. 1.
6. Wallace Stegner, in Maurice Sheehy, ed. : *Michael/Frank*, Dublin, 1969, pp. 96-7.
7. *The Backward Look*, London, 1967, p. 229.
8. *The Mirror on the Roadway*, London, 1957, p. 253.
9. The phrase appears in a quotation from Yeats' « Supernatural Songs » in *Towards an Appreciation of Literature*, Dublin, 1945, p. 57. O'Connor also uses it as the title of part IV of *The Mirror in the Roadway*.
10. *An Only Child*, p. 47.
11. *My Father's Son*, Dublin, 1968, p. 187.
12. Malcolm Cowley, ed. : *op. cit.*, p. 164.
13. *An Only Child*, p. 160.
14. *Ibid.* p. 176. See also Harvey Breit : *The Writer Observed*, London, 1957, p. 260.
15. *An Only Child*, pp. 194, 197, and *The Lonely Voice*, pp. 21-2.
16. *Stories by Frank O'Connor*, New York, 1956, p. VII, and Malcolm Cowley, ed. : *op. cit.*, p. 167.
17. Maurice Sheehy, ed. : *op. cit.* p. 152.
18. *The Lonely Voice*, pp. 187-201.
19. Harvey Breit : *op. cit.*, p. 260.
20. London and Dublin, 1945.
21. *Collection Two*, p. 12.
22. *The Lonely Voice*, p. 51.
23. *The Mirror in the Roadway*, p. 131.
24. *The Lonely Voice*, p. 124.
25. Deborah Averill : « Human Contact in the Short Stories » in Maurice Sheehy, ed. : *op. cit.*, pp. 28-37.
26. Malcolm Cowley, ed. : *op. cit.*, pp. 176-8.
27. *The Mirror in the Roadway*, p. 257.
28. *The New York Times Book Review*, October 12, 1952, p. 18.
29. Shevawn Lynam in Maurice Sheehy, ed. : *op. cit.*, p. 90.
30. *Stories by Frank O'Connor*, p. VII.
31. *Ibid.*, pp. VII-VIII.
32. *Modern Irish Short Stories*, London, 1957, p. XII.
33. O'Connor especially expressed his admiration for Synge in an Abbey lecture printed in Lennox Robinson, ed. : *Irish Theatre*, London, 1939, pp. 29-52, and for Somerville and Ross in *Towards and Appreciation of Literature*, pp. 8-10.
34. See « Guests of the Nation ».
35. « Peasants », « In the Train », « The Majesty of the Law ».
36. *An Only Child*, p. 237.
37. See *The Backward Look*, p. 227, and, for instance, « The Pretender », « News for the Church », « Legal Aid », « The Babes in the Wood », « The Masculine Principle » and « The Holy Door ».
38. See for instance, « Old Fellows », « The Drunkard », « Christmas Morning », « The Idealist » and « First Confession ».

39. Shevawn Lynam in Maurice Sheehy, ed. : *op. cit.*, p. 88. See also in the same book : Honor Tracy, p. 4, and Thomas Flanagan, p. 149.

40. *The Lonely Voice*, p. 21.

41. *Ibid.*, pp. 18-9.

42. See Gerry Brenner : « Frank O'Connor's Imprudent Hero » in *Texas Studies in Language and Literature*, X, Fall, 1968, pp. 457-69.

43. See « Guests of the Nation », « The Idealist », « Fish for Friday ».

44. See « Judas », « The Man of the House ».

45. « In Dreams : Does Seven Mean Conception ? » in *Vogue*, November 1, 1967, pp. 164 ff. ; see also the introduction to *The Mirror in the Roadway*.

46. Harvey Breit : « Talk with Frank O'Connor » in *The New York Times Book Review*, June 24, 1951, p. 14.

47. *The Stories*, pp. 312-67.

48. *Collection Two*, pp. 22-31, 94-104, 314-26.

49. *The Stories*, p. 123.

50. *Ibid.*, p. 127.

51. *Ibid.*, p. 125.

52. *The Mirror in the Roadway*, pp. 15-6.

53. *Towards an Appreciation of Literature*, pp. 7, 58.

54. Malcom Cowley, ed. : *op. cit.*, p. 173.

55. « A World of Fitzies » in *Times Literary Supplement*, April 29, 1977, p. 503.

56. *The Lonely Voice*, p. 157.

57. « A World of Fitzies », *op. cit.*, pp. 502-3.

58. *The Lonely Voice*, pp. 15, 19.

59. Vivian Mercier : *Great Irish Short Stories*, New York, 1964, pp. 13-5.

60. *Stories by Frank O'Connor*, p. VII.

61. See the introductions to *Modern Irish Short Stories* and *The Lonely Voice*.

62. See the epilogue to *The Lonely Voice*, and Richard T. Gill : « Frank O'Connor in Harvard », in Maurice Sheehy, ed. : *op. cit.* pp. 42-9.

63. « And It's a Lonely, Personal Art », *op. cit.*, p. 1:

64. *The Lonely Voice*, p. 218.

65. *Ibid.*, p. 25.

66. *Ibid.*, p. 218. A first version of « First Confession » appeared under the title « Repentance » in *Lovat Dickson's Magazine*, January 1935, pp. 58-70 ; a second in *Selected Stories*, Dublin, 1946, pp. 36-42 ; and a third one in *The Stories*, pp. 52-61.

67. Chekhov : *Letters on the Short Story, the Drama and Other Literary Topics*, ed. by L.S. Friedland, London, 1965, p. 106.

68. *The Lonely Voice*, p. 66.

69. Vivian Mercier : *op. cit.*, p. 17.

70. Malcolm Cowley, ed. : *op. cit.*, p. 169.

71. *Ibid.*

72. *Collection Two*, p. 56.

73. *The Stories*, p. 313.

74. *Ibid.*, p. 317.

75. *Op. cit.*, p. 8.

76. Malcolm Cowley, ed. : *op. cit.*, pp. 172-3.

77. *An Only Child*, p. 270.

78. P. Kavanagh in *The Bell*, XV : 3, December, 1947, pp. 11-22.

# SEAN O'FAOLAIN'S SHORT-STORIES
# AND TALES

## Guy LE MOIGNE

Over the last decades Sean O'Faolain, the « Doyen » of the « Irish Academy of Letters », has come to be recognized as that almost unique phenomenon in the intellectual history of his country, a man of letters. It is not easy to assign him a lower place in the post-Yeatsian era. Setting a pattern of marked excellence by his own fiction, especially his stories and tales, he has worked all his life to bring a parochial, nationalistic and clerical Ireland into the mainstream of modern culture. He prides himself on being a cosmopolitan without national prejudice :

> To me, now, Ireland is worth my attention only when it is the world. I have no least speck of local patriotism left in me (1).

He proved to be the most articulate spokesman on the issues that faced post-revolutionary Ireland and the contemporary artist. He realized from the outset of his literary career in the thirties — and consequently in his thirties since he is the age of the century — that the two sets of problems were inter-related and that retreating within an ivory tower was unthinkable under the particular circumstances. He became fully alive to the many responsibilities that were inevitably thrust upon the shoulders of every living artist who found himself struggling not only with the inescapable inner tensions of the creative process but also with countless external obstacles. During his seven years abroad (1926-1933), first as a beneficiary of the « Harkness Fund » at Harvard and then as a teacher in a College of Education in London, he had discovered that Ireland was to be the material of his creative work and his definite home. Dismissing thoughts of exile, he quickly embraced the challenge that awaited him on his return. The ambivalent relationship which he sustained with his native land that invariably failed to measure up to his exacting liberal standards contributed much towards the dramatic tension which is to be found in his earlier work. For some time the various pressures that were brought to bear upon the individual in a society still in search of its real identity and technique of living constituted the main substance of his fictional and non-fictional works.

It is mostly during that decade and the early forties when he was the chief-editor of *The Bell* (1940-1946), a literary monthly which attempted to fill the vacuum created by the disappearance of *The Irish Statesman* in 1930, that he earned his reputation as a man of letters. His stimulating and percipient social and political comments aimed at creating more breathing-space and giving a more international outlook to a country threatened by isolationism, the very conditions which he felt were prerequisites to the development of a genuine native art. Yet given the controversial nature of his concerns, what strikes us about his fiction is how subtly his conflicting sympathies are balanced, how indignation and the temptation of satirical writing are, except in very few cases, kept at a distance. Part of his achievement at a time when he felt strongly over a number of issues lies in the degree to which he did not allow himself to be distracted in his creative work by « those old Irish hobgoblins of Prudery, Hypocrisy, Deceit, Opportunism, Political Guile, Moral Cowardice and so on... » (2) that were given a severe trouncing in his editorials. In that respect his nonfictional writings, while helping him to move towards a more unified, varied, mature vision, served as useful outlets to the considerable strain exerted over him by an environment to which he was far from being reconciled, but with which he had passionately cast in his lot as a literary artist. « Ireland ! with all thy faults I love thee still », could he have written, if only he had chosen to translate some of his natural gifts into poetry.

During the ensuing years and the second period of his artistic career as a whole, i.e. roughly from the fifties onwards, his presence on the Irish scene became less conspicuous. Some critics yielding to oversimplification have gone as far as accusing him and other prominent writers such as Frank O'Connor of desertion. One has to admit that he hardly engaged in polemics any longer, which does not mean that he had departed from the astringent standards he had set for himself and his compatriots. The truth of the matter is that he has devoted himself more exclusively to his craft. He soon came to the decision that the short narrative was the medium that suited his temperament best, a half-hearted choice if one makes allowance for the three novels that had been published in the first ten years of his literary career and subsequent unsuccessful attempts at novel-writing. The earnestness of this profound involvement in literary creation is reflected in his critical work, including an authoritative study on the short story. But while perfecting his own art he has been active in the world of Irish letters and art. He continued, as he did earlier, encouraging young writers and helping them with advice. For two years (1957-1959) he acted as Director of the « Arts Council of Ireland ».

A notable feature of Sean O'Faolain's later life is that he left his home-base quite often, travelling widely abroad. This may have caused the kind of resentment alluded to earlier. In the fifties and sixties he spent extensive periods in American universities as a lecturer or a writer-in-residence. But most significant in his development were the consecutive trips to Italy in the late forties which were recorded in two intimate travel books, *A Summer in Italy* and *South to Sicily* (3). His first visit there in the summer of 1946 resulted in what he describes as his conversion to Roman Catholicism :

I was in fact exactly forty-six years old before I finally abandoned the faith of my fathers, and, under the life-loving example of Italy, became converted to Roman Catholicism (4).

Through his contact with the Italian way of life his objections to the Roman Catholic Church melted away. He found there no trace of that antihumanism which seemed to have corrupted Irish Catholicism. On each repeated visit to Italy he found himself overwhelmed by the sense of continuity between the past and the present, by the kind of harmony that prevailed between the body and the spirit. Some of the questions that had been tormenting him since his adolescence, especially after the revelation of his mother's misery, and that had been revived by his own night-marish experience during the Civil War, found a partial answer, self-acceptance, during an interview with a French jesuit priest on Easter-eve 1954 in New-York. One of the aims he had set for himself as a writer : « Il faut purifier la source », (5) following in this Mauriac's advice to would-be writers, was achieved partly through his own intellectual honesty and partly through what he believed was God's gift. Italy thus became the place of another crucial experience in his life, or to use his own striking phrase, of another « brimming moment » (6) whose forerunning signs and reverberations are variously expressed in his fictional work. As this image was recreated in subsequent tales, it grew into another « domination of place » that enriched considerably the topology of his work. For quite a few of his later stories have foreign settings involving, it is true, mostly Irish expatriates. But by and large, Sean O'Faolain is more successful at recapturing the Italian atmosphere in conjunction, one should add, with evocations of Irish scenes and places. The Italian experience contributed much to releasing that sense of inner discontent which had kept gnawing at his soul and had imparted to his earlier style some bite but also some bitterness. *Newman's Way* (7), published in 1942, embodies to a great extent the new qualities of imaginative sympathy already found in a tale of that transitional period, « Lovers of the Lake » and which were to blossom in O'Faolain's later stories.

This lifelong dedication to the writing craft is reflected in what one must describe as a considerable amount of fictional and non-fictional work (a most inadequate distinction, in fact, since in a few instances the boundary-line appears on close scrutiny to be rather elusive). The short stories sometimes, especially in the extremely creative period of the thirties, look like occasional accretions. Some critics have even blamed O'Faolain for being indiscriminately prolific, wishing that he had devoted more of his precious time to writing short fiction. That kind of statement is obviously based on the assumption that his other works are only derivative. Still, leaving aside the question of evaluating his achievement in those respective fields, the impression that prevails on moving from one work to another is one of unity and continuity. His literary production as a whole proceeds from a persistent quest for style and perception and for a synthesis of both. That basic concern is variously expressed in his versatile, many-faceted writing, whether he gives his main themes discursive treatment or imaginative embodiment. There is a very close interrelationship between his historical biographies, travel books, critical writings, essays, autobiography, his one play, *She Had to Do Something*, and his fiction. The insights which he gained through his relentless curiosity, whether he probed into the past of his own country looking for constructive political thought-patterns that would reconcile the revolutionary spirit with a pragmatic attitude or went exploring foreign cultures in a constant search for wholeness and unity, gradually transformed his vision and consequently his approach to short-story writing. One feels however that the interaction between the various genres is much more intricate. The reconstruction of the historical past of his country, for instance, in such biographies as *King of the Beggars* or *The Great O'Neill*, especially of those periods which he deemed highly significant, setting useful and essential guidelines for the future, gave free play to his fictional gifts and enabled him to develop new skills. The search for perception became inseparable from the search for a style that he could claim his own. All those works therefore played a decisive part in the emergence of that « personal way of seeing and saying » which one recognizes unmistakably as one moves from one story to another. Yet despite this variety of his literary pursuits it is through his stories that O'Faolain's development as a writer can be most fully traced.

The short narrative under its two species : the « short story » and the « tale », a much-quoted distinction which O'Faolain established in his preface to *The Heat of the Sun*, is indeed a genre to which he has remained faithful all his life. His exploration of the technical resources of that literary medium enabled him to treat with increasing subtlety and sophistication an ever-widening range of themes and subjects that reflected a persistent quest for a mature, articulate vision capable of holding together the many contradictions of man's nature including his own. Certainly no other tribute would be more appropriate to do justice to his achievement as a short-story writer than the one he himself paid to his forerunner and favourite model, Anton Tchekhov :

> ... he is one of the most heartening examples of skilful self-management, of the art of keeping the lines clear from beginning to end of the journey (8).

Sean O'Faolain's « love-affair » with the short-story has been going on now for over half a century. It began at an early age. He was in his early teens when he saw his first work in print. Other juvenilia, stories and poems, came in its trail and were published in Cork local papers. But it took him another decade before he found his own voice. He made a decisive breakthrough with the publication of « In Lilliput » — a story later included in *Midsummer Night Madness* (1932), — in *The Irish Statesman* of February 6th 1926.

> ... It was my first tiny success, yet showing already how through form or order I was liberated into myself, to good effect (9),

he commented later in *Vive Moi* !, as he painstakingly pinpointed the various stages in his slow development as a writer.

As his work now stands, his credentials as a professional short-story writer are based on the 85 stories and tales collected in the eight volumes which have been published at regular intervals since 1932. Not much would be gained by adding to O'Faolain's own canon the comparatively few minor pieces that might be gleaned in various papers and magazines, except perhaps the odd satisfaction of bringing the total number close to a hundred. As his later collection, *Foreign Affairs and Other Stories* (1976), shows, he still writes highly entertaining tales in a masculine, youthful prose. But all the same this is a small output compared with the twenty volumes produced by Guy de Maupassant in the space of fifteen years or the dozen stories or so that Anton Tchekhov could write within a year as he went through bursts of creative activity. Sean O'Faolain was to forestall that kind of objection in his preface to a selection of his stories which he published in mid-career :

> Story after story by Maupassant is journeyman stuff. I can now reread only the Chekhovs that I have ticked off on the contents page... I have learned in my thirty-odd years of serious writing only one sure lesson : that stories, like whiskey, must be allowed to mature in the cask. And that takes so much time !... (10)

In an interview given in the same period he added :

I truly don't believe that anyone can do more than about three of them a year. He can't, that is, if they are good ones... (11)

As far as he was concerned, this was a fairly optimistic estimate, for he was well below that target. This pace of production remained steady during the following years. The only noticeable change was that he displayed an increased predilection for the longer form of the tale more suitable for the new themes he was handling.

Sean O'Faolain could hardly be viewed as a capricious writer who works by fits and starts. By his constant advance and change in subject-matter and style, by his devotion to his craft, he has lived several lives in one. He is undoubtedly something of a bifrontal writer. Behind the artist whose style acquires increasing panache, bringing at times his stories movingly close to the lyric, hides a strong disciplinarian. He has constantly practised the kind of asceticism that enabled him to submit his writing to exacting formal standards. Besides obvious gifts of imagination and feeling he was endowed with a fine intellect which expanded considerably through academic training, something he has always been grateful for. Yet instead of stemming the creative impulse this formidable critical faculty helped him to marshal his sometimes contradictory natural gifts and impulses and thus to achieve progressively that unique balance between feeling and intelligence in a poetic mind. But at the same time it set him apart from those instinctive writers such as Faulkner, Gorki, Sean O'Casey etc..., whom he described in *The Vanishing Hero* (1956) as having more genius than talent, writing out of the depths of an inexhaustible imagination (12). In a recent self-portrait (13), he labelled himself as a « writer of talent », i.e. a writer dogged by that self-consciousness which Henry James saw as one of the distinctive features of modern writers. Concern with the formal requirements of his art played an important part in his development, but remained subordinated to a truthful, scrupulous translation of his groping search for a vision of life that would afford « cohesion plus variety », in other words, « unity of thought » (14). As far as the short narrative is concerned he is no experimental writer, except perhaps in some of his most recent tales where he makes sporadic attempts at updating his fictional idiom under the influence of contemporary American writers. He remains to a large extent a traditionalist.

He has adopted and made his own the modern form of the short story inherited from his Irish predecessors, George Moore and James Joyce, and their French or Russian forerunners.

This self-consciousness far from being detrimental to his artistic development impelled him to work out for himself the critical standards he desperately needed to protect himself from the prevailing complacency engendered by that Celtic foible, the art of indiscriminate praise. They were singularly lacking, as he often complained, in a country which remained « a paradise for the *homme sensuel moyen*, that untranslatable compound of sense, sensibility, and mere sensation, a purgatory for the artist, and a hell for the intellectual » (15). One of his characters, Pat Lenihan, on whom falls the burden of impersonating the fate of the artist in post-revolutionary Ireland, exclaims : « What's the use ? Who hears me ? ... Who could tell in this hole of a city whether I was good or bad ?... » (16). This was O'Faolain's own dilemma, although he was well on the way of resolving it. Following the early advice of Daniel Corkery and the pattern set by James Joyce, he went looking for models beyond the local sphere not in order to desert his native material but so as to enhance it and impart to it a universal relevance through a wider range of narrative and stylistic means. He went far afield in his exploration of Russian, French, English and American literature without neglecting the Irish tradition, learning from other writers' experience, measuring their achievement and probing into the personal and technical struggle involved in each case.

Of those influences the most decisive is undoubtedly that of Anton Chekhov with whom he is often associated in laudatory articles or reviews that occasionally describe him as « Chekhov in Erin ». This is probably stretching the parallel too far. Sean O'Faolain who made much of the Russian short-story writer in his critical writings is partly to blame for this. But his restatement of the question in a recent interview is useful in reminding critics that they should not follow blindly the leads which they are offered :

You know, people have talked about Chekhov and Turgenev and so forth, and certainly I learned from them. But the man who's really influenced me and whom I really admired was Shaw, who cut through all the sentimentality. He was able to hold quite tenderly the things that were important to him, and

still know that sometimes they had to be looked at objec-
tively (17).

Yet one cannot help but notice how strikingly close this evaluation runs to his earlier appraisal of Chekhov's blend of realism
and poetic feeling :

> What sometimes deludes the sophisticated is the poetry in
> which he seems to drown this banality, so that they see the
> beautiful mists and fail to see behind these mists the hard,
> mocking mind of the doctor, the moralist and the judge (18).

O'Faolain obviously praised in Chekhov the selfsame qualities
which he had been admiring in a fellow-Irishman but which were
this time invested in his own medium.

Such remarks passed on writers that have meant so much to
him reveal by implication the main dilemma with which he was
confronted in his own creative work. When O'Faolain's stories
strike us as being Chekhovian in manner or mood, he is not
merely imitating him but striving in his own idiosyncratic terms
after that balance between personal emotion and objective
treatment. This kinship became more conspicuous over the years
as O'Faolain moved towards more intimate, introspective
subjects, focusing his stories on increasingly complex shades of
feeling, bringing them sometimes close to the mood of a lyric or
of an elegy. But the influence of the Russian artist together with
that of other story-writers whom he studied appears much earlier
through the command which he gradually gained over his medium
of expression, as he began hovering around areas of experience
attuned to his own inflammable sensibility. In stories of the
mid-thirties included in *A Purse of Coppers* (1937) such as
« Sinners », « Admiring the Scenery », « A Meeting » or
« Discord », there is evidence of a subtler approach to short-
story writing. Some of them are elegiac in tone, they are all
saturated with a sense of dejection, of quiet despair. But at the
same time through the varied, imaginative interplay between
atmosphere and mood, between the past and the present they
acquire a much greater level of suggestiveness that goes along
with a tightened, less episodic structure. They stand in sharp
contrast to earlier stories in the same volume that suffer either
from heavy-handed didacticism in the case of « A Born Genius »

and, to a lesser extent, « A Broken World », excessive indulgence in slapstick comedy or satirical treatment in « The Old Master » and « Sullivan's Trousers », or from authorial manipulation of the kind found in « Egotists » and « Kitty the Wren ».

But despite their flaws and in particular their overexplicitness and occasional discursiveness these stories are not wholly unsuccessful. They indicate that O'Faolain is gradually mastering the techniques of a form more modern than the one consistently used in the tales of *Midsummer Night Madness*. The prose-line shows signs of greater simplicity, which in itself is no mean achievement when one considers his earlier predilection for lengthy, involved periods running at times one page long on the crest of romantic lyricism. This time scenic presentation, i.e. sequences of scenes linked up by short descriptive segments almost acting as stage-directions, tends to prevail over summary narrative. The long expository sequences of the first tales are likewise superseded by more abrupt openings that take us right into the heart of the action or of the situation or into some odd corner of the narrator's consciousness, thus imparting to the story a greater immediacy and directness. Through those stylistic and narrative innovations brought to the structure of the story as well as the tentative exploration of new modes such as comedy, satire and pathos, O'Faolain achieved a much greater concentration and compactness in his narratives. But one feels that the pendulum has swung to the other extreme and that the remedies used have been too drastic. A greater objectivity is achieved but at the expense of those emotional, poetic qualities that cause the reader of the first tales to overlook their occasional clumsiness and frequent mannerisms. The stories are much more compact, they show evidence of a more sophisticated craftsmanship, but by and large they rely too much on statement instead of working through suggestion and implication, which would make the experience of reading them much more rewarding. This failure is partly remedied in the following stories which improve considerably on those new skills, blending poetic suggestiveness and realistic treatment. O'Faolain thus hit upon a basic formula that enabled him to solve his artistic dilemma and which he kept developing and extending towards more refined and varied stylistic and narrative forms.

In view of the turn taken by his evolution over recent years one may wonder whether the more leisurely and traditional form of the « tale » has not been the genre that suited O'Faolain best. This was how he defined it in contradistinction to the short story proper :

> A tale is quite different. Like a small plane it is much more free, carries a bit more cargo, roves farther, has time and space for more complex characterisation, more changes of mood, more incidents and scenes, even more plot... It has its own problems, however, for the writer, whose toughest task is to orchestrate his Tale into a single, satisfying shape of flight (19).

There is in O'Faolain a suppressed novelist who needs a broader canvas than the one currently allotted to the short-story. In that respect he falls short of that complete self-abnegation which he considered as « the absolute essential of the modern short story » (20). He relishes the part of the narrator and carries it with gusto in the manner of the 18th century novelists and those writers who took the tradition into the following century. There is something Dickensian, for instance, in the touch of caricature based on animal imagery that almost invariably emphasizes the physical and moral peculiarities of his characters. He needs some space to give free play to those pictorial gifts which enable him to conjure place, atmosphere and scenery, to describe with artful casualness the dwellings and garb of his people. It is no surprise that in his critical writings he should draw parallels between his craft and the painter's art. His characters are fully realized as physical human beings rooted in their social and geographic environment, shaped by their own choices but also by the force of circumstance. « Reification », one of his favourite critical concepts, in other words, the painter's trick, is the only explanation for this illusion of reality. There is something profoundly healthy about his prose which combines sensuous imagery, romantic feeling and a robust sense of humour. It enhances the mystery and beauty of the gift of life. A most companionable writer, his aim is not only to instruct, but above all to entertain, i.e. share with the reader his own delight in man's physicality, inner resources and oddities.

More than the earlier stories the tales of the second period reveal O'Faolain's obsession with the classical ideal. There is sufficient evidence of this in the greater degree of contrivance in his plots as well as in the increased refinement of his idiom. The first feature has not escaped critics' notice. As Roger Garfitt pointed out :

> Perceptive as the stories are, their limitation is that rather than being drawn from the daily process of living they tend to be set at chance cross-roads somewhere on the edges of experience (21).

Likewise the complexity and ambiguity of the themes are gradually matched by a more ornate, florid idiom. This growing aestheticism sometimes goes to the point of affectation as literary and artistic reminiscences keep intruding. The story is viewed at a second remove, as it were, as we follow its reverberations through the narrator's mind, this at the expense of dramatic immediacy. In O'Faolain's hands the short story has grown into a highly civilized, sophisticated art, not to say aristocratic, meant for those select few who, in Malraux's words, are literature and art addicts. The stories as a result have a haunting quality, a kind of hypnotic effect. In the staccato opening of « The Inside Outside Complex », for instance, O'Faolain employs a short-hand style laced with slightly archaic, quaint words. This is bravura comic writing, and the element of exaggeration is, of course, part and parcel of the comic mode. For in most cases art, especially the writer's comic gifts and lyricism, disguises artifice. This more rambling form does not necessarily preclude suggestiveness. As one reviewer rightly emphasized :

> He knows exactly how much to explain and when to remain silent. « Who was it, » one of his characters wonders, « said the last missing bit of every jigsaw is God »... (22)

Few writers have emphasized as much as O'Faolain did that the business of writing is a slow, arduous process. He may be, as he himself put it, « a besotted romantic » in many respects, but he has all his wits about him when he talks about the creative process, dispelling all the romantic fallacies that are too often associated with that human activity. « Writing is a long, long lifetime study », he reminds us in *Vive Moi !* (23). Short-story writing is a craft. It cannot do away with time, the necessity of mastering skills, the necessity of growth and change. But what distinguishes it from other crafts is the extent to which it involves the self of the writer. The most difficult obstacles to overcome are not technical but personal, especially in the case of the short story which is essentially, as O'Faolain kept insisting, « an emphatically personal exposition » (24). W.B. Yeats's advice : « Write yourself into yourself » (25) kept ringing into his ears and urged him to seek out the means of attaining that balance between style and personality.

Quite understandably, when he fails in this, his stories lack the human depth and warmth that irradiate from his best stories and tales. They are not necessarily technical failures. They sound less convincing mainly on account of the choice of subject or even occasionally of setting, and in a few cases on account of the choice of satire, a mode alien to his own genius given to gentle teasing but hardly to derisive harassment of his fictional creations. This paradox will be found again and again. There are situations and themes close to his own personal experience which O'Faolain handles almost instinctively in a manner that often inclines us to forget the amount of painstaking work that lies behind those achievements. On the other hand, scenes that are, for instance, set in the destitute areas of his hometown, Cork, are not as shrewdly realized as in Frank O'Connor's stories. He is more at home with literate figures — teachers, clerical figures in the first period, and then professionals in his later stories and tales where the settings are nearly always urban and even cosmopolitan — characters belonging to the Irish middle-class. Seldom does his imaginative sympathy enable him to venture outside this narrow social spectrum. But there are a few success-ful forays, as in « Midsummer Night Madness » where the sympathies of the young narrator gradually veer towards that hated symbol of the Ascendancy, the pathetic figure of old Henn. Likewise if his use of demotic idiom may often sound contrived, it can occasionally be quite effective. One notable instance is represented by that fascinating artifact entitled « The Heat of the Sun », where literary reminiscences from *Cymbeline* play upon the beauty and the squalor of a pathetic encounter in the slums of Dublin between a young sailor ashore and a neglected wife whose husband, a mildly eccentric, garrulous barman, is dying in hospital.

But as a rule there are obvious limitations to O'Faolain's range of inspiration which are predetermined by his life-pattern and the moral, spiritual and religious questions that have kept obsessing him. Whenever he transgresses them, he seems to betray his own gifts. Should he strike out too far from his own home-ground, as it were, his stories are marred by artificiality, implausibility and contrivance. Fortunately failure is averted owing to his zestful sense of comedy. Besides those pitfalls were to be avoided as O'Faolain having overcome some of the moral and spiritual uncertainties that had bedevilled him began in mid-career drawing more extensively upon personal memories of childhood and youth, reviving some of the material previously used in his three novels, *A Nest of Simple Folk, Bird Alone, Come Back to Erin*, and dealing with themes intimately related to his own development as a human being. Paradoxically enough, he achieved a much greater measure of freedom by surrendering to the passion of memory, which fabled itself into art.

The use of autobiographical material is one of the most persistent features of his stories and tales. Any critic biassed against a biographical approach to literary works would have in O'Faolain's case to make important concessions just as Paul Valéry who initiated this modern trend had to in his comparative study of Villon and Verlaine :

But in the present case, he unwillingly admitted, the biographical issue cannot be dismissed. It has to be taken into account, and I must do what I have just condemned (26).

Confessions made by an artist, he added, are often far from being factually accurate. If he tells the truth, he does not tell the whole truth and he does not only tell the truth :

An artist selects his material, even when he confesses himself. And all the more so perhaps when he confesses himself. He tones things down or heightens them, here and there... (27)

O'Faolain has written a great deal about himself. Afraid of insincerity, he spent much of his life attempting to understand the deep contradictions within himself. His biographies and travel-books were, as is often the case, partly autobiographical. This he readily admits, in *South to Sicily*, for example, when he points out straightaway : « One travels inside oneself. It's all done with mirrors » (28). But it is mostly his account of the first thirty years of his life, *Vive Moi !*, and a recent self-portrait commissioned by *The Irish University Review* which have established him as a master of that peripheral fictional genre. The comment he appended to an overtly autobiographical story, « The Kitchen », first published in the same review, makes a rather successful attempt at drawing a line between autobiography and this dramatized version of a personal experience.

One of the aspects of the creative process that has engaged his attention most is doubtless the part played by memory. Many of his stories tend to be retrospective in some way or other. And in his characters' lives reminiscences are wedded with aspirations as they move uneasily towards some moment of greater awareness. The workings of memory are continuously scrutinized, most strikingly so in the title-piece of *I Remember ! I Remember !* which almost reads like a counterpart to Paul Claudel's dramatization of the opposition between « Animus » and « Anima », setting at variance factual memory and affective memory. This parable makes clear that in life as well as in art memories alone will not suffice. Imagination must reactivate and fecundate remembered images recent or remote and turn them into inspiring thoughts and works of art through an unexpected blend of memory and imagination. If O'Faolain's stories are so densely permeated by memories of his life including those recalled from books, these are remembered and remoulded into new creations.

Recurrent interferences between biographical facts and fiction reveal an oversubjective preoccupation which is however often transcended through dramatic detachment and humour, his two chief methods of objectivization. One must admit though that stories by O'Faolain remain above all pieces of writing « wrested from the tensions of his life » (29) and of his personality. As a result his vision of life is essentially agonistic. The various obstacles, either subjective or external, he had to come to terms with either during his formative years or during his career as a man of letters have led him to regard life as a succession of challenges. The theme that increasingly fascinated him was that of the limitations to individual self-fulfilment. Yet what imparts to this central obsession its particular urgency and poignancy is the knowledge of the « potential wholeness and integrity of human nature » (30) that had been forced upon him during those brief phases when he felt at one with himself and the world, for instance, as a youngster overcome by his first vision of love, (31) a youth taking part in the struggle for national independence « privileged to see men at their finest » (32) or as an adult joining the Empire of the Roman Catholic Church. Aching memories of those « few bright hours of grace » (33) reminiscent of the bliss of the paradise of early infancy when one lives « in the waking sleep of childish content, a hibernatory cocoon of total happiness » (34) will persistently haunt his fiction. His stories therefore frequently circle round a sense of loss, the emotional frustration caused either by the social pressures that are brought to bear upon the individual, by one's miscalculations or mismanagement of the business of life, or more fundamentally by man's time-bound condition. Many of his characters are burdened with feelings of nostalgia for blissful moments or missed opportunities at one stage or another in their past lives. The pathos of their lives reminds us very much of Boethius's maxim quoted by old Theo in *A Nest of Simple Folk* :

> *Fuisse felicem et non esse, omnium est infelicissimum genus* ; to have been happy at one time and then to be unhappy after, isn't that the greatest unhappiness in the whole world ? (35)

But this truth cuts both ways. As we are reminded in such stories as « Liars », « Feed my Lambs » or « Our Fearful Innocence », brief moments of fulfilment however ambiguous are treasured ever after and enable one to take an otherwise unpleasant and sterile existence in one's stride without being overpowered by despair.

What distinguishes O'Faolain from most of his contemporaries, and this is a constant feature of his work, is the fact that the theme of man's estrangement from his true self, his fellow-being and his environment is not absolutely taken for granted. There is no sense of irretrievability, for man can be redeemed. What perplexes him rather is the uneven course of man's life and the fact that he only seems to achieve « complete integrity... in moments as brief, if one compares them with the whole span of a human life, as a lighthouse blink » (36). O'Faolain's inveterate idealism goes against the grain of the tenets of the age.

The key-image in his work that embodies those ambivalent feelings is undoubtedly that of exile. He progressively extended it into an all-comprehensive metaphor of modern man's predicament. Like all organic images in an artist's work, it is deeply rooted in his own experience. Before actually leaving his country for a few years he had been like every Irishman both frightened and fascinated by that alternative. « Change your place, change your fate » may not always sound as a romantic fallacy especially when the individual finds himself confronted, as O'Faolain did, with the various strictures laid on him by faith, family and fatherland (37). This is no better at times than suffering from the pangs of actual exile. It is no surprise that in a story of the thirties, « The Born Genius », he came to describe Cork, his native town, as a « city of exile ». He was to make more explicit what he meant by this in *An Irish Journey* :

> Cork is no place for sensitive folk. I have known more men of real talent, who in another atmosphere might have been fruitful, become frustrated and warped in this city than I have ever met in any other of its size. To succeed here you have to have the skin of a rhinoceros, the dissimulation of a crocodile, the agility of a hare, the speed of a hawk. Otherwise for every young Corkonian the word is — « Get out — and get out *quick* » (38).

There is about O'Faolain a harsh streak. It is part of the survivor kit without which he would not have developed into a complete human being, let alone a full-fledged artist. But such pages largely eclipsed by lyrical celebrations of the hidden beauties of Cork are written obviously out of « that hatred born of jealousy without which there is no true love » (39). The image of exile in whatever guise it recurs through his fiction is always linked up with an ingrown tendency to perceive reality in dualistic terms, to respond to it both intellectually and emotionally.

Exile became an explicit concern of his second and third volumes of short stories, *A Purse of Coppers* and *Teresa*. They dramatize in various forms the condition of individuals whose emotional and spiritual development is almost invariably thwarted in the dispiriting scene of post-revolutionary Ireland. Their state of alienation is ascribed to the disruption of the social fabric and the lack of a workable alternative that would fill the Irish people with a renewed sense of purpose. In « The Silence of the Valley » characters belonging to the new generation are brought close to the remnants of an organic social tradition now almost extinct. Still the stories may at times convey the faint hope that the lonely people of Ireland can be reunited :

What image of life that would fire and fuse us all, what music bursting like the spring, what triumph, what engendering love, so that those breast mountains that now looked cold should appear brilliant and gay, the white land that seemed to sleep should appear to smile, and these people who huddled over the embers of their lives should become like the peasants who held the hand of Faust with their singing one Easter morning ?... (40)

In *Midsummer Night Madness*, O'Faolain's first collection of stories, the basic conflicts were already outlined. When one considers it in retrospect, it appears to a large extent as a kind of seminal work. It contains potentialities of development almost left untapped by the stories of the middle period too much concerned with local and historical conditioning. It makes more allowance for « the inevitable desires of the heart » (41) and the inner tensions of emotional growth. These tales of the Irish rebellion in which O'Faolain transposed the excitement and the nightmare of his involvement in the Civil War as a Republican pinpoint the various stages of growing disillusionment with Irish nationalism and the gradual release through love. They are steeped in luscious romantic imagery of the Irish countryside touched with the pathos of collapsing dreams.

Later stories extended the theme of loneliness and exile considerably as they revealed its psychological, moral and spiritual implications through a greater variety of modes using such ingredients as pathos, comedy and poetry in shifting combinations. Still the part played by external circumstances is not overlooked, but brought in with greater subtlety and complexity. It is seldom given the emphatic treatment it receives in « Brainsy », where the narrator confronted with the unrecognizable, corpse-like appearance of an old friend he had known earlier as a young man and a pal full of zest for life cannot refrain from thinking :

... why must everybody in Ireland live like an express train that starts off for heaven full of beautiful dreams, and marvellous ambitions and, halfway, bejasus, you switch off the bloody track down some sideline that brings you back to exactly where you began... (42)

This is all the same quite a successful story through its deft balance between poignancy and poetic symbolism. The concluding images leave a lasting imprint upon the reader's mind.

Stories and tales belonging to that period evince on the whole a much greater serenity and are much more subdued than during the first half of O'Faolain's artistic career. They reflect a change of outlook that came with the discovery that freedom lies in acquiescence. But this does not lead to smug optimism. There is still a strong undercurrent of nostalgia that seems to contaminate his work. The plaintive note which is often struck culminates in those elegiac moments that recur throughout his later prose.

The greater measure of self-acceptance led to a renewal of inspiration, a quickening of new creative energies, especially a refined sense of humour and comedy. They developed as he went on exploring the ambiguities of man's nature, the intricate workings of memory in *I Remember ! I Remember !*, the various shapes of passion in *The Heat of the Sun*, the pains of growth and change in *The Talking Trees*, the trickiness of the course of illicit love in *Foreign Affairs*, concerns which enabled him to achieve a more supple mixture of particulars and universality :

I would, then, in my late life-acceptance, embracing as much as I had the courage to embrace of all of life's inherent evil and weakness, try to write, however tangentially, about those moments of awareness when we know three truths at one and the same moment : that life requires of each of us that we should grow up and out whole and entire, that human life of its nature intricately foils exactly this, and that the possibility of wholeness is nevertheless as constant and enormous a reality as the manifold actuality of frustration, compromise, getting caught in some labyrinth, getting cut short by death (43).

He found at last that « concordance between temperament and subject » (44) in which the secret of the short story lies. He became increasingly fascinated with those inner obstacles to self-fulfilment which people tend to create through their boundless capacity for self-delusion, conveying the suggestion that a self-imposed moral and spiritual exile is infinitely worse than the one forced upon us by circumstance. Very often man brings the pangs

of emotional deprivation upon himself through his own foolish-
ness and folly. Middle-aged, affluent celibates, O'Faolain's
sad-eyed clowns, are often made to carry that burden. Many of
his recent stories that are cast in the comic mode display the
concerns of a moralist perplexed by his fellow-man's incompetence
in existential matters. He has chosen as his province the vagaries
of the human heart. His sense of fun always combines psychological insight with an extraordinary mixture of sound humour
tinged with gentle scepticism and the sentimentality of an
irrepressible romantic. His stories and tales belong to a tradition
which beyond Stendhal and Chekhov, two of his favourite
models, can be traced back to the sentimental works of the 18th
century, Mozart's operas and Sterne's prose-fiction for instance,
which Saul Bellow in *To Jerusalem and Back* described as
« comedies in which cries are torn from the heart » (45).

# NOTES

1. « A Portrait of the Artist as an Old Man » in *Irish University Review*, VI, 1, Spring 1976, p. 18.

2. « Don Quixote O'Flaherty » in *London Mercury*, XXXVII, December 1937, p. 170.

3. *A Summer in Italy*, London, Eyre & Spottiswoode, 1949 ; New York, Devin-Adair, 1950 ; *South to Sicily*, London, Collins, 1953. Published in the United States under the title *An Autumn in Italy*, New York, Devin-Adair, 1953.

4. « A Portrait of the Artist as an Old Man », p. 13.

5. *The Short Story*, New York, The Devin-Adair Company, 1951, p. 12.

6. *Vive Moi !*, Boston, Little, Brown & Co., 1964, pp. 95-6.

7. *Newman's Way*, London, Longmans, Green & Co., 1952, p. 17 : « Ham is another domination of place. Years and years after, when John Henry Newman was sailing past the island of Ithaca, he thought less of Homer than of Ham... » ; *Constance Markievicz, or The Average Revolutionary*, London, Jonathan Cape, 1934, p. 17 : « ... and all that is meant by place and position touches the pericardium of the imagination with a little mark that chafes and irritates for ever ». To understand what this concept of the domination of place meant in concrete terms for O'Faolain, we have at our disposal two indispensable guidebooks to the topography of his fictional world, *Vive Moi !*, ib. and *An Irish Journey*, London, Longmans Green, 1940.

8. *The Short Story*, p. 11.

9. *Vive Moi !*, p. 248.

10. *The Stories of Sean O'Faolain*, London, Rupert Hart-Davis, 1958, p. XII.

11. Lewis Nichols : « Talk with Mr. O'Faolain » in *The New York Times Book Review*, LXII, May 12, 1957, sect. 7, p. 26.

12. *The Vanishing Hero, Studies in Novelists of the Twenties*, London, Eyre & Spottiswoode, 1956, pp. 101-2.

13. « A Portrait of the Artist as an Old Man », p. 14.

14. *The Short Story*, p. 131.

15. « On Being an Irish Writer » in *The Spectator*, CXCI, July 3, 1953, p. 25.

16. « A Born Genius » in *A Purse of Coppers*, London, Jonathan Cape, 1937, p. 154.

17. W.L. Webb : « An Interview » in *The Guardian*, April 12, 1976, p. 8.

18. *The Short Story*, p. 104.

19. *The Heat of the Sun, Stories and Tales*, London, Rupert Hart-Davis, 1966, pp. 5-6.

20. « A Story and a Comment » in *Irish University Review*, I, 1, Autumn 1970, pp. 89.

21. Roger Garfitt : « Constants in Contemporary Irish Fiction » in Douglas Dunn, ed. : *Two Decades of Irish Writing, a Critical Survey*, Cheadle, Cheshire, Carcanet Press Ltd., 1975, p. 235.

22. Paul Gray : « Celtic Twilight », a review of *Foreign Affairs and Other Stories* in *Time Magazine*, January 26, 1976, p. 56.

23. *Vive Moi !*, p. 331.

24. *The Short Story*, p. 30.

25. *Vive Moi !*, p. 331.

26. Paul Valéry : *Oeuvres*, I, Paris, Gallimard, La Pléiade, 1957, p. 429 : « Mais, cette fois, le problème autobiographique est inévitable. Il s'impose et je dois faire ce que je viens d'incriminer ».

27. *Ibid.* : « Un artiste choisit, même quand il se confesse. Et peut-être surtout quand il se confesse. Il allège, il aggrave, çà et là... ».

28. *South to Sicily*, p. 11.

29. *The Short Story*, p. 8.

30. *Vive Moi !*, p. 225.

31. *Vive Moi !, p. 93-4.*

32. *Vive Moi !*, p. 225.

33. *Ibid.*

34. *Vive Moi !*, p. 9.

35. *A Nest of Simple Folk*, New York, The Viking Press, 1934, p. 157.

37. *Vive Moi !*, passim ; « A Portrait of the Artist as an Old Man », pp. 10-8.

38. *Vive Moi !*, p. 226.

39. *An Irish Journey*, p. 88 : «... that hatred born of jealousy without which there is no heat in love ».

40. « A Broken World » in *A Purse of Coppers, Short Stories*, p. 27.

41. « The Bombshop » in *Midsummer Night Madness and Other Stories*, London, Jonathan Cape, 1932, p. 180.

42. *The Talking Trees and Other Stories*, London, Jonathan Cape, 1971, pp. 196-7.

43. *Vive Moi !*, p. 226.

44. *The Short Story*, p. VII.

45. Saul Bellow : *To Jerusalem and Back*, New York, Avon Books, 1977, p. 76.

# TEST FLIGHT : BECKETT'S
# « MORE PRICKS THAN KICKS »

## Alec REID

As a people the Irish are said to have a great love of debate
and, if necessary, any true-born son of Erin can sustain a worth-
while argument with his own shadow. Be that as it may, we do
not here propose to question the propriety of including Beckett in
a book on the Irish short story. Incontestably Mr. Beckett is
Irish and, equally beyong debate, he is the author of *More Pricks
than Kicks*, a collection of ten short stories about Dublin written
in English and published by Chatto and Windus in 1934.

He was about twenty-eight at the time and although this is his
first full-length book, coming in chronological order after the four-
page poem « Whoroscope » and the seventy-two page monograph
*Proust*, he has never shown much affection for it. On publication
probably less than 200 copies were sold, the remainder were
destroyed by a German fire-bomb dropped on a London ware-
house some time during the last war and since then for more than
twenty years Beckett seemed resolved to leave the book in decent
obscurity. Only in 1966 did he sanction the limited reproduction
of a typescript intended for scholars and libraries, and a generally
available edition did not appear until 1970.

Much of *More Pricks than Kicks* is material originally destined
for a novel *A Dream of Fair to Middling Women* on which
Beckett had worked for two or three years before jettisoning it.
The ten stories are all concerned with one character, Belacqua
Shuah, whose adventures, if we may so dignify them, and whose

love life we follow from the university to the cemetery. Although each of the episodes is self-contained there are numerous cross-references within the stories.

Of the ten stories, one « Dante and the Lobster » deserves inclusion in any anthology of Irish short stories ; two others, « A Wet Night » and « What a Misfortune » are fine pieces of localised satire. The other seven all have their good things but do not merit much detailed examination.

In his study of Beckett, *The Long Sonata of the Dead* (1), Michael Robinson remarks that in their present form the short stories are uneven in quality and are evidently the work of a young man intent on exploring the possibilities of his learning and early impressions. Since Mr. Robinson himself was well under thirty when he passed this judgement it is tempting to dismiss it as an example of shallow calling unto shallow, but there is too much truth in the comment for that. *More Pricks than Kicks* is undeniably *juvenilia* with all the exhibitionism, the arrogance and the shallowness of a very clever, very erudite young man. But there is more to it than that. Maturity apart, in the lives of some artists there seems to be a watershed separating irrevocably the 'prentice work from the masterpieces. Just as few could have foreseen that « Mister John Keats », rightly trounced by *Blackwoods* for the Cockney vulgarities of his early poetry would leave behind him the *Poems* of 1820, so the Beckett of *More Pricks than Kicks* gives little hint of the future Nobel prize-winner. Beckett, the man, has changed from the promising young academic of the thirties to one who, to quote George Devine, « seems to have lived and suffered so that I might see and he was generous enough to pass it on to me ». Beckett as artist is no longer a cosmopolitan aesthete but a writer utterly committed to discovering the inner world of the self. The Dublin of Belacqua Shuah, hero of *More Pricks than Kicks*, is redolent of what now seems Edwardian euphoria. The gulf between *More Pricks than Kicks* and say *Molloy* or *Waiting for Godot* is no less than that which separates *Stephen Hero* from *Finnegans Wake*.

Of all the *genres* at which Beckett has tried his hand, the short story is probably the one which interests him least, certainly in the sense used by Sean O'Faolain when he described it as a piece of prose in which the tension is sustained. Tension is rarely found in Beckett's work, and where it does occur it is generated not by the content, the sequence of events, but by the writing itself in its constant attempt to say the unsayable, transcend the limitations of traditional form.

In examinations of the Irish short story certain ideas tend to come up again and again — What is the author's feeling for Ireland and the realities of Irish life ? Does he accept them or does he reject them ? Does Ireland become a character ? What are the author's feelings for the people he has created ? What are his relations with the reader ? The author of *More Pricks than Kicks* seems concerned only with the last two of these. Of Belacqua he has a good deal to say : « We were Pylades and Orestes for a period, flattened down to something very genteel, but the relation abode and was highly confidential while it lasted » (2). By nature, according to the narrator, Belacqua was « sinfully indolent, bogged in indolence » (3), while his mental and moral position, an attempt to separate himself as far as possible from the world around him, was equally pathetic and ignoble.

In his anxiety to explain himself, he was liable to come to grief. Nay, this anxiety in itself, or so at least it seemed to me, constituted a break-down in the self-sufficiency which he never wearied of arrogating to himself, a sorry collapse of my little internus homo, and alone sufficient to give him away as inept ape of his own shadow. But he wriggled out of everything by pleading that he had been drunk at the time, or that he was an incoherent person and content to remain so, and so on. He was an impossible person in the end. I gave him up in the end because he was not serious (4).

Even Miss Alba Perdue, the most sympathetic of Belacqua's lady-loves, was scarcely bowled over by him. Looking at him as he arrives at a party, bedraggled and slightly the worse for drink, she reflects that « she had never seen anybody, man or woman, look such a sovereign booby. Seeking to be God, she thought, in the slavish arrogance of a piffling evil » (5).

As for the reader, Beckett addresses him often enough in an almost conspiratorial tone, or as one needing enlightenment on detail :

« And the rosiner » said Mrs Tough, « will you have that in the lav too ? »

Reader, a rosiner is a drop of the hard.
Ruby rose and took a gulp of coffee to make room.
« I'll have a gloria » she said.
Reader, a gloria is coffee laced with brandy (6).

Even with such aids the book is not unfairly described by Katherine Worth as « one to defy translation » (7).

In feats of gallantry Belacqua is by preference a *voyeur* and only reluctantly a practitioner. Similarly Beckett seems more interested in the act of authorship in *More Pricks than Kicks* than in involvement with it. The very title was chosen, one cannot help suspecting, to stimulate the attention of the Irish Censorship of Publications Board, a body much in the minds of other avant-garde spirits of the time. If so, it succeeded.

Given Belacqua and his creator we should be content to look for amusement only. But this we find in plenty. Once we become attuned to a sardonic, detached point of view and to a very gifted writer light-heartedly trying his wings, we find there is a good deal of fun to be had. There is Belacqua in « Ding Dong » unassumingly seeking *Nirvana* in his favourite sombre hostelry only to be accosted by a beshawled female with « a white voice » who sells him two seats in heaven for tuppence each and bilks him of his small-change.

In « Love and Lethe » Belacqua and his « current one and only », a lady suffering from an incurable disease and finding the opportunities for gallantry decreasing as her desire for them sharpens, decide to end it all together. In the event, despite Belacqua's provision of a revolver, poison and a notice saying « temporarily sane » they make a botch of the business, ending up in each other's arms.

Then there is much satire of Dublin's provincial intelligentsia such as gathered at the party thrown by Miss Caleken Frica :

Two banned novelists, a bibliomaniac and his mistress, a paleographer, a violist d'amore with his instrument in a bag, a popular parodist with his sister and six daughters, a still more popular Professor of Bullscrit and Comparative Ovoidology, the saprophile the better for drink, a communist painter and decorator fresh back from the Moscow reserves, a merchant prince, two grave Jews, a rising strumpet, three more poets with Lauras to match, a disaffected cicisbeo, a chorus of playwrights, the inevitable envoy of the Fourth Estate, a phalanx of Grafton Street Stürmers and Jemmy Higgins... (8).

Another delight in the book, for those who find such things pleasurable, are the frequent erudite in-jokes, the tones of exact recondite scholarship in surrroundings of seedy disarray. Thus when Belacqua in « Fingal » takes Miss Winifred Coates who was « pretty hot and witty in that order » to the Hill of the Wolves looking down on Malahide Castle in North County Dublin, it is not long before he finds himself a very sad animal and we recall Galen and his *tristis post coitus*. In « A Wet Night » the sister of the hostess unveils the refreshments.

« Cup ! Squash ! Cocoa ! Force ! Julienne ! Pan Kail ! Cock-a-Leekie ! Hulluah ! Apfelmus ! Isinglass ! Ching-Ching ! »

A terrible silence fell on the assembly.

« Great cry » said Chas « and little wool » (9).

And the cognoscenti preen themselves as they recognise the headline from the copy books used in the National Schools, the works devised by Vere Foster.

Again there is the delight of parody. Only those with a good knowledge of James Joyce's « The Dead » will appreciate the Frica's party to the full but few readers will fail to enjoy the witty parody of the famous conclusion to that work. Beckett's arrogant self-confidence is astonishing :

But the wind had dropped, as it so often does in Dublin when all the respectable men and women whom it delights to annoy have gone to bed, and the rain fell in a uniform untroubled manner. It fell upon the bay, the littoral, the mountains and the plains, and notably upon the Central Bog it fell with a rather desolate uniformity (10).

Closely associated with this zest for parody is the young man's exuberant enjoyment of his own linguistic powers. Later Beckett was to achieve a style of chastened, chilly economy. In *More*

*Pricks than Kicks* he luxuriates in verbal excess, delighting for example in sustained passages of the mock-heroic, exulting in his verbal energy. And at moments, almost against the grain we find an imagination and an intellect at work :

> The groundsman stood deep in thought. What with the company of headstones sighing and gleaming like bones, the moon on the job, the sea tossing in her dreams and panting, and the hills observing their Attic vigil in the background, he was at a loss to determine off-hand whether the scene was of the kind that is termed romantic or whether it should not with more justice be deemed classical. Both elements were present, that was indisputable. Perhaps classico-romantic would be the fairest estimate. A classico-romantic scene (11).

Despite such moments, the stories as a whole do not have the stamp of authentic genius. On their showing, Beckett could fit snugly enough into an Irish tradition of verbal brilliance with little behind it, another fashionable Dublin literary wit. Once only in *More Pricks than Kicks* a deep, more lasting note is sounded, strangely enough in the first story, « Dante and the Lobster ». Here we meet Belacqua for the first time as he wrestles with an obscure passage from Dante's Purgatory. When the Angelus rings, he closes his book and turns to « the three great obligations of the day, lunch, lobster and his lesson ». The first of these inspires a mock heroic account of how Belacqua prepares and organises his meal, two rounds of thoroughly toasted bread smeared with mustard and then taken to the grocer's for their filling, a piece of gorgonzola, thence to a rather low pub where Belacqua can enjoy them in peace. Lunch is a ritual which can be easily violated but on this day it goes well. From the pub, Belacqua makes his way to a fishmonger's to collect a lobster, already wrapped up, which he and his aunt will eat that evening. The fishmonger assures him that it is « leppin fresh ». Then comes the Italian lesson with Signorina Ottolenghi, « a lady of a certain age who had found being beautiful and young and pure more of a bore than anything else » (12). While he is with her the lobster, left on a hall table, is almost snatched away by a cat belonging to Mlle Glain, a French teacher in the same institute. Eventually without hurt it reaches the kitchen of Belacqua's aunt where Belacqua discovers to his horror that when the fishmonger had described it as « lepping fresh » he was speaking no more than the truth. Even now it is still alive.

« What are you going to do ? » he cried.
« Boil the beast » she said, « what else ?»
« But it's not dead » protested Belacqua « you can't boil it like that ».
She looked at him in astonishment. Had he taken leave of his senses ?
« Have sense » she said sharply, « lobsters are always boiled alive. They must be ». She caught up the lobster and laid it on its back. It trembled. « They feel nothing » she said.
In the depths of the sea it had crept into the cruel pot. For hours in the midst of its enemies, it had breathed secretly. It had survived the Frenchwoman's cat and his witless clutch. Now it was going alive into scalding water. It had to. Take into the air my quiet breath.
Belacqua looked at the old parchment of her face, grey in the dim kitchen.
« You make a fuss » she said angrily « and upset me and then lash into it for your dinner ».
She lifted the lobster clear of the table. It had about thirty seconds to live.
Well, thought Belacqua, it's a quick death, God help us all.
It is not (13).

The last short sentence is a master stroke, breaking in like the trump of doom to scatter our facile, self-induced indifference to the diabolical actions afoot. Here is Beckett speaking in his authentic, unmistakable voice, austere, insistent, unrelenting. It is hard to know if he is addressing the reader, or any audience at all, or whether this is not the voice which we shall hear in all the later work, a voice speaking for man into a universal darkness simply because it cannot stay silent. Here are the originality, the compassion, the sheer mastery which, as the Nobel prize jury said, have enabled Beckett to elevate human wretchedness to the level of art.

But this lies far ahead. In 1934, Beckett was still a young man though, as Joyce said of him, of undoubted talent. The war was to come with two years' work in the French Resistance in Paris and three in hiding for his very life. There will be a switch from stories to novels, from English to French, and a change of style from the early highly polished pedantic elegance and excess to an earthy violent incoherence, a demotic economy, somehow saying far more. Amazingly *More Kicks* will lead to *Lessness*.

*More Pricks than Kicks* is only a start, light-hearted, clever, amusing, notice served that here is a writer of wit, ready to laugh, in a slightly condescending way perhaps, at the world around him, but above all, at his own learning and at himself.

# NOTES

1. Michael Robinson : *The Long Sonata of the Dead*, London, Rupert Hart-Davis, 1969.

2. Samuel Beckett : *More Pricks than Kicks*, London, Chatto and Windus, 1934, pp. 44-5.

3. *Ibid.*, p. 44.

4. *Ibid.*, pp. 45-6.

5. *Ibid.*, p. 106.

6. *Ibid.*, p. 119.

7. Kathleen Worth, ed : *Beckett the Shape Changer*, London and Boston, Routledge and Kegan Paul, 1975, p. 8.

8. Beckett : *op. cit.*, p. 88.

9. *Ibid.*, p. 87.

10. *Ibid.*, pp. 112-3.

11. *Ibid.*, p. 278.

12. *Ibid.*, p. 15.

13. *Ibid.*, pp. 19-20.

# MARY LAVIN

## Séamus DEANE

Mary Lavin's work seems naturally to command the reader to
respond, as most of her commentators have done, to a certain
purity of execution, of phrasing, and, perhaps more peremptorily,
of the kind of concentration which we properly associate with
deep and patient study. The object of study in her case is, very
simply, the nature of love. Sometimes its validity is tested,
although this is rare. Sometimes its bitterness is revealed, and this
is frequent. More often again, its endurance is made manifest in the
form of an iron stoicism or in the shape of an ethereally intense
conviction. At all times, there is a deep engagement with the social
environment, although that environment is often more restricted for
the central character than it is for the narrator, these two being very
seldom identical. In fact, the restriction of people's lives in these
stories is best confirmed for us by the number of celibates who
inhabit them. The celibacy may be enforced by death — Mary
Lavin writes with great force about the widowed — or chosen as a
vocation by priests or by laymen or women who entertain a love the
world cannot respond to satisfactorily. All the forms of celibacy are
for her forms of fidelity to a lost love, whether it be lost in the past
or lost in the sense that it was never attained. Despite this,
sexuality is a strong and pervasive presence, breathing pantheistic-
ally through the Irish (particularly the County Meath) landscape,
erupting in the arms of the lovers as a cascade of daffodils (as in
'Happiness') or becoming a sensual image of their anticipated

Morally, this is a severe world. Although Mary Lavin has,
psychologically, an empathetic closeness with even the most
brutal or selfish characters, she candidly denies them moral
sympathy. Sympathy is for lovers. To earn it, they must
overcome all barriers — of class, of family, of temperament. They
must elope, take risks, « learn », as Clem says in « The Gar-
dener », « to distinguish » (3). Out of love for his children and,
generally, for the innocent, he killed his wife. It is that kind of
distinction which the extraordinary sensibility of the lover must
have the courage and lucidity to make. However, the feeling that
someone has been judged is not coercive. It more usually comes
as a kind of aftertaste. The stories are not morality tales ; they
adjudicate by implication, not by pronouncement. A great deal
depends, therefore, on the tone of the narrative. I once referred to
it as having a « nefarious sweetness » and see no reason to
question that ascription (although it is less evident in the most
recent volume *The Shrine and Other Stories* (1977) than it had
previously been). Indeed the tone so beautifully blends the
elements of sympathy and judgement that we can only wish that
union (as does the field of meadow-grass in 'Asigh') (2). Whether or
no it be said that these erotic tensions are embodied in or trans-
ferred to the details of landscape, it is difficult to think of this action
as a solely literary device. It bespeaks the attitude towards
sexuality characteristic of the Ireland of the last half-century. It is
not, in other words, just a technique of conscious or unconscious
sublimation. Insofar as these stories are concerned with the oblique
exposure of powerful feelings, we sense that their power is closely
related to the social and psychological habits of social suppression
and secrecy. There is no attempt, really, to criticise this typical
aspect of Irish social life, although one can infer a certain amount of
disagreement and bitterness towards its inevitable consequences.
Mary Lavin very largely shares the mores of her society. The
question for her is, given those mores, by what means do people who
behave in accord with them, deal with the anxieties and longings for
which no direct, outright expression is available ? She is concerned
with the preservation of dignity and worth in very unlikely and
often demeaning circumstances. The subtlety of her scrutiny and
the assurance with which she controls her narrative indicate the
presence throughout all her work of a firm moral criterion by which
worth can be judged and in accord with which people can come to
embody such worth. That criterion is fidelity to the vocation of love.

Mary Lavin had consistently found an appropriate narrative form in which to cast it. A writer who is so involved in the domestic, practical world is committed by that involvement to the demands of verisimilitude, even in the way in which the story is told. Occasionally, these demands are not met and the result is disquietingly artificial.

The awkwardness I refer to is most often found in those stories which are reported through an intermediary. In « The Mouse », for instance, the story of Lelia, Mina and Arthur is told by a mother, who has recently renewed her friendship with Lelia, to her daughter, who is intrigued by the hidden tale of Lelia's lost lover, Arthur. The mother and Lelia are, as usual, attracted to one another by the enforced celibacy of their present state. The mother's husband is dead, Lelia's Arthur forsook her for another woman, Mina. Yet Lelia remains faithful to the love she had for him ; and, more wonderfully, continues to believe in the love he had for her. At any rate, after many years of silence, Lelia finally tells how it all happened to her new-found friend. The mother, in turn, tells it to her daughter whose curiosity had provoked the whole confession. But the confession is reported verbatim. We are listening to Lelia's voice, disguised as the mother-narrator's voice. Although there is an effort to set the scene, to give a physical foreground, so to speak, to the telling of the story, we are conscious of a certain clumsiness and certain improbability in the whole matter. The mother may be cross, shivering with cold, she may fill the kettle for a cup of tea, but we know that these actions are merely efforts to disguise the fact that she is no part of the story's moral fabric, but is merely a fictional device. The same applies to the daughter. As a consequence, the story lacks that surety of tone and address which we meet with in such perfect stories as « At Sallygap », « An Akoulina of the Irish Midlands », « Asigh », « A Memory », « Happiness » and « Senility ». It is when Mary Lavin cannot find a satisfactorily probable way of getting the story told that she lapses into an excessive enumeration of small actions and physical details which have no direct bearing upon the story itself. The reader is diverted from the feeling in the story by the mock-cosiness of its address. It is possible that this kind of flaw is one endemic to short story writers. The fact of publishing story after story in magazines leads the author as much as it does editors or readers to expect of himself a certain kind of story. All the best short story writers — Tchekhov, Henry James, Babel, Kafka — produce works which are in some respects a stereotype, in some respects a caricature of their best stories. I think that Irish writers are probably more prone to this failing than are most authors, for there is a certain expectation in their audiences (especially their American audiences) about what an Irish short story is like. The pressure of editors and audience is a very real one and Mary Lavin now and again succumbs to it, just as Frank O'Connor, far more often, also did. In Mary Lavin's case the house style of *The New Yorker* sometimes shows through. When it does, the effect is not good.

Even if this be so, « The Mouse » has moments which remind us of other, more enduring aspects of her work. Take, for instance, Lelia's description of her last moment with Arthur :

> I remember almost everything about that day as if it was a painting, and I was outside it, instead of in it. I remember a man with an ass and cart came down to the bank of the stream where we were sitting, with a big barrel to fill for the cattle grazing inside the ramparts. Well, I suppose anyone would remember a thing like that, but I remember every detail of it, and how when the barrel was filled, and he was leading the ass up from the stream, the wheels of the cart rocked, and little silver drops of water were tossed up in the air, and they seemed to hang in the air for a minute, like a spray of tremble-grass, before they fell back into the barrel. Fancy remembering that all those years ! And I remember, just close to Arthur's face once, where he was lying back in the grass, a little black insect... (4)

This is, to some extent, a set piece. It is description saturated by grief, but formally so. The grief arises both from the situation itself and from the innocence of Lelia, however willed we may feel that to be. The acuity of her perception renders the depth of her loss. If we compare that to another passage from a different story, we can see how subtly the description of landscape can operate with, in this case, a retrospective force. The story is called « Asigh » :

> Closed in by summer, the fields were deeper and lonelier than ever, and the laneway that led out to the road was narrowed by overhanging briars and the wild summer growth of bank and ditch (5).

This is a story of love frustrated by a father's brutality and by a lover's hard-nosed common sense. It is also a study of sexual pathology and its manifestation in social attitudes. Most memorable though, is the girl's longing to find an outlet for the love which has stirred to life inside her. If not through her suitor Tod Mallon, or even through the quiet vengeance of love for the father who destroyed her life, then at least, vicariously, through her brother and his girl-friend, Flossie Sauran. But that longing is disappointed too. We leave her as we found her, lost amid the stiflingly rich fields of Meath, emotionally starved in the midst of plenty. The world depicted here is a cowardly one, and its harsh male authority is shown to be the product of half-sensed but wholly submerged sexual longing. But it is the girl who is the primary victim. Her impulse is to give love, not merely to have it. On all sides, the gift is betrayed by people unworthy to receive it. Such stories reach the level of parable. They exemplify a great deal about Irish social life but so powerfully embody it in terms of natural description and narrated event that we feel the convergence of every detail towards a single, powerful impression. The landscape, as described above in the opening sentences of the story, incorporates in itself the claustrophobic loss of the young girl. In this case, we are aware of a venomous economy in the telling and a stiff resistance to any easing or sentimentalisation of the theme. Mary Lavin's women may be heroic ; but their stature does not diminish their unhappiness ; it is instead the consequence of that unhappiness.

It is, therefore, a mistake and an exaggeration to speak of Mary Lavin's stories as though they were, *au fond*, a version of Irish pastoral — a notion put abroad by many of her reviewers. Although love is their subject and the Irish landscape, lyrically evoked, is often their environment, there is a candid bitterness, an unforgiving spirit in many of them. The most notable fact about love is its wastage.

« Oh, how had it happened ? How could love be wasted and go to loss like that ? » (6)

Those who waste it are terribly punished, like the vacuous academic James in « A Memory » ; those who suffer from its loss are haunted like Bartley Crossen in « In the Middle of the Fields », or Vera in « One Summer », even Bedelia in « The Little Prince ». Widowhood, bachelorhood, spinsterdom, childhood, old age and death — these are the states in which Mary Lavin tests love's validity. Marriage too, but marriage in her stories is always anticipated, brought to a sudden end or is a form of living death. It is not a state in itself but one from which her people seek refuge or to which they aspire. Although it is a fixed institution, it is rarely inhabited in the present tense by a living soul. Physically too, the act of love is always, so to speak, postponed. It is indeed surprising how very seldom such intimate stories are involved with physical intimacy. A touch or a kiss may mark the physical horizon of a love affair. This may be taken to indicate a certain prudery, but I hardly think so. Instead it would seem to indicate a highly spiritualised conception of love which governs the selection of physical detail — whether of the body or of the surrounding world — in most of these stories. Sexuality is denied, not by the narrator, but by her characters. Because of this denial, its effects are oblique and savage. We have here an analysis of Irish puritanism, not a monument to it.

The true lover fights against the world. Widows fly from those who remember the dead husband ; other people's versions of the beloved make him and the love he bore unreal. Vera Traske in « The Cuckoo Spit » and Mary in « In a Café » experience this. That which is given in love — perhaps no more than the memory of a face — is precisely what the world wishes to take away. Love is phantasmal, yet the only reality ; the world is actual, yet not at all real. Innocence and simplicity are the emotional stigmata of the lover, but they only show up in the presence of loss. In these stories, the deepest passions are the most disappointed. As celibacy is the recurrent image of loss, fidelity is the recurrent virtue characteristic of that state. Marriages may be made in heaven, but when they are so they are rarely realised on this earth. Or at least, to make the point truer to the stories, their realisation is always in the past. Marriage is the past tense of love. It survives, though, as an order of values which contrasts with the meaner values of the loveless world, whether that be middle-class Dublin, the rural world of County Meath, the faded gentility of the Anglo-Irish or the shopkeeper world of the village. Conflict is inevitable and many of these stories demonstrate the various shapes which it can assume. The great virtue of the lover is to maintain the integrity of passion, the great vice, to violate or betray that integrity. It is worth emphasising that passion is not subdued or granted a merely desultory role. Passion is kept intact by celibacy, just so long as we understand the celibacy to be a form of fidelity and not as merely a repudiation of the physical.

The conflict I have spoken of can sometimes, as in a story like « Brother Boniface » take a very simple form (7). In that story, the world of the shop and that of the monastery are clearly seen as opposites to one another, but they are not in any deep sense inimical. Brother Boniface's uselessness in worldly matters is merely proof of his contemplative saintliness in an other-worldly realm. More often, we find that these stories pit two different types against one another. One type is ethereally gentle, consumed by passion so completely that his or her physical presence is slight ; the other type has a more dominant, even a grosser, physical presence and an accompanying set of worldly values. Women in particular often fulfil the roles of Martha and Mary, with painfully contrasting fates as their reward or punishment. One thinks of Mary and Sis in « A Tragedy », Bedelia and Liddy in « Frail Vessel » Mae and Essy in « Second-Hand ». But perhaps it is « An Akoulina of the Irish Midlands » which best exemplifies this contrast. This is one of Mary Lavin's finest stories, a small masterpiece which is not at all overshadowed by its reference to Turgenev.

Still, it would be false to think of this body of work as conducive to a simple kind of type-casting. We are almost always aware of the small, irreducible pressures of Irish social life being exerted in a variety of ways upon individuals who are in part formed by that pressure, who in part embody it themselves and who, less often, have a conception of themselves which is independent of the formative influences of their environment. In some easily identified ways we can follow the evolution of Irish society in the last forty years by noting some social indications in these stories. An aspect of Irish middle-class feeling, the so-called « Fairyhouse Tradition », towards the movement for national independence is nicely caught in « The Patriot Son » ; « Scylla and Charybdis » gives us a small, reverberative instance of the social distance between the gentry and their employees ; « A Fable » uses the relationship between the Big House and the village as a ground for a parable about Beauty and Belief ; the increasing importance of the university world for the middle classes is evident in stories like « The Lucky Pair », and the more recent « The Shrine ». We learn that Tod Mallon in « Asigh » « was one of the first in the countryside to own a motor-car ». In « The Mock Auction » Mrs. Lomas's respectable Protestant world collapses in squalid ruin in the period of transition between travel by pony and trap and travel by motor-car. Then there are other stories — « Trastevere », « Villa Violetta », « A Memory » —

which belong to a less enclosed, more obviously contemporary Ireland and Europe, one akin to that with which Sean O'Faolain concerns himself, with a good deal less assurance, in his most recent volume, *Foreign Affairs* (1976).

As we observe the mutations of social life in these stories and compare these to the near-intransigent preoccupation with love which gives them their moral stability, we gain an insight into Mary Lavin's role in modern Irish writing. She is not, in any technical sense, an innovator. Equally, the reader is not troubled by the traditional form of her fiction any more than he would be by the same phenomenon in O'Connor, O'Faolain or O'Flaherty. The short story has remained comparatively free from that radical experimentation which is more usually (if not often successfully) tried in the novel or in poetry. Perhaps traditionalism is native to the form itself, or rather native to the relation established in Ireland between this form and Irish society. Literature is by a long way the senior art form in this country. As such, it has always self-consciously assumed to itself the responsibility of registering Irish life — metaphorically or otherwise — in ways which in other cultures would be fulfilled by political and sociological commentary. The poverty of Irish intellectual life (slightly less profound now than used to be the case) makes so many compensatory demands on Irish literature that it restricts the area for experimentation which we find so vast and open in other cultures. Although much Irish writing is concerned with alienated lives, it is not itself a literature of alienation. For that one needs to go to Eastern Europe or the United States. Society and literature retain their intimacy in Ireland to such a degree that our best literature is still, in the widest sense of the term, social.

When we add to this the fact that the short story, no matter how elusive its mode of narration may be, rarely if ever loses its desire to pass judgement, to create at least the fiction of a moral world, then the form's traditionalism is perhaps more easily understood. In Ireland too the tendency to adjudicate has always been most pronounced in those writers who take a local area as an object of such penetrating scrutiny that its recurrent features attain an almost allegorical status. They become so familiarised that we learn to « read » them as short-hand notations for certain kinds of moral attitude or idea. Mary Lavin's fields, Joyce's streets, George Moore's rooms become transparently familiar as moral arenas, although to be sure they have also an exact and acute physical presence. Judgement is refracted through the particularity of detail, giving us the spectrum of a story.

Yet Mary Lavin wears her Irish rue with a difference. Only Elizabeth Bowen equals her in the exercise of a peculiar kind of authority — the authority of the artist as a woman. Neither is doctrinaire on account of her sex. But each is highly sceptical of the importance of the « male » worlds of politics and work. There is no such thing as a career in the lives of their people ; careers become vocations, and the vocation is always understood as a devotion to the complexities of human feeling. I think that because of this we never find in the work of these two women the kind of aggressive, domineering relationship to the world which is so typical of the many artist heroes in modern Irish writing. The pronoun « I » loses its customary importance in their work. The singular individual's relationship with the mediocre world is not their concern. Instead, as we read, we become aware of a very closely meshed nexus of feelings in which their protagonists are bound. Men are not men of affairs but men who have had or are having affairs. With this, there is a less hectoring and less anxious search for brilliance, charms, the edgy phrase-making of the conventional Irish short-story writer. (One would have to make an exception in Mary Lavin's case for stories like « The Green Grave and the Black Grave » or even « The Great Wave », which strike me as professional Irish stories). Narratives may focus on an individual but not to the degree that we become diverted from this centre by the eccentric individualism of the narration itself. It is for instance only rarely that Frank O'Connor found a subject other that his own personality. He did not so much write stories as search in his work for a way in which to write with a Cork accent.

But Mary Lavin could not be accused of having a style in that sense of the word. More precisely, she deploys a rhetoric, just so long as we retain for the latter word its traditional and honourable meaning. Style is what we speak of when an individual seeks to discover in words the unique flavour, the particular mode of performance of his own sensibility. In rhetoric, the object is not the display of self, but the deployment of language for the sake of illuminating a particular situation or problem. One is the romantic, the other the classical mode of writing. Mary Lavin is classical. Her ethic is communal ; the writing bears witness to commonalty in its traditional address, syntax and tone. Love, after all, is the great classical, not romantic, subject. The great romantic subject is the self. Love demands relation. Relation requires the exercise of certain controls which can become values, like those of loyalty, truth - telling, self-restraint.

Of course the dishevelled Irish community of which Mary Lavin writes does not embody these virtues. However she perceives in that community a peculiar combination of traditionalism and of rootlessness. Social institutions like the Church are powerful, yet artificial. The loyalties of people are strangely disturbed by its presence. Like the villagers in « Sarah », they experience a curious ambiguity :

> There was greater undestanding in their hearts for sins against God than there was for sins against the Church (8).

The public practice of traditional beliefs is not often possible in such a society. Its ambience is sympathetic, its final decisions are loveless. For Mary Lavin the basic values are practised by the minority of lovers, almost all of them abandoned, almost all of them faithful to that which has caused them so much pain. They are the constituency of the elect in whom the human value of society is embodied but against whom its inhuman impulses are directed. The celibates become martyrs in the end. Like Liddy in « Frail Vessel », who in her abandonment has still the better, spiritually, of her grossly competent and respectable sister Bedelia, they can murmur, « Even so... Even so » (9). Great stories concentrate on individual moments but they articulate communal values. Mary Lavin has given us an astonishing number of these.

# NOTES

1. *Happiness and Other Stories*, London, 1969 ; Boston, 1970.
2. *A Memory and Other Stories*, London, 1972 ; New York, 1973.
3. *Collected Stories*, Boston, 1971, p. 419.
4. *The Great Wave*, London and New York, 1961, pp. 37-8.
5. *A Memory and Other Stories*, New York, 1973, p. 67.
6. « Brigid » in *The Stories of Mary Lavin*, Volume Two, London, 1974, p. 152.
7. *Tales from Bective Bridge*, Boston, 1942.
8. *Bective Bridge*, pp. 54-5.
9. *The Stories of Mary Lavin*, Volume One, London, 1964, p. 8.

# PRIVATE WORLDS : THE STORIES
# OF MICHAEL McLAVERTY

## John FOSTER

The short stories of Michael McLaverty enjoy a firm but
muted reputation. Critics frequently praise but rarely pursue
them in prolonged discussion ; the praise as a result has about it
a hint of lip-service and the formulaic. The great affection in
which he is held to the contrary, McLaverty it seems to me has
been somewhat damned with faint critical effort. The author has
not, of course, been highly visible to an Irish public that likes its
writers to be seen and heard as well as read, and this apparent
diffidence may not be unconnected to the critical privacy
McLaverty's fiction has maintained. Moreover, only thrice* has
McLaverty invaded the relative privacy of little magazine
publication with collections, only one of which was published
outside Ireland and all of which contain some duplicate stories :
*The White Mare* (Newcastle, Co. Down, 1943), *The Game Cock*
(New York, 1948 and London, 1949) and *The Road to the Shore*
(Dublin, 1976).

But where privacy ends and privation begins is a moot point in
any discussion not merely of the publishing and promotion of
McLaverty's stories and of the critical response to them, but also

---

* McLaverty's *Collected Short Stories*, with an introduction by Seamus Heaney,
were published in Dublin by The Poolbeg Press in 1978. The volume contains 23
stories. (Eds.).

of the very themes and forms of those stories. In several senses which account for their fineness and durability as well as their limitations, McLaverty's stories constitute small private worlds whose relationships to the larger public worlds beyond are — to a degree unusual in an Irish, particularly Northern Irish writer — implicit, oblique, problematic. I would like here to linger on those relationships and to suggest the guises which McLaverty's private and privative vision assumes and some of the forces that perhaps compel them.

Through the eyes of his characters, McLaverty is used to noticing such things as most writers do not, lowly details of the physical world available to all of us but largely invisible or contemptible once we have lost, as McLaverty has not, the near-sightedness of childhood and love : the squeaking of the father's boots in « Evening in Winter » that is a sure sign to the small son that the boots haven't yet been paid for ; the old man in « Uprooted » who sits in the priest's sitting-room, « his eyes fixed on the chair-dents that were like paw-marks in the polished linoleum » ; the young narrator's memory in « Pigeons » of being awakened of a morning : « My eyes would be very gluey and I would rub them with my fists until they would open in the gaslight. For a long while I would see gold needles sticking out of the flame, then they would melt away and the gas become like a pansy leaf with a blue heart ». Observation of such modesty and delicacy is a kind of revelation where we least expect it, amidst the daily and the commonplace, and so is mingled public surface with private vision. The observations have the passive quality of presentations — hardly to the characters, as they would be to a Stephen Dedalus, presentiments — and rarely help the characters to know themselves better, for there is no critical or psychological intelligence (not even that of a narrator since grown up) to pierce the muffled, inchoate, insulated effect ultimately conveyed as a quality of existence by McLaverty's stories.

Rarely, too, is a character's observation or insight relayed to another character and so it remains personal, heard only by the eavesdropping reader. This gives McLaverty's stories a curious quality of soliloquy that goes beyond what we would normally expect in the short story form. In privacy, the meanings of events, of places, of people and of things become talismanic, and their remembrance or experience a personal rite like the telling of beads. In « The Poteen Maker » the science master repeats over and over again one lesson in Science (unknown to his pupils he is really distilling illicit whiskey) « which he called : *Evaporation and Condensation* ». A nuns' outing in « The Road to the Shore » ends in minor catastrophe when a cyclist collides with their car ; they take the cyclist to hospital and are told that his wound is « only a slight abrasion and contusion » : « Sister Clare made no remark when she heard the news but as the wheels of the car rose and fell on the road they seemed to echo what was in her mind : *abrasion and contusion, abrasion and contusion* ». Sister Clare's expropriation of book-learning is no less private than Sister Paul's sad memories of her father's death and of a childhood garden in which grew winter poplars : to Sister Paul the poplars seen on the outing from the car grow in the past, to Sister Clare they grow in a scientific present but one which has its own kind of privately enjoyed poetry : *augustifolia, laurifolia, balsamifera, tremula, tremuloides*. Sister Clare's musings in the car cannot fail to remind us of the narrator's memory in « The Game Cock » of returning as a boy from a cockfight and a day in the country during which his uncle explained that the local Big House is in ruins because the ladies and gentlemen took the land from the people and God cursed them : « I was glad when (my father) was ready for home and gladder still when we were in the train where I made the wheels rumble and chant : ... *They took the land from the people ... God cursed them* ». For McLaverty and his characters, not only the world but also the word becomes private.

In the word is frequently contained the past which even when vividly recalled, as is Sister Paul's, has the mesmeric quality of a freshly remembered dream meaningful only to the dreamer. The nuns listen politely but vacantly to Sister Paul's memories, only the wise Reverend Mother guessing the paining depth of their nostalgia. On a train journey — trains and boats and cars are important in McLaverty's stories, as they bear his characters off into an old landscape of the past or a new landscape of emotional discovery — the husband in « After Forty Years » recalls in front of his wife a young married woman whom despite his denial he loved and who was drowned two score years ago ; his wife is vexed by his reminiscences and becomes jealous and peevish as they assume, like the noise of the train, the exclusive power of soliloquy. He ends his recollection with a blessing on the long dead young woman. « He leant back against the headrest and closed his eyes. His wife continued her knitting with grim speed, the train rattling loosely on its journey through the night ». At its most potent, the personal past enthrals a McLaverty character, as it does Annie in « The Schooner » who lives in the daily and yearly hope that her husband of three months who went to sea years before and never returned, presumed drowned by her relations, will come back to his Rathlin Island home. The futility of her patience is imaged in the symbolic re-enactment of the husband's loss when Annie permits a boy visiting the island from Belfast to sail the model schooner her husband made — for her it has become a private and poignant symbol — and it is washed out of the harbour and vanishes. Captivation by the past is almost invariably in McLaverty's stories captivation by a blurred sense of that personal loss the past entails. On occasions a narrator by telling the anecdote that is the story re-discovers part of his past — a kind of submerged geography, lost or sunken island, re-charted on the map of consciousness — and in so doing reaches the brink of understanding what it is that has been lost. Unlike real-life anecdotes told to entertain, the narrator's anecdote is, we feel, being told for the first and last time, for its progress is indistinguishable from the growing, painful and enriching sense of self-discovery felt by the narrator. Yet in McLaverty the approaching self-discovery is never quite fulfilled, either because obliqueness and understatement are McLaverty's formal preference in this matter or because the essentially private nature of the self-discovery forbids too public and direct an expression (compare the diffidence of McLaverty's narrator in, say, « Pigeons » with the brashness of Frank O'Connor's narrator in, say, « My Oedipus Complex »). Both are likely the case. In any event, such stories use the past to colour a present that is more private than public. This is paradoxically true of « The Poteen Maker ». In the death of Mr. Craig, the retired, small-town schoolteacher who had once taught the narrator the secret of distillation in the disguise of a Science lesson on evaporation and condensation, we sense the passing of a whole way of life, but a way of life that precisely allowed greater privacy and freedom for eccentricity and charming inefficiency than the progress that threatens the world the narrator now inhabits :

On my way out of the town — I don't live there now — I passed the school and saw a patch of new slates on the roof and an ugly iron barrier near the door to keep the home-going children from rushing headlong on to the road. I knew if I had looked at the trees I'd have seen rusty drawing-pins stuck into their rough flesh. But I passed by. I heard there was a young teacher in the school now, with an array of coloured pencils in his breast pocket.

As a creator of character, McLaverty is happier with children than with adults, though a successful compromise is for him to have a grown-up narrator remember his boyhood. A riskier device, but one that comes off in that excellent story « Pigeons », is to have a young narrator recall recent events in his own vocabulary and youthful tone. The result, which might have been a patronizing and coy story, is in « Pigeons » a memorable piece of poignant ventriloquism. More than half of McLaverty's stories primarily concern children, and the writer is — as befits the schoolteacher he was for his working life — entirely at home in the private world of childhood. If the past as theme and setting, submerged beneath the bullying demands of the present, is in accord with an extension of Frank O'Connor's theory that the short story is a genre of and about « submerged population groups », so too is McLaverty's cast of children, since children could be thought of as one of O'Connor's submerged populations. McLaverty's youngster is psychologically if not actually an only child — « The Circus Pony » is unusual in its noisy childhood camaraderie — and inhabits lonely stretches of imaginative terrain from beyond which come (as obscure threats) garbled or uncomprehended signals from the foreign and public world of the adult (« *They took the land from the people ... God cursed them* »). Rathlin Island off the northern coast of Antrim, where McLaverty spent some of his own childhood, has been with its lonely cliffs, tarns and mountainy paths a perfect setting for the insulated lives of his child characters who graduate into adulthood with the greatest reluctance and the scantest understanding. Often they travel from noisier Belfast to the silences of Rathlin as though travelling from the public to the private or from the present to a physically timeless world, at once past and present. Such a landscape McLaverty's characters forsake only by external compulsion, as in « The Game Cock » and « Uprooted », or by internal compulsion, as in « Look at the Boats » or by mysterious compulsion, as in « The Schooner », but never do they forsake it willingly or happily. This is what makes « The

White Mare » so painful and so characteristic, for in this story an old man's stubborn fidelity to the land is sabotaged by his sister who betrays his white mare's comparable fidelity by selling her behind the old man's back. On the other hand, « The Wild Duck's Nest » is a brief story of triumphant fidelity, for the wild duck whose nest on Rathlin Island young Colm discovers and whose single egg he caresses does not, despite the bullying chant of his friend Paddy (« You had it in your hand ! ... She'll forsake it ! She'll forsake it ! She'll forsake it ! »), desert her nest, but returns to lay a second egg. The private joy of boyhood nestles safe amidst a larger and vulgar world of betrayal and conflict as the duck's eggs nestle safe amidst the soddy islets, sighing reeds and the prying attention of such as Paddy. It is as if the wild duck is the boy's secret sharer as he goes his own way in the quiet exile of the imagination.

In a fashion that shrinks the possible scope of his canvas, McLaverty's characters seem to pass directly from childhood to old age, leapfrogging the years of strength and accomplishment when imagination might be fruitfully wedded to realistic self-assessment. The youths in his fiction who have crossed into the adult and public world, such as Johnny in « Pigeons » and Alec in the novel *Call My Brother Back* (1939), both of whom « died for Ireland » during the Troubles of the 1920's, seem prematurely, almost preternaturally old. With old people the writer has nearly as much empathy and gift for creation as with children ; his old people, indeed, inhabit a kind of childhood and are pathetic even when, as in « Mother and Daughter », « Six Weeks On and Two Ashore » and « Stone », they are not attractive individuals. Always, to the point of sentimentality, McLaverty conceives his submerged population of the old in compassion and understanding. Aunt Suzanne in the story of that title takes privacy to the length of secretiveness in the home of her brother-in-law where she has been brought to look after the children of her dead sister. Her furtive drinking in her locked bedroom is an escape from loneliness and the pain of her deformed leg but when discovered by her brother-in-law leads, in a scene of Dickensian sentimentality — from which it is rescued only by the alacrity with which her youngest nephew apparently disremembers her departure — to her banishment from his hearth.

It is in the privacy of the hearth that many frail attempts at happiness are made by McLaverty's characters, though most of the characters seem ready to settle for humdrum contentment. McLaverty is on top of his material when creating domesticity which he implicitly defines in the homeliest sense : only rarely, in the relationship of Frank and Delia Coady in « Six Weeks On and Two Ashore » for instance, does McLaverty broach sexuality as a source of anguish or fulfilment. The innocent propriety of his characters is doubtless to some extent an authentic reflection of life among devout Catholics (the husband in « After Forty Years » tells his wife it would have been *impossible* for him to have been in love with the young fellow-teacher he is recalling, « and she with a wedding ring on her finger ») and it is arguable that McLaverty is merely respecting the privacy of his characters when it comes to matters sexual. But equally there is little doubt that McLaverty has to some extent connived at that burdensome propriety by failing to explore alternative ways of thinking and feeling and acting, ways that already existed in reality among the people who are his fictional models, or to interpret less neutrally the writer's task, seeing it not merely as one of recording but also of shaping, transmuting, pressing in imagination and thought outwards and onwards (in « After Forty Years, » for example, we are hardly meant to regret that the husband did not declare his love for a married woman, but are merely pointed in the direction of vaguely wishing that things might have been different).

On other family affairs McLaverty's loving eye is capable of sporting a shrewd and ironic glint. The titular hero in « Father Christmas » is a timid and obsequious little man who is coaxed by his wife to wear a bowler hat to an interview for the job of Santa Claus in a department store, a job applied for by the local and becapped unemployed. He is the kind of fellow who voluntarily removes a sticky caramel paper from the store manager's heel (a characteristically McLaverty detail) and when given the job cannot bring himself to complain that the boots he has been issued are painfully too small. He carries his public humiliation determinedly home to his wife and children, where his rage is melted by a hot fire and a wife whose clever flattery barely hints at a domestic tyranny that makes of Santa's hearthside a dubious harbour. Less subtly dubious is the reward of the titular heroine in « The Mother » who resists tyranny of the opposite kind, that of a selfish suitor who seeks to seduce her from her hearth. When the widow chooses over the suitor a conviction that she can turn a cramped domestic life with two demanding children and a father in the workhouse into some kind of happiness, she does so in the deeper anguish of surmised hopelessness.

Yet when domesticity is spurned, as young Peter cheerlessly spurns it in « Look at the Boats », one feels no guarantee that freedom has been attained. McLaverty's people inhabit spaces that are essentially private, be they house, classroom, field or train carriage (the widow in « The Mother » manages to make even of the workhouse a place safe from the prying eyes and ears of the everpresent neighbours), and beyond them the larger world exists only as a confused message or conjecture (1). In Belfast young Peter reads aloud « the enormous black letter printed on the shipping sheds : G-L-A-S-G-O-W, L-I-V-E-R-P-O-O-L, H-E-Y-S-H-A-M. » For McLaverty the writer as well as for young Peter, these places exist only as labels in Belfast, and we do not follow Peter at story's end past the Copeland Lighthouse on his way to England and an unknown fate. The Belfast shipping sheds are an apt symbol of the limits of McLaverty's geographic spread and his reluctance to leave the privacy of Ulster as his fictional universe. While it would imply a resonance he does not achieve to say that McLaverty instead of imagining what lies the far side of the shipping sheds has struck, in the manner of Seamus Heaney's Irish pioneers, « Inwards and downwards », it is certainly true that McLaverty has made of Rathlin Island and the back streets of Belfast the « important places » Patrick Kavanagh made of Mucker and Shancoduff. In McLaverty one has the impression of despised and overlooked people, places and events raised into art with almost the ministering devoutness a missionary raises into spirituality despised and overlooked primitives in some remote corner of the world, and for the writer one has the admiration reserved for those who self-impose some privation or other in the service of a higher ideal, in McLaverty's case the modest, crafted story that gently vibrates with the larger meanings of art.

The name of Turgenev is sometimes mentioned in connection with McLaverty, but though the Irishman shares the Russian's deceptive simplicity and has a similar eye for rural detail, he does not have Turgenev's spaciousness nor the dominating awareness maintained by Turgenev's sportsman. To mention Frank O'Connor, Liam O'Flaherty and *Dubliners* is to illuminate portions of McLaverty's canon of stories, but one feels uneasy about imposing public influences upon what seems to have been a rather private, even lonely movement towards an odd breed of excellence. If McLaverty is parochial in form as well as theme, it is in the praiseworthy sense championed by Patrick Kavanagh (2). The public issues of Irish life are sometimes there in the stories, but are so mutely, obliquely, even ironically. The universality of war is far more important in « Uprooted » than the specific war intended — is it World War One or World War Two ? — and the universal pain of having one's local roots destroyed far more important than the universality of war. In « Father Christmas », urban unemployment is but a shadowy though necessary presence. Indeed, in McLaverty's best stories, for example « Pigeons » and « The Game Cock », McLaverty will ironically reverse or undermine an initial illusion or fantasy that is too publicly Irish for such a private visionary as the writer to accept. The governing irony in « Pigeons » is the disparity between the public abstraction « Ireland » for which Johnny dies and Frankie's mundane but life-enhancing concern for the safety of the pigeons he has inherited from his dead brother. « The Game Cock » registers the uncle's vengeful satisfaction that the cruel Ascendancy fell, but in the chanting of an essentially private repetition of his satisfaction by his homebound nephew (« *They took the land from the people* ») is hinted a great emptiness of spirit, a sense of opportunity tragically squandered by the boy's own people, perhaps even the notion of a lost paradise (3).

This is not to say that McLaverty abandons the Northern Catholics, especially the poor countrymen and slum-dwellers, who seem to constitute for him a hidden Ireland beneath the public surface (always offstage) of Protestant Ulster, a leaderless and submerged population cut off from their southern compatriots who have now, one feels, grown foreign to them : often we overhear McLaverty's children being taught, like the devout in penal times being reminded by the fugitive priest of their faith, chants and sayings about Ireland which seems so distant a country as to be imaginary. Yet — perhaps because of this indeed — stories like « Pigeons » and « The Game Cock » arguably install a myth of the beauty and freedom of the Irishry less vulnerable and more poetic than the more public myths of manifest Irish destiny and inevitable Irish unity which McLaverty silently abandons. If he seems a diffident champion of his Ulster Catholic heritage, it is because his priority is the human heart whose corners are inaccessible to the affairs of kings

and state, for even when such affairs cause grief, as they do in
« Pigeons » and « Uprooted », it is the exclusive privacy of grief,
the heart's self-nourishing, that begs McLaverty's attention.
When the old man in « Uprooted » returns to the farm he was
forced by the army to quit, he finds the old familiar landmarks
razed in the interests of an airstrip and stands amidst a lifeless
vacancy ; the story ends with his eyes resting on the untouched
church and the white headstones in the graveyard, the last,
solitary and private reminders of his loss and of his final end.
Vacancy does not normally worry McLaverty's people overmuch
since their private worlds they carry with them. So many of them
in any case spend their time rummaging on « waste ground », a
forgotten people inhabiting barren edges of Belfast, only
exceptionally conscious of their social privation (the present
Troubles have since helped to re-discover them as the Troubles of
the 1920's did not), but also a people perversely content to be
forgotten if they are to be remembered only by their Protestant
fellow-northerners. More often they are conscious of the private
losses that inspire their creator's elegiac stories. Occasionally one
of them will have the arrogance to try and make his private world
public and enduring but McLaverty, in a teacherly manner that
reveals the limits of his own rebellion against the human
condition, undeceives him. Old Jamesy Heaney in « Stone » fears
anonymity after death and taunted for his childlessness decides
to have his name endure, inscribed on what he plans to be the
largest stone monument in the graveyard, larger even than the
locally famous McBride stone : « It would be his stone that the
people'd talk about when he'd be gone ; and visitors to the island
would look at it and read the name, James Heaney ; a great man
they'd whisper amongst themselves ! ». But his name in such a
form is destined to be merely a futile talisman, as private in his
mental repetition of it as the words that hypnotize Sister Clare
and the narrator of « The Game Cock ». A momentous storm
strikes the island and when old Heaney visits the graveyard after
it subsides he finds a change as great as that found by the old
man at the end of « Uprooted ».

Outside the graveyard on the hill he halted. Slyly he walked
to the gate and entered. And then his eyes bulged and he
stiffened with awe. He looked for the McBride stone ; it was
gone ; a great vacancy held the sky. The monument lay in

fragments on the top of the grave and crosses were tilted or blown down.

Slowly Jamesy backed away. His eyes stared at the great carnage of stone. He left the gate open and made off for home again. The dog stood sideways on the top of the hill, waiting for him to turn, but he went on and on, going quickly, afraid to look back, while behind him the children screamed in delight as they gathered the sticks washed up on the stormy shore.

The storm is McLaverty's answer to a character who tries to transgress the boundaries of his creator's fictional universe. Jamesy Heaney is left for the moment without even a private world because he attempted to gain a public one, and is mocked by the figures of the children, content with this godsend until they grow into a more personal, less merited loss.

# NOTES

1. Unlike many Irish writers, McLaverty shows no interest in the public house. Of the stories I have read, only « Aunt Suzanne » uses the public house as a setting, and then it only occupies the attention of a five-line paragraph and is clearly another private space (neither patrons nor barmen are glimpsed).

2. Like Kavanagh, McLaverty commemorates the vitality of Ulster colloquialisms and dialect words but which in McLaverty's case belong to a linguistic area north of Kavanagh's Monaghan : dunt, barge — for scold — clabbery, slutthery, throughother, etc.

3. I discuss « Pigeons » and « The Game Cock » more fully in *Forces and Themes in Ulster Fiction*, 1974.

# FROM LISTOWEL WITH LOVE :
# JOHN B. KEANE AND BRYAN MacMAHON

Patrick RAFROIDI

Listowel is probably the most widely known of all Irish small towns, partly because « Writers' Week » has given the world a timely reminder that it was the home of George Fitzmaurice, Maurice Walsh, Brendan Kennelly and a few more, partly because the principal of its national school was, from 1941 to 1975, no less a man than Bryan Mac Mahon, and also because the owner of one of the many pubs to be visited there is John B. Keane.

The two men have one or two things in common apart from their geographical origin. Keane was Mac Mahon's pupil, like everyone in Listowel and quite a few in the rest of Ireland and the United States. Both also share certain North Kerry characteristics, even if they are not quite the same, together with the fact that their fame rests on genres other than the short story : Bryan Mac Mahon's most recent successes have been a novel (dramatised later) : *The Honey Spike* (1), a genuine picaresque narrative set among the tinkers, and a translation from the Irish : *Peig*, the autobiography of Peg Sayers of the Great Blasket Island (2), while John B. Keane's main impact has been as a playwright from *Sive* (3) to *The Crazy Wall* (4) through *Many Young Men of Twenty* (5), *The Field* (6) and over a dozen more plays. Both finally have come or come back of late to story-telling, Keane with a whole series, on which more details will be given anon, Bryan Mac Mahon with a collection — *The End of the World and*

*Other Stories* (7) which reprints former pieces from *The Lion Tamer* (8) and *The Red Petticoat* (9) but also contains material not yet published in book form.

Here, however, the parallel should cease, in favour of one of those academic oppositions that even French scholars no longer dare attempt since the New Mandarins have taken over and that yet, in this case, must prove illuminating.

For, to start with, no two authors provide such clear-cut examples of the Dionysian and the Apollonian : *vide* the wild Bacchic spontaneity which animates John B. Keane's *Letters — of a Successful T.D.* (1967), *of an Irish Priest* (1972), *of an Irish Publican* (1974), *of a Love-Hungry Farmer* (id.), *of a Matchmaker* (1975), *of a Civic Guard* (1976), *of a Country Postman* (1977) — as well as the accompanying series (not, however, in epistolary form) made up of *Strong Tea* (1963), *The Gentle Art of Matchmaking* (1973), *Is the Holy Ghost Really a Kerryman ?* (1976) (10), and the quiet, subdued mood, the discreet classicism which schoolmaster Mac Mahon cultivates, even though his readers have learnt to regard his still waters with a wary eye.

This first contrast should ultimately be to the advantage of the latter ; but it does not, for all that, imply condemnation of the former (at least not in our opinion, for high-brow critics have little to say in favour of the 'popular' author Keane). Being 'of the people', John B's art is in fact very much in touch with that of the storytellers of the past, and of all those Irishmen of to-day, those wonderful talkers and over-imaginative narrators that you meet in pubs and elsewhere. 'Stage-Irish'? Undoubtedly. But perhaps it is high time to remind our Hibernian friends that in the eyes of all sympathetic and yet objective foreigners at least being 'stage'does not imply being fundamentally less 'Irish'. Such popular art does not, it is true, shine through literary nuance and it is no difficult task to isolate passages, in John B. Keane's works, where comedy or melodrama intrude in a rather ponderous way.

It is quite understandable, for instance, that one should prefer Shaw's handling of the Pygmalion myth to this more vulgar version of it, from *Letters of an Irish Parish Priest* (11) :

The High Valleys,
Lochnanane.

Dear Father O'Mora,

I am a married woman whose family is done for and all gone
their ways abroad in the world from their home in the High
Valleys. My husband and I were always united and happy until
two months ago he got a parcel from his brother Martin in
Chicago. First I thought the contents was a rubber boat or the
like but I found out in time it was a rubber woman that could
be pumped up with air or filled with warm water until it
became the size and shape and colour of a fine figure of a
young woman exactly the same in appearance as Dolores
Viago, the famous film star that was in voyage to mars. She
has glass eyes, dark with long lashes exactly the same as the
real Dolores and when she is squeezed she sighs like a real
person from some gadget under her oxter. My husband has
gone crazy over her, taking her to bed and talking to her
and buying the like of a watch for her and some nice clothes
and underwear. I do not know what to do Father. There are
more cases than me here in the High Valleys which was always
a holy and contented place where the Rosary is never missed
in any house even still but he puts Dolores Viago in the
trimmings and puts her alongside him and says a decade in a
woman's voice, by the way it would be her talking. He answers
in his own voice and I answer too for the sake of quietness.
Others have their false women too but it was my brother-in-
law Martin that sent the first one. Then they all started
writing for one. I only saw one other. She is the image of
Mrs. Freddie Fox-Pelley who rides the horses on T.V. except
she hasn't a stitch of clothes on her.

Will you guide us Father out of this evil pass. Pray for us
Father. Our men are shoving into the years and are turning
a bit foolish. Frighten them Father know would they forget
this nonsense.

Yours faithfully,
Noreen Hannassy (Mrs.).

Or that the following episode should not strike anyone as better than *Clochemerle* :

The Elms,
Louchnanane.

Dear Father O'Mora,

I have never troubled you up to this but I feel that you are the only one I can turn to. I am, as you probably know, a spinster and I live in retirement here at the Elms with my housekeeper Josephine Lalor.

Recently a local drunkard, Sammy Seller has been causing me some annoyance and embarrassment not to mention the embarrassment he causes other people. I cannot quite bring myself to tell you what it is wrong but I suppose I had better begin somewhere.

On his way home he persists in urinating at the entrance to the avenue leading to my house. He exposes himself for long periods and even when the children are on their way home from school or old ladies are passing he refuses to button himself. It is all dreadfully embarrassing and I am afraid to go to the Guards in case they might expect me to act as a witness to this sordid and revolting business. You are the one person I feel I can trust.

The other evening he was there so long that my housekeeper Josephine went down the avenue. I feel I oughtn't tell you how she addressed him but it has to be told.

'Get out of here you tramp', she screamed at him. 'and stop showing off your dirty oul' drumstick while you're urinating.'

'That's what it's for', he called back at her, 'for urinating. That's what I got it for. It helps get the water out'. What are we to do, Father ? Please help us.

Sincerely yours,
Cliona O'Gairca. (12)

It is also likely that you will feel rather embarrassed if you have cried over the letter John Bosco Mc Lane, the 'Love-Hungry Farmer' wrote to his friend Frank O'Dell just before he shot himself. It does serve its sentimental purpose, but the style is completely out of keeping with character and situation, and the final verdict is bound to be one of inflated mawkishness.

Tubberganban House,
Tubberganban.

My dear Frank,

I am going to seed. I no longer care. I no longer worry. Before me is a bottle of whiskey and whatever the night may bring. We have been long-time friends you and I and one of my great regrets is that we did not see more of each other since our schooldays. The cold wind of winter howls without and harries the sedge and willow and I dearly wish that I had sons to share my fireside and a sweet wife to share my bed. To-day I gave some schoolgirls a lift as far as Killarney where I went to purchase whiskey. I wonder if they will ever know how deeply they gashed my last vestiges of pride. I doubt if they could ever grasp the extent of my humiliation as I listened to them titter and giggle in the seat behind me. None of the three would sit in the front seat. You would swear I was some kind of dirty old man. Sometimes the tittering and the giggling erupted into unbridled scoffing and laughing. I was glad when they left the car. I watched them as they threw backward looks at me and covered their open mouths with their palms. I hope the days hold fine for them. So this is what I now am, the butt of schoolgirls who know my plight and who are too young to have pity. They see me as I am. They know but they don't know everything.

They don't know the crying, whimpering loneliness of nights without end, the barrenness of summer days when all the world is singing but one has no note left to join in. They don't know the woeful futility of trying to grasp the evasive wisp which is the loveliness and beauty of women. Only my God and I know what my hell is like.

Oh woman why are you so merciless, so heedless, so thoughtless ? What heinous crime have I committed that I should be sentenced to misery by your lack of concern, your lack of compassion. What awful unknown misdeed have I unwittingly perpetrated to incur your eternal failure to understand a man's need. Oh the good you could do with the slightest effort. You hold the key to the happiness and hope of outcasts like myself. Without you there can be nothing. The door to love is barred and bolted by your lack of comprehension.

And now Frank the flames in the hearth reach higher into the chimney. A lone bright spark is swept upwards by the draught.

Oh sprightly bright spark retain your fire and mount the midnight wind. Ride the heavens and circle the seas till you alight upon the lap of a lonely heart like mine. Somewhere, somehow, there has to be someone who would understand and care. The whiskey is gone to my head. The truth is I don't care anymore.

I don't matter anymore. I don't count and if I don't matter nothing matters, nothing whatever. If I don't count nothing counts. I hope you understand Frank. I will not be writing to you again. My deep love to your good self and to all your care.

> Your old schoolmate,
> John Bosco McLane. (13)

The fastidious critic may well turn up his nose at this, but the fact remains that, here as elsewhere, there is an enormous vitality, that vitality which is the mark of a true writer even if, to be great, he must also bank up its flow, as it were, and restrain its vehicle of expression. What a pity John B. Keane doesn't take his time, at least with his pot-boilers ! If he had written fewer of those and more stories of the type collected in *Death Be Not Proud* (14), his status would be quite different.

It might be interesting, to work out this point, to compare the passage just quoted and « The Hanging » (15) where the situation is basically the same but where the careful technique erases all excess : the minute time-pattern, the description of the dangling body through a child's consciousness, the awesome economy of words. Besides, John B. Keane manages, within the frame of thirteen small pages, to delve into the spirit of collectivity as well as of the individual, and he is obviously better at that.

*Death Be Not Proud* is a fascinating collection to compare with the author's plays whose main themes are taken up, from the realistic description of the peasant's hunger for the land (« Death

Be Not Proud », « The Fort Field ») reminiscent of *The Field*, to the interest in the supernatural (« 'You're on Next Sunday'») that already appeared in *Sharon's Grave* (16).

« The Change » deserves, perhaps, a special mention. It is also a perfect story born of a very fleeting image (a sports car stops for a second in an Irish village, a girl steps out to change her clothes and reveals part of her beautiful body, the change of clothes changes the lives of all the staring villagers), retaining instantaneousness and yet having duration. But it is worthy of mention for another reason : it symbolizes one of Keane's fundamental attitudes.

In an interview he gave in 1975 (17), Bryan Mac Mahon is reported to have said something like :

> Our problem is how to achieve the mating of Peig Sayers with the pilot of a jumbo jet.

Yet, Bryan Mac Mahon can be suspected of having much more interest in Peig than in the jet. Although he obviously doesn't reject change out of hand, he gives the impression that his heart is in the past, the Gaelic past of glory, and his reaction to the great feud about what the second Irish television channel should be was typical. Should B.B.C. be chosen, he prophesied that

> Abdication of everything concerning our national identity would be the outcome (18).

I have no idea what John B. Keane's personal position is on this particular problem or on the compulsory teaching of Irish which his senior countryman defends in the same interview. But I remember a Brendan Behan-like outburst by one of his characters in *Many Young Men of Twenty* (19).

> Well, we don't give a tinker's curse about the Civil War or your damn politics, or the past. The future we have to think about (...)
> Keep the Irish language and find jobs for the lads that go to England. Forget about the Six Counties and straighten out the twenty-six first.

Change is evidently one of John B. Keane's main concerns and,

as for his place in the Irish tradition, it definitely is, not only
with the storytellers of old, but with the wicked satirists, the
ancient pioneers of 'la contestation'.

What a difference when we turn again, for good, to Bryan Mac
Mahon and not from this point of view only.

Here we have a meticulous artist who could even, at times, be
reproached with overpolishing his pieces. They occasionally read
like passages in an anthology of 'proses' and 'unseens' :

> When they came out of the station they saw the trees. From an
> old oak depended the tattered remnants of summer finery now
> eked out in ragged brown bunting ; a mendicant beech held out
> in emaciated hands the last of its unspent coppers, the furze
> was flecked with in-between-season gold.
> (...)
> Under their feet it was prune and orange and vermilion, with
> sometimes a lichen blazing up in a brilliant green. The leathery
> heather swished hungrily around their boots. The large white
> bones of fallen and stripped trees were flung here and there in
> the campus of the cutaway. The sun had bleached them and
> the wind had antlered them... (20)

Bryan Mac Mahon is a traditionalist, and not solely in matters
of style. He also cultivates myths, both classical, like the myth
of Eurydice movingly revived in « The Gap of Life » (21), and
Irish, as in « King of the Bees » (22) where the Celtic and the
Graeco-Roman combine to remind us of the spirit of a short-story
by another 20th century humanist, from the neighbouring isle
this time, E.M. Forster's « Other Kingdom ». The scene is a very
ordinary one : a pub, once again, where a young red-haired
travelling-man has placed a bet with the villagers that he could
summon all the bees of the neighbourhood ; ordinary remarks are
passed too, but then gradually the setting changes to provide for
the voice of prophecy and the miracle :

> Villagers continued to enter : they resembled actors entering on
> cue to take part in the climax of a drama. In the silence that
> followed an old man shut his hanging hips and said loudly :
> « Once every century he comes ! King Maoibu of the Bees is
> born again ! » (23)

After which the mysterious youngster who has « the curse o' the road on him » will duly disappear into the unknown.

> Standing at the hall doorway the women watched him go. He passed under the bee-skip, then shrugged himself free of houses and faced for the bluff beyond which outer Ireland lay prone (24).

But what is even more striking and perhaps, more surely than anything else, places the author in a literary world different from Keane's and, indeed, from that of to-day in general, is his lack of protest, the fact that he is and remains fully integrated in a universe where the physiological and spiritual laws are so binding that to question them would be for him perfectly useless and even evidence of an infantile mind.

It would be a complete mistake, however, to try and pin down Bryan Mac Mahon too closely to any of the assertions we have made. Although he may remain rooted in the past and pay only lip service to the inevitable mutations of the age, his fictional world displays a variety of interests and approaches and is not easily labelled.

Even in the first (descriptive) passage quoted above, one word, one image, resulting from the realistic observation of the country-man blot out any impression one may have of the 'purple patch`, the touch of the artist in an ivory tower. The vivaciousness and discreet dialectal edge of the dialogue reinforce this feeling.

More typical than his ability to revive them is Bryan Mac Mahon's celtic propensity and highly personal gift for transforming everything into myths as in « The End of the World » (25) where a child, taking an obscure prophecy literally, organizes an armed vigil in anticipation of the last judgment, or as in the wonderful « The Kings Asleep in the Ground » (26) where all the glory of the Gaels wells up in the souls of the prisoners, especially in the soul of the youngest captive, although he has just been overcome by despair.

As for his integration into the surrounding universe and society, it comes neither from a lack of imagination nor from sanctimonious acceptance. It is rather an assimilation of and a fusion with the forces of nature, complicity with life, repro-duction, death, a serene sensuality, a tranquil love. Certainly not the integration of the complacent yes-man, but rather that of the sage.

# NOTES

1. New York, Dutton, 1967 ; London, Bodley Head, 1967.
2. Dublin, Talbot Press, 1973.
3. Dublin, Progress House, 1959.
4. Dublin & Cork, Mercier Press, 1974.
5. Dublin, Progress House, 1961.
6. First performed 1965 ; Dublin, Progress House, 1966.
7. Dublin, Poolbeg Press, 1976.
8. Toronto, Macmillan, 1948 ; London, Dent, 1958.
9. New York, Dutton, 1955 ; London, Macmillan, 1955.
10. All titles : Mercier Press.
11. Pp. 65-6.
12. Pp. 46-7.
13. *Letters of a Love Hungry Farmer*, Dublin & Cork, Mercier Press, 1974, pp. 87-8.
14. *Death Be Not Proud and Other Stories*, Dublin & Cork, Mercier Press, 1976, 94 pp.
15. Id., pp. 25, foll.
16. Dublin, Progress House, 1960.
17. 'Elgy Gillespie talks to... Bryan Mac Mahon`, *The Irish Times*, Thursday, August 14, 1975, p. 8.
18. Id, ibid.
19. Robert Hogan, ed. : *Seven Irish Plays*, Minneapolis, 1967, p. 404.
20. Bryan Mac Mahon : « Ballintierna in the Morning » in *The End of the World*, Dublin, Poolbeg Press, 1976, pp. 24-5.
21. Same collection.
22. Id.
23. Id., pp. 129-130.
24. Id., p. 132.
25. Id., pp. 7, foll. (title-story).
26. Id.

# PATRICK BOYLE'S TRAGIC HUMANITY

## Henri-Dominique PARATTE

The world of Patrick Boyle exudes at the same time deeply humane impressions, and the constant feeling that human life — whether in Ireland or elsewhere — is a grim, cruel and tragic game, that matches the strife in the animal kingdom, that hovers constantly between cruelty and innocence. The Irish quality in Boyle's stories has little to do with fear of the supernatural, with that « deep core of superstition and fear of the unknown, going back through the centuries » (1), that gave birth to so many Irish tales of terror, that other side of those gross exaggerations in Irish comedy that begot the stage Irishman and his followers. Most of the time, the stories are centered around an individual at a time of crisis — the issue of which can be either tragic or trite —, or around a conflict between a married couple or within a whole family. All of these people are living lives any of us might live in an Irish setting. And, through the author's flair for recording Irish ways of speech, we discover a world of small towns, of villages, of isolated farms. The works of this manager of the Ulster Bank in Wexford, Eire, include a tragic novel of personal decay, *Like Any Other Man* (1966), in which James Simpson, a middle-aged district manager of a small bank in Western Ireland, a powerful ox of a man, deeply in love with young Delia, finds himself compelled to give up all types of physically exhausting activities after suffering from a retinal hemorrhage ; and collections of short stories, *At Night All Cats*

*Are Grey* (1969) (2), and *All Looks Yellow to the Jaundiced Eye* (1969).

Let us select the stories from the latter collection, and see in what kinds of environment they are set. « All Looks Yellow to the Jaundiced Eye » takes place on a farm, with mountains to the east ; « Interlude » in a small town ; « Dialogue » in a country parish on the western seaboard of Ireland ; « Rise Up, My Love, and Come Away » takes us to the Knocklangan Lake, through Ballysillon graveyard, with a scene remembered from the past taking place on the Claran strand ; « Sally » depicts a love affair in the villages of Drumkeel and Bundoran ; « Three Is Company » is set in the country, close to the sea ; and a similar setting — either small towns or villages — is to be found in most stories, except for « The Rule of Three », an adventure in Dublin at Christmastime, and « Shaybo », in which we are introduced to the homosexual life of Dublin city through discussions in an underground jakes. One major feature of Patrick Boyle as a short-story writer is a flair for unforeseen events that suddenly break the routine of a rather dull daily life.

The first striking trait is the recurring symbolism provided by animal life. This may sometimes be used for comical purposes, for instance in « The Betrayers » (3), at the beginning in particular, when Willie Nesbitt tries to tame a horse while seducing the girl Cassie at the same time, a counterpoint that will, in the long run, turn comedy into tragedy :

> The mare was a lovely creature... Cassie too looked a thorough-bred... Willie Nesbitt gave his verdict as we watched her carrying water back from the well :
> « She's a well set up wee cuddy, all right. As neat a pair of hocks as you'd wish to see. They're two of a kind, herself and the pony » (4).

Such words will indeed prove true, although not in the sense that Willie Nesbitt hoped for : the pony will, in the end, run free, because at the same time Cassie started betraying him with a local policeman, a man he does not hesitate to compare to a brute beast :

> Yon man's only half-human, that's what he is. With a mane of hair as thick as a badger's running down the small of his back.

He would put you in mind of a stinking old conger squirming about in the bottom of the boat, trying to jook every belt you make at him with the butt of the tiller before you'd give him the sea-bed (5).

There is a high degree of animal savagery in man and in woman, and this often comes to light in a love-hate relationship. The young girl in « Go Away, Old Man, Go Away » keeps teasing her old husband in a most cruel fashion, doing nothing to hide the fact that she prefers the young lovers she runs to at night, playing nookey along the banks of the river. Mrs Kipoor in « Square Dance » has chosen a similar type of activity, as though the animal life of man was to take place outside respectable social commitments. Her daughter, on the other hand, is described by one of the characters as « a class of a watchdog » (6). Mr Hunter, a comic middle-class character, is described to us as a creature close to a squirrel, « small, weak and inoffensive » (7), although we are warned that the turn of events may in the long run prove tragic, as :

... in squirreldom the impotence of the weak is their most dangerous weapon (8).

For, despite humor, tragedy has the final say in most of the stories, and the animal world is often used to reinforce the violence building up from the start. The best instance of this is the unrelenting movement towards suicide that takes place in « All Looks Yellow to the Jaundiced Eye ».

We know, from the start, that something is wrong, but we are plainly unable to see what it is, and so is the narrator :

It is curious how the first manifestations of disaster can pass unnoticed (9).

We are immediately thrust into that ambiguous space where man loses his bearings, where he experiences feelings that coincide with the weather, and with the reactions of the animals to it. The uneasiness shown by the cows, the sulky behaviour of the sheep, the unrelenting heat-wave do add to the overall impression that something is not as it should be. A lost man confronting Fate has little chance of knowing what will happen.

The very landscape achieves a blurring effect :

> Shimmering spirals rose from the baking ground distorting the landscape so that all clarity and sharpness of outline were lost (10).

Other forerunners (11) can be noted, and the more we feel an impending doom threatening the main character, the more the animal world reacts to it, in strange, unpredictable ways :

> ... I noticed the peculiar flight patterns of the birds... Of course there was no significance to the erratic behavior of wild creatures. But still (12).

The flight of the birds is followed by an ominous scene in which rabbits skip, caper, leap and dance in erratic ways, before a clearer warning is issued by that surprising prophet, a blind sentinel rabbit stamping the ground. This is followed by a worse omen :

> This strange immobility was disquieting. I could presage something much more alarming (13).

This silence looks indeed like the silence of death after the frantic activity that comes before the end : and it is hardly surprising that the series of murders taking place in the story start then, with the inexplicable, senseless murder of the rabbit by the dog, a murder which Boyle describes, without passion, without any personal intervention, but with a neutral realism — that we shall find in other stories, like « Rise Up, My Love, and Come Away », or « The Rule of Three » — :

> There was a flurry of tiny vicious paws. A yelp of pain. A second's pause as the dog sprang back, shaking its head violently. Then it pounced. Pinned the rabbit to the ground. Mauled it fiercely, until all struggle ceased. Grabbed it by the neck and shook the limp body furiously from side to side, only desisting when flesh and fur came away in its teeth (14).

Coming back to his farm under the blazing sun, the man is caught up, little by little, in a mysterious frenzy that prompts

him to kill the rooster, then a hen, then the dog Bran, as if
something had to be done, as though an urgent purpose had to
be fulfilled :

Twice more I brought the flailing blade down on the dog's skull
before the awful howling was silenced. And twice more again
before the hind legs stopped twitching (15).

Similar examples of cruelty towards animals can be found in
other stories : the epic fight between the badger and the dogs in
« Meles Vulgaris » ends with a scream of agony from the
wounded badger that keeps resounding in the mind of a middle-
class husband in bed with his wife :

Lying wide-eyed and sleepless, he tried to close his ears to the
appalling sound. It was no use. The voice of the dying badger
refused to be silenced.
For all these years it had resounded in his memory with the
urgency of a trumpet call — the wild defiant shout of an
animal ringed about with enemies (16).

There may be in this use of the animal world a deep feeling
that there is a similarity between a life in which fighting and
solitude are the rule, and human life, in which the union of two
persons is the basic expression of the love-hate relationship that
cannot break solitude, although it is a necessary fact of life,
despite the many frustrations that it creates. This parallel is
clearly stated while the dogs fight with the badger, in that old
primitive ritual which does not make sense from a rationalistic
perspective :

If both had not been so mired and bloodied — the badger's
slender elegant head being so plastered with blood and clay
that the parti-coloured striping could no longer be discerned — they could have been tricking together harmlessly. Or
dozing in the sun. Or even coupling (17).

Life is, after all, a complex of alternatives : sanity/insanity,
life/death, love/hate ; and a single moment of crisis can resolve
the human problem in a definite way. So the main character in
« All Looks Yellow to the Jaundiced Eye », before killing himself,

strangles his wife in a way that is both gentle and dispassionate, as though both could not take it any more, as though the balance of life had been broken even before the final act :

> Her grey-blue eyes, now wide with anxiety, glittered with unshed tears. Impossible to credit that these familiar and well-loved features masked the high cheekbones, the thin cruel lips, the slitted eyes, of an alien... Gently, tenderly, I shifted my hands till they gripped her neck, nipping the scream that rose building in her throat (18).

In the country in which Bridget Cleary was burnt and tortured by her husband and friends for being possessed by the fairies (19), there remains little doubt that such cruelty is possible, and that the environment, both moral and physical, has a part to play in it. Life, as Boyle sees it, can be highly comical at times, but there is always a tragic element that pervades even moments of relief, sympathy or joy. For instance, the character of Musky in « The Window » claims our sympathy, and yet he will be singled out by the preacher as an individual whose conduct is « vulgar, scandalous and intolerable » (20). He may be a stinking half-wit, and yet his exaggerated praying and his physical problems are much more human and appealing than the cold, dispassionate, scolding tone of the preacher, if only because they provide us with an opportunity for laughing, for a relief from our condition :

> If you can imagine a guinea-hen with the power of speech you will have some conception of the dramatic effect of Musky's sucked-in screech : « Gooooohhhhh ! » followed by the rest of the pious ejaculation in a loud relieved voice : « Ye big un by ! » (21).

These characters are often cast out of communities, either because of their conduct, or because of some physical peculiarity. This is the case of Andy Foster, the cobbler, in « The Port Wine Stain », who keeps being treated as a leper by adults and children alike, although the narrator tries, for a while, to make friends with him, playing cards, but not knowing how to give him some form of kindness. This was also, to some extent, the case of James Simpson in the novel *Like Any Other Man*, singled out as he was by his physical problem :

Once more Simpson recounted the onset of the first haemorrhage... The olive-green cluster of spots. The coalescence of these spots into one vivid green whole... « It was shaped like a bird. A parrot, to be exact. The comb. The beak. The tail feathers. All outlined in purple » (22).

Sometimes the peculiarity is a trait common to a whole group, making the story a highly comic one : this is in particular the case in « Myko », in which Myko Connors, a bartender and manager of a funeral undertaking business, is conned by two tinkers and left with the rotting corpse of old Maggot Feeney in his yard :

At the thought of that disreputable tomtit — never a creature of fixed abode — coiled up, in an odour of respectability, in a corner of the graveyard, with maybe a granite headstone over him erected by his sorrowing relatives, I could do nothing else, God forgive me, but laugh... (23).

At times the petty social hypocrisy that reigns in a priest-ridden country of small towns and villages becomes evident, not in an unbearable way as a socially committed writer would describe it, but in a funny manner, which a highly human story-teller knows how to tackle. In « Dialogue », a curate with progressive ideas — not supported by the arch-conservative local community — finds relief from the dogmatic rebuking of his bishop in the person of his dog :

« It seems », said the Bishop, his manner diffident, placatory, « it seems that you take the dog everywhere... ». « You even take him into the confessional box, it appears. This action is grievously resented. One lady, well-known to me for her piety and generosity, assures me that once, at confession, when she was saying the Act of Contrition, the dog poked its nose against the grill and growled at her. She was most perturbed. » He staggered forward...
« Eeeeeeeeeeooooooow ! » the dog screeched.
Father Dempsey rushed to him, chafed the lifted paw.
... He reached back with his free hand and slapped gently but firmly the Bishop's trousered legs.
« Bad Bish ! Bad Bish ! » he said. « Kicking poor Bran ! » (24)

Social mores may compel individuals to look for ingenious ways out of tricky situations. In « Interlude », Molly and Jim, surprised in an embarrassing situation by the landlady's daughter after playing nookey in Molly's bed, have no other way out than to pretend that they are engaged — and to attend the following celebrations. But, as we go along, the mock engagement quickly becomes a real one for Molly, a change of mind that Jim cannot understand, and which nearly breaks their relationship :

Impatiently I grasped her, lining with urgent hands her body against my own. I kissed her, lips mashing on teeth till the taste of blood was in my mouth. Groaning with desire, I buried my face in her hair, her neck, her rudely exposed breast whilst the blood pounded madly in my ears.
Struggling fiercely, she broke away from my arms.
« Now-now Jim », she panted, « Behave yourself ».
... I grabbed her hand.
« But why ? » I begged.
« We're engaged. That's the why » (25).

A different situation arises in « Three Is Company », in which the attitude of the man, Frank, corrupts what might have been a brief and pleasant fling on the beach. There is criticism of social life in Boyle's stories, in particular of the coldness it can create in any person : we notice it in « Sally », where the main female character plays the piano well, but without feeling, or dances like an athlete, before giving herself to a friend of her lover, dancing with him with unprecedented ease and animal grace. This coldness can be found in « Three Is Company », when Frank learns how Maeve used one of his most poetic statements for one of her cheap novels :

She had plundered his fancies for a phrase. « The fanned-out feathers of a peacock's tail ». It was to have been the spring-board for a poem. But now it must be cast aside as a cull. For it was shop-soiled. Shoddied by misuse (26).

The passion for poetry shown by Frank (but hidden from others) reveals another feature of Boyle's characters : they try, at one and the same time, to achieve some kind of relationship with others (thus fulfilling the expectations of society), while preserv-

ing a dynamic core of personal identity. When, in a love relationship, this balance is achieved to some extent by both partners,
we may fall into some modern Irish version of « marivaudage » :
in « At Night All Cats Are Grey », the main character, back
home from a pub crawl, tries to remember what happened the
night before, and ends up playing a game with his wife in which
both will be satisfied, although for different reasons : she because
he will agree to play golf with her and her best friend, he because
he wishes to carry on a love affair with her friend, started under
strange auspices the night before. Sometimes, however, we meet
a protagonist whose social situation is, by all standards,
satisfactory, but who can cope no longer with the stifling of
other, deeply personal, aspirations. In « Rise Up, My Love, And
Come Away », a young wife and mother, amazed by her own
conduct, escapes and decides that there is little in this world of
enough value to keep her from committing suicide in Knocklangan Lake :

> The wind is rising, coming in fresh from the East, flattening
> nettle, docken, and scutch grass with the rustle of starlings'
> wings. Flurries of rain come in its wake, driving the loiterers
> helter skelter through the cemetery gates. I shiver. Better for
> you to go now. Why delay ? What is there to keep you here
> any longer ? (27)

There are, indeed, unknown forces at work, that can make
human beings move like puppets. The young woman in the latter
story dresses up to go on her last errand with the greatest
possible care, and even imagines her own funeral in Ballysillon
graveyard, the social gossip around her sudden, unbelievable,
unexplainable act. But is she in the control of an external fate, or
driven by inner distress ? One story leads us to a partial answer :
« The Rule of Three », in which a young man comes to Dublin for
Christmas (a bad period indeed), and is led by a series of
coinciding events to remember the old saying of his mother that
« Everything goes by threes » (28). He tries to save a guillemot,
and fails ; then, on the same beach, fails to rescue a stranded
seal ; then misses the opportunity to spend the night with a
young woman to whom he was directed by chance alone, before
going back home and marrying a girl called Dorothy. Somehow,
he thinks, there might be a plan behind such chance sequences ;

perhaps they are intended to stir up men to act as human beings
and not from social habit :

> In some obscure way I felt that it was no accident that had
> brought the two of us together this day. It was the inexorable
> working out of a Divine Law of Numbers. A unique and never-
> to-be-repeated chance had been offered (29).

Fate is present in the religious motto on the grave in Ballysillon graveyard : « The Lord giveth and the Lord taketh
away » (30). But the quality of strangeness in Boyle's stories
comes from some unknown space, which is faced by the
protagonist in that same story :

> So what prompted me to act as I did ? What sudden impulse
> sets a body veering about like a weathercock ? (31)

That particular strangeness may be the ultimate reason which
prompts a man like Julian (Maeve's husband in « The Rule of
Three ») to spend weeks at a time drinking in village pubs ;
which prompts old men to drink, at wakes as in « Oh Death,
There Is Thy Sting-a-ling » (32), or as a habit, as the father does
in « Home Again, Home Again, Jiggety-Jig » (33) ; which
enables the old maid, in « Blessed Are the Meek », to ask her
dying mother for the signature which will enable her to draw
money from the bank, turning her last moments into a cruel
agony. Frustration, loneliness, oddity : there is much of these in
the tragic quality that pervades Boyle's works. But, at the same
time, there remains, as a solace, this deep human quality that
lets us laugh with old Shaybo in an underground jakes of Dublin
city, which turns the youngest son in « Home Again, Home
Again, Jiggety-Jig » into an ally of his father against the
pharisaic attitude of her mother and his oldest brother (who is to
be a priest), that leads the young character in « The Window » to
believe that the Apostles on the stained-glass window are not
people of his kind :

> These whey-faced men had been house-bound all their lives,
> perhaps chained to book-littered desks or to counters clotted
> with silks or furs or great bars of yellow gold. They had never
> seen a tall mast reel across the sky or heard the creak of

straining timber or felt the pulse-beat of a tiller. They had never learned the kindly tolerance of those indentured to the sea (34).

# NOTES

1. Jim McCarry, ed. : *Irish Tales of Terror*, London, Fontana Books, 1971, p. 9.

2. *At Night All Cats Are Grey* was originally published by Mac Gibbon and Kee, Ltd, London, 1966. The collection was published in paperback edition in two volumes : *At Night All Cats Are Grey, and Other Stories,* London, Panther Books, 1969, and *The Betrayers, and Other Stories*, Panther Books, 1969. References are from the paperback edition.

3. « The Betrayers » in *The Betrayers*, London, Panther Books, 1969.

4. *Ibid.,* pp. 66-7.

5. *Ibid.,* p. 101.

6. « Square Dance » in *The Betrayers*, ed. cit., p. 115.

7. « Suburban Idyll » in *The Betrayers*, p. 133.

8. *Ibid.*

9. « All Looks Yellow to the Jaundiced Eye » in *All Looks Yellow to the Jaundiced Eye*, London, Mac Gibbon and Kee Limited, 1969, p. 5.

10. *Ibid.*, p. 10.

11. Helen Creighton : *Bluenose Ghosts*, Toronto, McGraw-Hill-Ryerson, 1957, p. 1 : « Forerunners are supernatural warnings of approaching events and are usually connected with impending death ».

12. « All Looks Yellow to the Jaundiced Eye », *op. cit.*, p. 11.

13. *Ibid.*, p. 12.

14. *Ibid.*, p. 13.

15. *Ibid.*, p. 17.

16. « Meles Vulgaris » in *At Night All Cats Are Grey*, London, Panther Books, 1969, p. 106.

17. *Ibid.*, p. 99.

18. « All Looks Yellow to the Jaundiced Eye », *op. cit.*, p. 19.

19. The story of Bridget Cleary is known to be the last witch-burning in Europe ; it is commonly known as the story of the Clonmel Witch. This story, which took place in Ballyvadlea in 1895, is told in Jim McCarry, ed. : *Irish Tales of Terror, op. cit.*, pp. 54-60. Needless to say, there is no mention of fairies in Boyle's stories.

20. « The Window » in *At Night All Cats Are Grey, op. cit.*, pp. 70-1.

21. *Ibid.*, p. 69.

22. Patrick Boyle : *Like Any Other Man*, New York, Grove Press Inc., 1966, p. 269. This novel was seized by Irish customs but released after examination by the Censorship Board.

23. « Myko » in *At Night All Cats Are Grey, op. cit.*, p. 84.

24. « Dialogue » in *All Looks Yellow to the Jaundiced Eye, op. cit.*, p. 49.

25. « Interlude » in *All Looks Yellow to the Jaundiced Eye, op. cit.*, pp. 38-9.

26. « Three Is Company » in *All Looks Yellow to the Jaundiced Eye, op. cit.*, pp. 38-9.

26. « Three Is Company » in *All Looks Yellow to the Jaundiced Eye*, p. 135.

27. « Rise Up, My Love and Come Away », *Ibid.*, p. 99.

28. « The Rule of Three », *Ibid.*, p. 65.

29. *Ibid.*, p. 75.

30. « Rise Up, My Love, and Come Away », *op. cit.*, p. 87.

31. *Ibid.*, p. 91.

32. *At Night All Cats are Grey, op. cit.*

33. *Ibid.*

34. *Ibid.*, p. 72.

# JOHN McGAHERN'S « NIGHTLINES » : TONE, TECHNIQUE AND SYMBOLISM

### Terence BROWN

Thomas Kilroy, playwright and novelist, provided the critic of Irish fiction with one of those clarifying and organising generalizations which illumine much that one has almost unconsciously accepted, when he wrote in 1972 :

At the centre of Irish fiction is the anecdote. The distinctive characteristic of our « first novel », *Castle Rackrent*, that which makes it what it is, is not so much its idea, revolutionary as that may be, as its imitation of a speaking voice engaged in the telling of a tale. The model will be exemplary for the reader who has read widely in Irish fiction : it is a voice heard over and over again, whatever its accent, a voice with a supreme confidence in its own histrionics, one that assumes with its audience a shared ownership of the told tale and all that it implies : a taste for anecdote, an unshakeable belief in the value of human actions, a belief that life may be adequately encapsulated into stories that require no reference, no qualification, beyond their own selves (1).

This tone of voice, a voice redolent, despite many momentary doubts, of basic social certainties is a tone that sounds recognizably in the anecdotal fiction of William Carleton, in the tales of Somerville and Ross, later in the episodic sequences of Kavanagh's *The Green Fool*. This is a fiction that has roots in an enclosed oral culture, in the countryman's regard for the tale, for « experience passed on from mouth to mouth and intelligence that comes from afar » (2). It is a fiction that, delighting in objectivity, is undisturbed by the subjective or the psychologically complex, unless they can be embodied in concrete actions.

This Irish tone, unselfconsciously rejoicing in linguistic afflatus, survived the shift in the early twentieth century from the tale of countryside and farm, to the story set in shop, convent, school and presbytery, set in short in the *petit bourgeois* world of post-revolutionary Ireland. It survives as the dominant tone of the Irish school of short story writers, in O'Faolain, in O'Connor, in Mary Lavin. So the following opening, from an O'Faolain story, « The Old Master », is entirely characteristic of the mode :

> When I was younger, and so, I suppose, in the nature of things, a little more cruel, I once tried to express John Aloysius Gonzaga O'Sullivan geometrically : a parabola of pomposity in a rectangle of gaslight. The quip pleased everybody who knew the reference — it was to his favourite stand, under the portico of the courthouse, his huge bulk wedged into the very tall and slender doorway.
>
> I said *gaslight* because John Aloysius rarely came to work before the afternoon, when they lit the gas in the dim entrance hall, and its greenish, wateryish light began to hiss high up in the dome. There he would stand, ten times in the afternoon, smoking, or watching the traffic, or gossiping with some idling clerk. He had a sinecure in the fusty-musty little law library, a room no bigger than a box. He used to say, in his facetious way, that he left it often because he exhausted the air every half hour (3).

In this we note the slightly garrulous pleasure in the act of telling the tale ; the rhythms and syntax (« smoking, or watching the traffic, or gossiping with some idling clerk ») are those of a voice preparing for a protracted discourse, welcoming digression and expansion, proffering intimacy. This is a world that has time for anecdote, for the kind of tales in which landscape and milieu can be rendered, almost gratuitously, in passages of sustained rhythmic ease, where they are as much aspects of how the world is, in its timeless permanency, as the narrative events are the objective revelations of the unchanging vagaries of human nature. So, the Irish school of short-story writing, that an unwary critic might too readily assume to be a school of provincial realism, seems to me to have its sources in an oral culture's delight in tale-telling, in anecdote.

But while the Irish short story may have its roots in an oral culture (many of the stories seem written as much for performance as for silent reading in the arm-chair) it also begins to move away from the objectivity of tale, touched as it almost invariably is by romantic subjectivism. So, in O'Connor and O'Faolain we often encounter a central character who is a sensitive outsider in society, or he is an adolescent experiencing anguished dissatisfaction in a provincial environment. And in Mary Lavin, at her best, strangeness of incident suggests a romantic intensification of feeling amidst the small-town banalities, while in her less successful works grotesquerie of character or event hints at gothic moods.

For the young Irish writer beginning to write in the 1960's, especially the writer who chose the Irish provincial world as setting for his work, this narrative tone for an Irish fiction must have seemed inevitable as must a technique of realism tinged with romanticism. As Kilroy further reminds us :

> I am attempting here to discuss the experience of writing fiction in modern Ireland... The contemporary Irish writer of fiction must surely be aware that his local heritage differs in kind from that of an English or a French writer. Its difference has to do with the emergence of Irish fiction, both novel and short-story, from a culture which already had its native, long-standing, oral tradition of fictionalizing experience, a mode that has continued to challenge the composition of literary fiction even to the present day (4).

The case of John McGahern is exemplary. His first published novel *The Barracks* (1963) manages its fiction in a narrative tone recognisably within the tradition I have been identifying. The prose is reflective, expansive, open syntactically and rhythmically to accumulation of event, deed, detail of milieu and to narrative comment. It is a prose untroubled by doubts as to the value of its own movements and procedures as it confidently renders the way things are in the provincial milieu that is so intimately known. So *The Barracks* opens :

> Mrs Regan darned an old woollen sock as the February night came on, her head bent, catching the threads on the needle by the light of the fire, the daylight gone without her noticing. A boy of twelve and two dark-haired girls were close about her at the fire. They'd grown uneasy, in the way children can indoors in the failing light. The bright golds and scarlets of the religious pictures on the wall had faded, their glass glittered now in the sudden flashes of firelight, and as it deepened the dusk turned reddish from the Sacred Heart lamp that burned before the small wickerwork crib of Bethlehem on the mantelpiece (5).

Tone and strategy here are not so distant from the idioms and rhythms of story-telling. One notes in particular the conversationally-managed movement away from particulars to sociable generality (« They'd grown uneasy, in the way children can ») establishing an audience that is allowed to contribute its knowledge to the narration before the narrator returns with ease to the details of a specific world.

Some of McGahern's best writing is in this assured conventional mode. The implicit, uncomplicated belief in the value of recounting allows for extended passages in which the novelist possesses his world, characters in their settings, landscapes and actions, with the unselfconscious confidence of a story-teller absorbed with his material. In passage after passage in his three novels McGahern concentrates on the particularities of the Leitrim, Roscommon border-country (passages which, extracted from their context, read remarkably like the openings of Irish short-stories).

> It started to rain as he gulped his meal, the first drops loud on the pane, and it was raining steadily by the time they were on their way to the field.
>
> Between the lone ash trees, their stripped branches pale as human limbs in the rain, Mahoney worked. The long rows of the potatoes stretched to the stone wall, the rows washed on the top by the rain, gleaming white and pink and candle-yellow against the black acres of clay ; and they had set to work without any hope of picking them all. Their clothes started to

grow heavy with rain. The wind numbed the side of their faces, great lumps of clay held together by dead stalks gathered about their boots (6).

As with the conventional Irish short stories, those of O'Connor and O'Faolain, this objectivity in McGahern is somewhat disturbed by romanticism, for in his three novels the central character is a sensitive adolescent or young man whose feelings in the midst of a constricted provincial environment are the central points of interest. But the traditional temper, tones and techniques in McGahern's fictions are disturbed in a further much more important way ; McGahern is aware of an urban and fragmented culture encroaching upon the stable, provincial, rural world upon which in Ireland the anecdotal, orally-based tale ultimately depends. When the earlier writers took account, as they did occasionally, of the modern urban world it was without any real sense that the encounter with novel experience might require significant aesthetic innovations. They continued indeed to write as if literary modernism had nothing to teach them. McGahern does not.

It is evident even in his most conservative novel *The Barracks* that McGahern, while confident and skilled in portraying the provincial world he knows, recognises a need for modern Irish fiction to meet more stringent demands. It must be attentive to the recent major social changes in the country, in an art that more appropriately reflects the complex psychological currents that stir in its turbulent waters. So McGahern is consciously experimental in his work, welcoming the resonance of image and symbol to the enclosed worlds of rural and small-town Ireland, taking his protagonists away from their childhood farms and fields to the confused cultural settings of modern Dublin and London.

McGahern, as symbolist, is absorbed by the potency of ritual, particularly by the Catholic rituals associated with death, with burial and with Holy Week. In his three novels, imagery drawn from these various rites is employed to ground his fiction in a deeper sense of the way things are, than was the case in traditional Irish short stories and novels. The imagery serves to imply a metaphysical dimension to experience, unknowable except in the mysterious patterns that ritual reveals in life itself, inducing in the participants of ritual an emotional awareness of metaphysical depth. Memory and meaning, myth and mystery, passion and pattern, seem controllable for the protagonists of the novels and for the author himself only through the mediation of rite and symbol.

> Before the post-office the people knelt in the dry dust of the road for Benediction. The humeral veil was laid on the priest's shoulders, the tiny bell tinkled in the open day, the host was raised and all heads bowed, utter silence except for the bell and some donkey braying in the distance. Kneeling in the dust among the huddled crowd it was hard to fight back tears. This was the way your life was, you belonged to these people as they to you, you were linked together. One day that Sacred Host would be your burden to uphold for them while the bell rang, but it was still impossible to join in the singing as the procession resumed its way, only listen to the shuffle of boots through the dust. Wash me ye waters, streaming from His side, it was strange, all strange and the candles burning against the yew trees in the day (7).

Such moments, however, run grave tonal risks, dependent as they usually are in the novels on the imagery of a specific church and tradition. For the novelist, writing out of a culture where these images are almost unconsciously understood, must uneasily recognise that in the wider world, where he will most probably find his readers, these familiar properties will suggest not the mystery of ultimate things but the curiosity of the primitive, the exotic. So at times in McGahern's works one senses that the descriptions of rite and custom operate less as symbols than as passages of local colour. There is a note of explanatory insecurity in these passages, a tendency to tonal uncertainty.

It is in his collection of short-stories, *Nightlines* (1970), that we see McGahern attempting to resolve this problem. In this volume McGahern seeks to write short-stories exploiting symbolist possibilities without depending on the traditional metaphors of church and religion. He seeks symbols within the physical properties of his fictional environments, in event and deed. So the symbolism is unobtrusive, tonally contained within the movements of narration, without any sense of the insecurity occasioned when, as in the novels, more explicit symbolism is attempted.

McGahern's short-stories, like his novels, occupy a middle-
ground between the conservative traditionalist mode and
modernist experiment. Where O'Connor and O'Faolain wrote their
tales of enclosed provincial worlds, McGahern also senses that a
short-story must in part depend on such hermetic self-sufficiency.
But the social conditions that allowed the earlier writers to
explore a stable, self-confident Irish world no longer obtain. So
McGahern writes of artificially self-contained worlds. He sets a
story in a railway carriage, in a school, on a London-Irish
building site, in a guest-house, in a police-station, on a boat in
the middle of a lake, in an isolated house on the Mediterranean.
In most of them a sensitive central character, so familiar from
Irish fiction in general and from McGahern's novels in particular,
suffers in an unpleasing milieu. In « Wheels » an adult returns to
the pain of his provincial origins. In « Coming into his Kingdom » a child experiences the discomforts of sexual awakening.
In « Hearts of Oak and Bellies of Brass » the narrator struggles
to anaesthetise his cultural and emotional awareness with back-
breaking labour ; in « Strandhill, the Sea » the narrator is a
troubled kleptomaniac ; in « Lavin » he is an adolescent
discovering homosexual feelings and sexual disgust ; in « My
Love, My Umbrella » he is a young Dubliner enduring the
agonies of an unrequited passion, in « The Recruiting Officer » an
alcoholic, failed Christian brother, eccentric and tired rebel.

In *Nightlines* the tone of traditional Irish short-story-telling is
not entirely forsaken either. At moments, in fact, one suspects
the author's nerves fail him in his literary experimentalism and
he falls back on familiar, proved techniques. So in « Wheels », at
the opening of the collection, we encounter a very curious blend
of prose-impressionism with a structure reminiscent of a much
more direct and anecdotal kind of short story.

Grey concrete and steel and glass in the slow raindrip of the
morning station, three porters pushing an empty trolley up the
platform to a stack of grey mail-bags, the loose wheels rattling,
and nothing but wait and watch and listen, and *I listened to
the story they were telling* (my italics) (8).

Elsewhere the anecdotal Irish speaking voice is heard quite
clearly, as in so many discursive Irish tales.

There was no reason this life shouldn't have gone on for long but a stupid wish on my part, which set off an even more stupid wish in Mrs Grey, and what happened has struck me ever since as usual when people look to each other for their happiness or whatever it is called. Mrs Grey was Moran's best customer. She'd come from America and built the huge house on top of Mounteagle after her son had been killed in aerial combat over Italy (9). (« Christmas »).

McGahern's short-stories are most interesting when these tones and techniques are avoided, when the processes of his prose combine an unsentimental apprehension of the physical world with symbolist resonance and where he manages to generate the symbolic charge of his tales without dependence on the dynamism of a traditional religious or cultural symbol system. In his novels the rituals of the Church provided that charge ; in *Nightlines* McGahern turns to imagery of wheel, river, sea. The wheels of the first tale are the wheels of a train bearing a man back through his past across the Shannon and also the « ritual wheel », the repetition of a life in the shape of a story that had as much reason to go on as stop. And the collection ends with a character, who has recognised that life « is all a wheel », contemplating the Shannon as it flows to the sea. Roger Garfitt has suggested that « McGahern sometimes seems more Buddhist than Catholic » (10) and sees the imagery of the Wheel as possibly owing something to that tradition. But, if this is so it functions in a much less obtrusive way than does the Catholic imagery of the novels.

It is in the detailed interrelationship of the facts of McGahern's stories, the blend of event, physical milieu and meaning that McGahern's symbolism is least obtrusive and, I think, most effective. Each story employs one or two central images which, as Henri D. Paratte remarks, « offer a symbolic frame to his vision of reality » (11). That vision is austerely metaphysical but reductively so as the human world of desire and meaning is set against images which suggest iron physical law, machine-like inevitability, cruelty, decay, the ritual wheel which breaks all backs as it turns. The world of these stories is a world of chain-saws, hooks, chains, ice, flame, shovels, metal, shot, coffin-wood, bait, mallets, chisels, rusting tools, iron-bolts, whips with metal tips, glass inseminating plungers, knives, pumps, concrete lavatories, ticking clocks.

The framing images of each McGahern story contain within them accumulations of detail and fact which further serve to symbolise the writer's ambiguous, metaphysically bleak vision of reality, though they do so without any suggestion of overt symbolist technique. It is only on a close examination of these works that a reader realizes how far he is here from the direct, unself-conscious discourse of the traditional tale-taller, how much he is in the hands of a skilled, very self-conscious imagist. For in McGahern the moments of traditional tone distract from the modernist techniques.

« Hearts of Oak and Bellies of Brass » is a sketch of life on a building site in a London summer. The workers are Irish and the central character is a countryman who has sold his sensitivity for the dulled, unfeeling security of life as a wage-slave, which anaesthetises pain and fear of death :

I love to count out in money the hours of my one and precious *life*. I sell the hours and I get money. The money allows me to sell more hours. If I saved money I could buy the hours of some similar bastard and live like a royal incubus, which would suit me much better than as I am now, though apparently even as I am now suits me well enough, since I do not want to die (12).

His ambition is, as he puts it, « to annul all the votes in myself ». This he does in accommodating himself to the regular, monotonous violence of the building site, its gratuitously violent language, the sexual animality, the sudden eruptions of physical force. Through the story, imagery of machines plays a crucial role in establishing a sense of monotonous dehumanization. A steel hopper, metal buckets, a brass medal bearing a worker's number, the « back of the hopper bright as beaten silver in the sun » and, centrally, the sharp, silver blade of a shovel, serve as metaphors of a dangerous physical violence, a dehumanised instinctual energy in the story. The movements of the shovels further suggest the sexual drives that find release only in violence of tongue and in prostitution.

The familiar tirade would continue, predictable as the drive and throw of their shovels...
The hooter went. The offered breasts withdrew. A window

slammed. « The last round », someone said.
The mixer started. The shovels drove and threw : gravel, sand, gravel ; gravel, sand, gravel, cement (13).

The wheel of labour turns in this tale. It is sensitivity and human hope that are broken by its mechanical, grinding revolutions.

As the hopper came down again he shouted in the same time, « Shovel or shite ; shite or burst », and the shovels mechanically drove and threw... It'd go on as this all day (14).

The longest piece in the collection is « Peaches ». It is also the story where the texture of the narrative is most dense with symbolic intimations of the kind I have been identifying. The plot is fairly straightforward. A moderately successful novelist is living in a rented Spanish villa with his Northern European wife. The relationship is in crisis. Creativity is at low-ebb. Neurosis and tension dominate the conversational exchanges, while the smell of a decaying shark on the beach, referred to at various points in the work, suggests the decay of marital compatibility. But there are many other details which embody the story's meanings. The relationship is as infertile as the man's (throughout they are « He », « She ») imaginative powers. So there are frequent functionally ironic images of containers being filled to overflowing with liquid. A swimming pool is filled by a pump — « the three started to watch in the simple fascination of water filling the empty pool », water is poured into clay jars, a wine glass is filled « to the brim from the Soberano bottle », peaches in an orchard are sprayed by a « machine on metal wheels ». This latter image resonates with another important image complex in the tale — that of machines as artificial and uncreative. The pool is filled by a pump ; the woman is obsessed with the possibility of machines replacing people, electric light seems a poor substitute for the religious-sexual mystery of candle-flame, a Vespa scooter is dangerous, risky. The movement of the story in this world of significant patterns of detail can be readily studied in the passage where the couple make love. Section V111 of the piece begins with the image of the decomposing shark ; the couple take a swim and in the sea they move to sexual union. But afterwards their lovemaking on the clinical « white sheet of the bed » is crude, acquisitive. Instead of the imagery of sea where they « let

the waves loll over them » the man postpones his orgasm by
« trying to make up what each gallon cost of the load of water
that had been put in the pool that morning ». Then he « held her
close for her to pump him until she came ». The fraught tension
of their infertile, uncreative sexual coupling is then suggested in
the tense dialogue with its syntactic bluntness :

« Why do you want ? »
Our relationship would get much better.
But how would it do you good » (15).

The conversation and the section end with the machines, the
reductive images of sterility, danger, of cold metaphysical
austerity, that are the frightening equivalents of the rotting
shark, the ripe peaches proffered as tokens of lust at the story's
climax.

« We'll be happy », the man said.
Later, as he got the Vespa out of the garage, he heard the
clean taps of her typewriter come from the upstairs room (16).

The economical skill of passages such as this in *Nightlines*,
with their subtle blend of image, dialogue and action suggest the
degree to which McGahern has moved away from the expansive,
anecdotal mode of much Irish fiction to tautly economical stories
as metaphysically resonant as his novels, but without their overt
traditional symbolism and techniques.

# NOTES

1. Thomas Kilroy : « Tellers of Tales » in *Times Literary Supplement*, March, 17, 1972, p. 301.

2. Denis Donoghue : « The Problems of Being Irish » in *Times Literary Supplement*, March 17, 1972, p. 291.

3. Sean O'Faolain : *The Finest Stories of Sean O'Faolain*, Bantam Classic Edition, 1959, p. 83.

4. Kilroy, *op. cit.*

5. John McGahern : *The Barracks*.

6. John McGahern : *The Dark*, Panther, 1969, p. 21.

7. *Ibid.*, pp. 43-4.

8. John McGahern : *Nightlines*, Panther, 1973, p. 9.

9. *Ibid.*, pp. 30-1.

10. Roger Garfitt : « Constants in Contemporary Irish Fiction » in *Two Decades of Irish Writing*, Carcanet Press, 1975, p. 223.

11. Henri-D. Paratte : « Conflicts in a Changing World » in *The Irish Novel in Our Time*, eds. M. Harmon and P. Rafroidi, Publications de l'Université de Lille III, 1976, p. 319.

12. McGahern : *op. cit.*, p. 45.

13. *Ibid.*

14. *Ibid.*, p. 38.

15. *Ibid.*, p. 101.

16. *Ibid.*, pp. 101-2.

# NOTES ON CONTRIBUTORS

André BOUÉ : formerly lecturer at the University of Lille (1961-1970) is now Professor at the Sorbonne (Paris IV) where he holds the chair of « Littérature et Civilisation britanniques des XIXe et XXe siècles ». He is the author of *William Carleton, romancier irlandais* (1973).

Terence BROWN : Director of Modern English at Trinity College, Dublin. Has published *Louis MacNeice : Sceptical Vision*, and *Northern Voices : Poets from Ulster*. He is currently at work on a study of Culture and Society in post-Treaty Ireland. He is the secretary of I.A.S.A.I.L. and a member of the Royal Irish Academy's sub-committee for the study of Anglo-Irish literature.

Roger CHATALIC : teaches at the Université de Bretagne occidentale, Brest. Engaged in a study of Frank O'Connor. Has written in the *Cahier du Centre d'Etudes Anglo-Irlandaises* of the University of Rennes.

Anne CLUNE : is Lecturer in English at Trinity College, Dublin. She is author of *Flann O'Brien : a critical introduction to his writings*. She is currently at work on a study of Anglo-Irish Prose Fantasy. She is an executive committee member of I.A.S.A.I.L. and was a member of the Cumann Merriman Bicentennial Committee.

John CRONIN : is Senior Lecturer in English at the Queen's University, Belfast. He is the author of *Somerville and Ross* (1972) and *Gerald Griffin, 1803-1840 : A Critical Biography* (1978).

Seamus DEANE : Teaches in the English Department, University College, Dublin. Publications include two volumes of poetry *Gradual Wars* (1972), winner of AE Memorial Award for Literature, and *Rumours* (1977). Has also published critical essays on various topics. Founder editor of Irish journal *Atlantis*, 1969-74.

Guy FEHLMANN : Professor of English at the University of Caen. Has published : *Somerville et Ross témoins de l'Irlande d'hier* (1970) and co-edited : *France-Ireland, Literary Relations* (1974).

John Wilson FOSTER : Born in Belfast ; lives in Canada where he is an Associate Professor at the University of British Columbia. Author of *Forces and Themes in Ulster Fiction* (1974) and numerous articles on folklore theory, Irish literature and eighteenth-century poetry. He was one of the contributors of *The Irish Novel in Our Time* (1976).

Maurice HARMON : Teaches at University College, Dublin. Editor of the *Irish University Review : a Journal of Irish Studies*. Recent publication : *The Irish Novel in Our Time* (co-editor, 1976), *Select Bibliography for the Study of Anglo-Irish Literature and its Backgrounds. An Irish Studies Handbook* (1977) ; *Richard Murphy : Poet of Two Traditions* (1978).

Brendan KENNELLY : Professor of Modern Literature at Trinity College, Dublin. Has published two novels and nine collections of poems. Winner of the A.E. Memorial Prize for Poetry, 1967. Editor of *The Penguin Book of Irish Verse* (1970).

Declan KIBERD : Sometime lecturer at the University of Kent at Canterbury, is now lecturer in Irish at Trinity College, Dublin. In addition to articles on the literature and politics of Ireland, has written a study of *The Merchant of Venice* and a number of stories and poems. His *The Inner Exile of J.M. Synge* is shortly to be published. At present he is preparing a critical introduction to the major Irish writers under the title *Styles of Irish Will*.

Guy LE MOIGNE : teaches at the Université de Bretagne occidentale, Brest. Is currently engaged on a study of Sean O'Faolain's fiction.

Jean LOZÈS : teaches in the English Department of the University of Toulouse — Le Mirail. Has written for the journal *Caliban*. Is preparing a work entitled : *Joseph Sheridan Le Fanu : Irlandais et Humaniste de l'Imaginaire.*

Seán LUCY : Professor of Modern English, University College, Cork, since 1967. His main publications include : *T.S. Eliot and the Idea of Tradition* (1960), *Love Poems of the Irish* (ed. 1967), *Five Irish Poets* (ed. and contrib., 1970), *Irish Poets in English* (id., 1973). Was chairman of the I.A.S.A.I.L. Conference in 1973.

David NORRIS : is lecturer in English at Trinity College, Dublin. He is currently at work on a study of James Joyce. He is Chairman of the Dublin James Joyce Committee and a trustee of the James Joyce Foundation.

Henri-Dominique PARATTE : Assistant Professor, Acadia University. Has contributed to previous *Cahiers Irlandais*. Presently engaged in comparative literature programmes, with particular emphasis on francophone literatures. To be published : *La Mer Ecartelée, La littérature romande*. Revised for publication : *Mythe et Roman, l'exemple irlandais*.

Patrick RAFROIDI : Professor of Modern English and Anglo-Irish literature, Vice-Chancellor of the University of Lille, founder and director of C.E.R.I.U.L., Chairman of I.A.S.A.I.L. (1976-1979), editor of *Etudes Irlandaises* and ʹ *Cahiers Irlandais* ̀. Recent publications : *Précis de Stylistique anglaise, Irish Literature in English : The Romantic Period.*

Alec REID : Taught at T.C.D. for some years, was a drama critic for the *Irish Times* and has lectured widely on Beckett in North America and in Europe. He was a co-editor of *Time Was Away : The World of Louis MacNeice* (1974) and author of *All I Can Manage, More Than I Could : an approach to the plays of Samuel Beckett* (1968), both published by The Dolmen Press of which he is a Director.

Donald TORCHIANA : Professor of English, Northwestern University, has published : *W.B. Yeats and Georgian Ireland* (1966), *English Literature 1660-1800* (1972). His *English, Irish and American Essays* have been collected and he is currently working on *Dubliners* and on *J.B. Yeats's Letters*. A member of several learned societies and a Consultant, Royal Irish Academy, is General Editor of the Modern Irish Writers Series at Northwestern University Press.

# OUVRAGES PARUS

## LITTERATURES ET CIVILISATIONS ETRANGERES

ETUDES ANGLAISES
— Renaissance

*Le bouffon sur la scène anglaise au XVIe siècle*, Victor Bourgy.
*John Milton. Pensée, mythe et structure dans le Paradis Perdu*, Armand Himy.

— Centre du XVIIIe siècle

*Elizabeth Inchbald et la revendication féminine au XVIIIe siècle*, Françoise Moreux.
*Aspects du féminisme en Angleterre au XVIIIe siècle*, Paul Denizot, Françoise Moreux, Michèle Plaisant.
*L'excentricité en Grande-Bretagne au XVIIIe siècle*, Etudes rassemblées par Michèle Plaisant.
*Jardins et paysages : Le style anglais*, André Parreaux et Michèle Plaisant, éditeurs.
*Regards sur l'Ecosse au XVIIIe siècle*, Etudes réunies par Michèle Plaisant.

Collection *"Tables rondes et colloques"*

*La femme en Angleterre et dans les colonies américaines aux XVIIe et XVIIIe siècles*, Actes du colloque tenu à Paris les 24 et 25 octobre 1975.

— Centre d'Etudes Victoriennes

*Politics in Literature in the Nineteenth Century*, ouvrage dirigé par Pierre Coustillas.
*La Nouvelle Bohème (New Grub Street)* de George Gissing (1891). Traduction de Suzanne Calbris et Pierre Coustillas.
*Victorian Writers and the City*, ouvrage dirigé par Jean-Paul Hulin et Pierre Coustillas.

— XXe siècle

*Les élections de crise en Grande-Bretagne*, sous la direction de Monica Charlot.

ETUDES AMERICAINES

*Myth and Ideology in American Culture*, ouvrage dirigé par Régis Durand.
*Le discours de la violence dans la culture américaine*, ouvrage dirigé par Régis Durand.

ETUDES IRLANDAISES
— Etudes Irlandaises

*L'Irlande et le Romantisme*, Patrick Rafroidi.

*Charles Robert Maturin (1780-1824), l'homme et l'oeuvre*, Claude Fierobe.

*William Butler Yeats. Les fondements et l'évolution de la création poétique*, Jacqueline Genet.

— Cahiers Irlandais

*Aspects of the Irish Theatre*, Patrick Rafroidi, Raymonde Popot, William Parker, editors.

*France-Irland, Literary Relations*, Patrick Rafroidi, Guy Fehlmann, Maitiu Mac Conmara, editors.

*The Irish Novel in Our Time*, Patrick Rafroidi, Maurice Harmon, editors.

— Irish and Anglo-Irish Texts

*The Boyne Water*, John Banim.

*The Rivals and Tracy's Ambition*, Gerald Griffin.

— Traduit de l'Irlandais

*Les occasions perdues (The Trusting and the Maimed)*, James Plunkett.

*Chrétiens, demain (Le Visiteur) (Catholics)*, Brian Moore.

*Les Vivants et les Morts*, Mary Lavin.

ETUDES GERMANIQUES

*L'évolution politique de Bertolt Brecht de 1913 à 1933*, Fred Fischbach.

ETUDES ITALIENNES

*La ville dans la littérature italienne moderne : mythe et réalité*, J. Basso, M. Pantaloni, M. Tanant, V. Caprani, J. Venturini, D. Cohen-Budor.

ETUDES IBERIQUES

*Les idées sur l'Amérique Latine dans la presse espagnole autour de 1900*, Guy-Alain Dugast.

*Recherches sur le monde hispanique au XIXe siècle*, études rassemblées par Jean-Louis Picoche.

*Nationalisme et cosmopolitisme dans les littératures ibériques au XIXe siècle*, Centre d'Etudes Ibériques et Ibéro-Américaines du XIXe siècle.

*Lettres inédites de José Maria de Hérédia à Alfred Morel Fatio*, publiées et anotées par Jean Lemartinel.

Collection *"Tables rondes et colloques"*

*Aspects du XIXe siècle ibérique et ibéro-américain*, Actes du XIIe congrès de la société des hispanistes français, Lille 1976.